MemOz Bible

Methods & Suggestions To Enhance Bible Memory

I will not forget Your Word
—Psalm 119:16

Ken Remember

MemQz Bible

Methods & Suggestions To Enhance Bible Memory

Copyright © 2018 by Ken Remember

Cover Design by John Phillips Graphic Design

ISBN: 978-1-7328325-0-3

MemQz Publishing
Hixson, TN 37343
https://memqz.com

Why Bible Memory Cues?

You search the Scriptures because you think that in them you have eternal life (John 5:39)

Hi, I'm Ken Remember. I hope this book will help you remember the books and chapters of Bible topics you know and love.

Of course you can find them with a computer or device, but it takes some time to power up and then google the *right* terms—the ones from the Bible version you read them in.

But why do this all the time? Your brain is subject to the "use it or lose it" threat the rest of your body is. Since recall naturally diminishes with age even when brain disease is not a factor, why not improve it with freshly-built circuits? All exercise strengthens, doesn't it? Besides, you already have a good memory! Why not add God's eternal Word to it, something you *"can* take with you!"

And *use now!* God's Word claims to be *truth* (Psalm 119:160; John 17:17), *wisdom* (1 Corinthians 12:8), *eternal life* (John 5:39; 6:63; 1 John 1:1), *light* (Psalm 119:105), *power* (Psalm 119:11; John 17:17; James 1:18), *peace* (Psalm 119:165), *hope* (Psalm 130:5), and *encouragement* (Romans 15:4) . . . all in *this* life.

"But the Bible's so huge!" you say. "How can I remember the 'where?'s of even the topics I know? There are so many!"

Yes there are, but aural, visual, and conceptual factors can help you remember the books and numbers. Consider Jesus' feeding fish to 5000 and 4,000 people on separate occasions. Where are these two events in the Bible?

We don't know the *kind(s)* of fish Jesus served but we can invent some to serve as memory cues, for *example:* **Shark Plate** (Mark

8), **Fluke Dine** (Luke 9), **Codfish** (John 6), **"Gaff Some Swordfish!"** (Matth[ew] 14)—"**Sooo (5,000)** many fed!"

These **Aural Cues** *roughly rhyme* with sounds in book titles and chapter numbers. They're also **Conceptual Cues** related to the subjects we're trying to remember: shark, fluke, cod, and sword are *species of fish*, and "plate" and "dine" both relate to *eating*. "Gaff" is close enough to Matth[ew] for our purposes but you'll think of better terms and when you do, they'll be IQz.

For books we'll extract a string to rhyme with, for example *em* or *en* for the *en* in Genesis, *ex* for Exodus, etc.

Aural Cues

We'll use these cues to rhyme with the vowels of numbers.

0	Ō	No, hope
1	Uh	Won, one
2	oo ū	To, new, few
3	Ē / ē	Seek, eat
4	Or	For, more
5	Īve / Īfe	Strive, life
6	i	Fix, hiss
7	E/e	Set, less
8	Ā	Ate, raise
9	īm īn	Time, sign

From 10 up we'll *rhyme either the composite*—for example 10 = "when" or "tend"; 11 = "leaven" or "left in"; 12 = "tell" or "self"—*or each number*—10 (one oh: for example "one goat"). Occasionally we'll shorten a multi-syllable word to sound out the single vowel of the number, for example b[e]lief = b'lief = "bleef" to rhyme with 3; or the two-syllabled "belief" (buh + leaf) can stand for 13 (one-three). "Serene" is one of the few words close to "thirteen."

Occasionally we'll mispronounce a vowel. For example, B**a**rak appears in Judges 4, so it would help if his name rhymed with 4. In a case like this we'll put the "a" in brackets (B[a]rak) to suggest you pronounce it "Borak" as in **Four**ak.

Visual Cues

Visual Cues *are letters that look like the numbers of chapters*. For example, Mark's **Shark Plate** might have been B^{8}ullshark or B^{8}lueshark (B = 8, chapter 8). Luke's **Fluke (Dine)** may have been pounded into g^{9}efilt-fish. John's **Codfish** has a "d" (backwards b = 6) in its co**d**^{6} and there are two subspecies: b^{6}lue and b^{6}lack cod. Finally, we know Jesus multiplied fish so I^{1}chthus M^{4}ultiplied takes us to Matthew **14**. Icthus is Greek for fish.

Generally we'll use visual cues secondarily to aural cues, cuing just chapter numbers. But these too will be conceptually linked to biblical topics, some tightly some loosely. Hopefully the mix of *approximate **sounds**, **sights**,* and **concepts** derived from biblical subjects will direct us to the books and chapters they're in.

The next page lists the letters we plan to use to *approximate the appearances* of numbers. We'll use both small and capped letters which in a few cases are inconsistent, but it will expand vocabulary for *conceptual* cuing. For example, the small **b** in **b**^{6}oat" (Noah's ark) can represent Genesis **6** where the Flood **b**^{6}egins while a capital **B** represents Genesis **8** where the Flood **B**^{8}reaks!

These contrary uses of the same letter will seem confusing at first but with use you'll be surprised how many your mind learns to treat as *separate distinct letters!*

0	o O c C u U D Q
1	l i J
2	n v V T y
3	F H k K N Y z Z m ω
4	A E M W x X
5	S s
6	b d G
7	L T J
8	B R
9	g q p P e

The letters were picked to maximize the number of conceptual links. This contrasts with memory systems that use only consonants and often just one letter per number, consequently restricting the vocabulary available for concepts and proper names. One common system, for example, uses a scripted small "f" for an 8 which is fine, but script is regrettably on a downslide, the capital B looks at least as good if not closer to the 8, and, most importantly, there are more "B" than "F" words in the dictionary.

Following are some visual criteria for the choice of letters to represent numbers.

Shape—the open-curved **C/c** and **U/u** and the bounded curves **D** and **Q** represent **0** (zero) in addition to **O/o** which obviously will be used more often.

S is a "**S**hoe-in" for a **5** (five). No competition! *Italicized **L** and **T*** are used for **7**. In addition to **B**, **R** may be used for **8** since its bottom right line can be curved left to shape it into the B that stands for 8.

Number of lines—l and **i** and **J** have **1** line; **n, v** and **T** have **2**; **F, H, K, N, Y** and **Z** have **3** (to which we added the less used small **m** and omega (**ω**) which rotate into 3s. **E, M, W** and **X** have **4** lines (though arguably X could be 2). "**A**" appears to have a crooked 4 embedded in it when you rotate 4 slightly left, so we used this exception too.

Mirror Images—The **b** and **d** for **6** (**G** too), and the **g, p,** and **q** for **9** (**e** too, a backwards 9).

We'll do some strange things with letters, even misspell a term to locate its chapter as, for example, Babell[11] (the "Genesis" of multiple languages) or reverse it to get the number order for the chapter as in l[1]on-B[8]aby for "Babylon" in Revelation **18**.

You won't appreciate all the cues because, frankly, *I don't!* Although I've tried to stick to a general method, there is no "best job" to this and I hope you will take the results as a "Quick Start" to making up your own cues. You'll do better than I in this venture if you creatively tailor your Qz to unique features of your own memory. So, while I think the overall model is decent, when you come to a bad cue, rather than curse it on Media please just improve**/**replace it.

The colored eBook, offered at a discount if you buy this printed version, includes navigation links to hop around faster.

Unless you really want to, don't read this book cover-to-over. I suggest you pick a favorite book of the Bible then read the cues before each chapter to anticipate topic breaks. You may want to consider a handful from the New Testament like John, Romans, Hebrews, and Revelation which are theologically dense.

Then you may want to memorize topics, persons, and events in historical books like the Torah (Genesis through Deuteronomy), the Samuels, Kings, and Chronicles, the Gospels, and Acts. Finally, you may want to add the prophetic and wisdom books. In the long run you may want to know Bible topics from cover to cover.

A few books don't have book cues because of their brevity and/or consistent, overriding theme. For example, proverbs are arranged *topically* since each chapter in the book is filled with so many. Neither Proverbs nor Chronicles have *book* cues since both are action related. Proverbs' ethics are summarized by nouns (principles) or verbs (actions). Chronicles essentially "chronicle" events so 1 Chronicles has verbs for events (e.g. fight) and **2** Chronicles has infinitives (e.g. **To** fight).

Here's an example from Genesis of what you'll find in the pages ahead:

Chapter	Topic	Rhyme Cue	Visual Cue
[03]	**The Fall** : *Entry* of sin into world :	F³all

May the Lord help you recall biblical topics and locations to put them to good use for every occasion. Visit us at **memqz.com** where we'll post articles on the biblical perspective on memory.

—Ken Remember

This I recall to my mind, therefore have I hope
(KJV Lamentations 3:21)

Old Testament

New Testament

OT   Genesis   NT

[*en* *em* *Genesis* = "beginning"]

[01] Creation : God ***Sends Sun/Genesis Sun*** : l^{1}et *there be* l^{1}ight!

[02] Adam and Eve : ***Sends Two*** into garden : **T^2**wo: *male/female*

[03] The Fall : ***Men Free*** *themselves from God* **//** ***Entry ("Tree")*** *of sin into world* : ***Genesis Free****dom* **//** **F^3**all **//** *Tree of the* **K^3**nowledge *of good and evil*

[04] Cain Kills Abel : ***Genesis Sword*** *(1st murder)* : **M^4**urder/**A^4**bel

[05] Adam to Noah : ***Descendants/Men Thrive*** : **S^5**uccessors

   God Takes Enoch (24) : ***Men Fly? //*** ***Sent Live*** to heaven: **S^5**ent *to* **S^5**ky *(heaven)*

[06] Noah : ***Men Pick*** *animals in pairs* : **b^6**easts **//** **b^6**oat **//** **b^6**uilds

[07] Flood Begins : *God* ***Rends Heaven*** : **T^7**orrents **//** *FL^7*ood

[08] Flood Ends : ***"End Waves!"*** : *Flood* **B^8**reaks/A**B^8**ates

[09] Rainbow Covenant : ***Blend-Sign*** *to all generations* (12) : **P^9**romise: *"No more* **g^9**ushers!*"* **//** **g^9**orgeous *rainbow*

[10] Nati^{1}o^{0}ns Descend from Noah : ***Genetics/Men Trends*** *up* : l^{1}ands **O^0**verrun

[11] Babel : ***Men Elevate*** *Tower;* ***One-Tongued*** **>: 1^1** l^{1}anguage **>** Babel**l^{11}** > l^{1}ots l^{1}anguages

[12] God Calls Abraham (1-9) : ***Sends One To*** *new land* : ***Heaven Tells*** him: l^{1}eave **n^2**ow!"

   Men Meld *together* (4) : l^{1}ot **T^2**eams *up with Abraham*

OT   Genesis   NT

[12] **Famine in Canaan** : *God **Ends The Food** in Canaan* : l[1]and n[2]on-productive: ***Men Fell** in Canaan/**Men Dwelt** in Egypt*

[13] **Lot Leaves Abraham** : *Men Veering/Steering away* : l[1]ot's H[3]erds-men *argue that* l[1]ot's F[3]locks *are not getting* l[1]otsa F[3]ood *so* l[1]ot F[3]arewells!" l[1]ot H[3]ikes *away but* l[1]ot's K[3]idnapped *by enemies*

[14] **Abraham Rescues Lot** (1-16) : ***Abram is/Men Warring** to rescue Lot.* l[1]ot M[4]akes *it out;* l[1]ot E[4]xtracted

M[4]el[1]chizedek (17-24) : *Abraham gives him a **Tenth From War** :* l[1]oads M[4]elchizedek *with spoils* **//** *Mechizedek is king of Salem (Shalom: Hebrew for Peace):* "l[1]ord M[4]ake-peace"

[15] **Abram's Sons "Stars"** (1-6) : ***Benefits: Sons Thrive** :* l[1]ike S[5]tars *in the heavens. But first they will* l[1]ive S[5]lavery / l[1]sraeli S[5]laves *in Egypt for 400 years (13-16).*

[16] **Ishmael the "Wild Donkey of a Man** : *Men Kick[s]ing* : l[1]shmael b[6]rays

[17] **Circumcision** (1-14) : ***Men Severing** small circles of skin* : l[1]imited *T*[7]rim

Covenant with Isaac & Sons (15-27) : ***Benefits*** : *Sons Several* : l[1]saac *T*[7]estament

[18] **Sodom's Sins** : *Men Raping/Hating* : l[1]ntensely B[8]ad

[19] **Gomorrah's Sins** : *Men Binding men* **//** *Men Declining* : l[1]ntense g[9]ratification/g[9]reed/g[9]luttony/g[9]uilt **//** l[1]usty g[9]omorrah

***Men Dining** with Lot in Sodom turn out to be angels—these **Men Blinding** attackers*

OT   Genesis   NT

[20] **Abraham Offers Half-Sister-Wife to Abimelech** : *Lend-A-Sis Many* times *(here, 12:13, and 26:7)* : n^2uptial O^0ffer

[21] **Abraham's T^2wo I^1ads** (1-21) : *Men: Two Sons* : V^2irtuous I^1saac *to Sarah* (21: 19) *and* V^2ile I^1shmael *to Hagar* (16)

  Ishmael (10-21) *Sent To Sun* (desert) : *God* V^2isits I^1shmael *and mother in the desert and promises to make him a nation*

  Well-Water Treaty with Abimelech (22-34) : *Men To Shun Well* (30) : T^2reaty $I^1$and (23-32)

[22] **Abraham Offers Isaac** : *Sent To Wound his only son* / *Sent To Prove his faith* : *"T^2ouch n^2ot the boy!" God says*

[23] **Sarah Buried in Hittite Tomb** : *Men To Weep* (2) : T^2erritory H^3ittite / T^2omb H^3ittite

[24] **Isaac Sends Men to Nahor to Find Wife** : *Send/Men To Nahor / Men To Lure wife* : n^2ahorian W^4ife *(Rebekah)*

[25] **Abraham Buried with Sarah** (7-11) *Men To Drive his body to Sarah* / *Sent to Wife's tomb* : T^2omb S^5arah

  Jacob and Esau (19-28) *Men To/Two Strive in the womb* : T^2wo S^5trive // n^2ations S^5trive

  Esau Sells Birthright for Lentil Stew (29-34) : *Lentils to Drive men apart* : V^2eggie S^5tew // T^2estament S^5old // T^2ransfers S^5hares *of inheritance*

[26] **Famine Forces Isaac to Gerar** (1-11) : *Men "Food-Trip" to Gerar* : T^2o G^6erar

  Attempts To Trick Abimelech with his wife (like his father) : T^2rick "b^6im"

OT   Genesis   NT

[26] **Water Fights (17-34) :** *Men To Pick* fights over water wells for their herds **: T^2**hirst **b^6**attle **:** *Men To Give* water rights with **T^2**reaty **b^6**etween *Isaac and Abimelech* **: T^2**reaty A**b^6**imilech **/ T^2**reaty **b^6**enefits *both parties*

[27] **Esau Sells Birthright for Venison Stew** (1-46) **:** *"Venison Stew Heaven"* **:** n^{2}abs ***L^7**egacy **/ V^2**enison **L^7**adled*

[28] **Jacob's** (1-9) **:** *Sent To Take* a bride **T^2**o **B^8**etrothe **/ T^2**o **B^8**eersheba **/ T^2**o **B^8**ethuel 's *house in Paddan Aram*

   Ladder-to-Heaven Vision (10-22) **:** *Angels **Sent To Face** God // **Sent Through Gate/To Face** God //* **T^2**op **B^8**efore *the Lord*

[29] **Jacob** (1-17) **:** *Sent/Men to Find/Bind* a bride **: T^2**o **g^9**et *bride*

   Laban (18-20) ***Meant To Bind*** *Jacob to 7 years of service for Rachel but Jacob got Leah first* **: T^2**wo **g^9**irls, *local custom*

   Laban > *7th and 14th year //* n^{2}o **g^9**ive-away *wives*

[30] **God Closed Down Rachel's Womb** (1-22) **:** *Gen**era**tion He Closed down* **: N^3**o O^{0}ffspring **// K^3**ids 0^0. But later ω^{3}omb-O^{0}pened *by God:* **Gen***era*tion]**Working**

   Laban Keeps the Best Animals (25-43) **:** *Laban Is A Dirty dealer* **: K^3**eeps 0^0-defect *animals. **Sends Blurry/Dirty/Wormy** ones—striped, speckled and spotted (defective ones)—to Jacob*

[31] **Jacob and His Wife Free from Laban** (1-21) **:** *Jacob is Free From Laban* **:** *God* **m^3**andates **J^1**acob's *return to his* **N^3**ative **l^1**and **//** *They* **F^3**lee **l^1**aban

   Laban Chases Them for Idols (22-55) **:** *Laban Is Scurry-Run after Rachel who* **H^3**eisted **l^1**dols **// H^3**ousehold **l^1**dols

OT   Genesis   NT

[32] Jacob Offers Meat to Esau (1-21) : *Sends Peace Food/Meat To Esau (peace offering)* : **H³**am **T²**o Him **//** **F³**locks/**H³**ogs **T²**oo

Wrestles Angel (22-32) : *Jacob Is Beat Blue* : **H³**ip **T²**orn

[33] Esau Responds : *"Plen-ty Meat I have!"* (9) : **F³**ull **F³**locks **//** **H³**earty **H³**ogs **//** **m³**uch **m³**eat. *But Jacob insists that he take them*: **F³**raternal **H³**ello!

[34] Jacob Arrives in Shechem : *Shechem Is Th[e] Lord of Shechem that subdues Dinah* : **F³**emale **M⁴**ishandling.

[35] Jacob Revives Worship at Bethel (1-8) : *Jacob Is Revived for worship* : **F³**orms **S⁵**hrine *(builds altar)*

God names Jacob Israel (9-15) : *Gent Re-"lifed"* : **N³**ew **S⁵**ignature

God Renews Abrahamic Covenant with Jacob (11-15) : *Benefits Revived* : **F³**aithfulness **S⁵**ustained

Jacob's Many Sons (22-26) : *Man-y Lives* : **N³**umerous **S⁵**ons

[36] Esau's Many Sons : *Many "Es"-Kids*, :**N³**umerous **b⁶**oys

[37] Coat of Many Colors (3) : *Man-y Sections of colors* **//** **H³**ues **/** **H³**alftones ***L⁷***ots

Sheaves Bow to Joseph (5-11) : *Men-sheaves Slavin* : **K³**neeling ***L⁷***eaves

Joseph Sold by Brothers (18-30) : *Men-Thieves Settlin him for money* **/** **m³**arket ***J⁷***oseph; **m³**edianites ***T⁷***ake *him to Egypt*

[38] Onan Spills Seed (8-10) : *Onan/Men-Seed Waste* : "**N³**o **B⁸**oys **//** **N³**o **B⁸**irths *for me!*"

OT   Genesis   NT

[39] Potiphar's Wife and Her > (1-18) **:** *"Men-Designs" on Joseph / Joseph Is Resigned to purity* **: H³**eadmaster's **g⁹**al

Joseph Arrested/Imprisoned (19-23) **:** *Joseph Is Behind bars* **: H³**e's **P⁹**enned *up/"***P⁹***risoned" // "***H³***ooseg⁹owed"*

[40] Joseph Interprets Two Dreams (1-23) **:** *Joseph Is Sorting out dreams in* **Pen Ph[a]raoh /** *"Senses" Story* **: M⁴**aster **O⁰**neirocritic (*oneiros* [dream] + *critic* [judge])

[41] Pharaoh Needs an Interpreter: *Sends For One!* (14) **: M⁴**aster **I¹**nterpreter

Joseph Becomes Lord of Egypt : *Joseph Is "Lord 1"* in *Egypt /* **E⁴**gypt's **I¹**ord

Men Store Tons *of grain for the coming 7-year famine /* ***Store Buns/Crumbs*** *too?* **: W⁴**arehouse **I¹**egumes

Joseph Is Born Sons *in Egypt* **: M⁴**anasseh / Ephrai¹m

[42] Jacob: "To Egypt for Food!" : *Jacob's Sons/Sent For Food* : E⁴gyptian **V²**ittles**/V²**eggies

[43] Jacob: "Return for Meat!" : *Jacob's Sons/Sent For Meat* : E⁴gyptian **H³**ogs**/F³**locks**/m³**eats

[44] Benjamin's Accused of Stealing : *"Benjamin's Stored Ore for himself!"* **:** *Silver* **M⁴**etal **M⁴**ug *hidden in sack:* **M⁴**etal **E⁴**mbezzled

[45] Joseph Reveals Himself to his brothers (1-8) **:** *"Joseph's Sibs: "Your alive!"* "**M⁴**y **S⁵**on's *Alive!" Jacob shouts.*

Joseph Tells Family to Move > (9-28) **:** *Benefits For Life in Egypt!* **: M⁴**ove **S⁵**outh!

OT   Genesis   NT

[46] Joseph : *Sends for Sibs* (5)—*his brothers (and his father)* **:**
"**M**[4]ove **b**[6]rood *to Egypt!*"

[47] The Famine : "***Spend for Seven*** *years all you have for <u>my</u>*
grain!" **: E**[4]gypt ***L***[7]*anguishes **/*** *Pharaoh owns their property*
and lives **: W**[4]ealthy ***L***[7]ord!

[48] Joseph > *Blesses His Born Babes from Egypt* **: E**[4]phraim
B[8]lessed *and* **M**[4]anaseh **B**[8]lessed

[49] Joseph > *Blesses His Born Line Entirely* **:** *all Twelve Children*

Joseph > "***Blessings/Benefits For Mine* : M**[4]y **g**[9]enerations

[50] Joseph > "**You intended** *evil* **but God** *good!*" (20) **:** *Meant*
***Shifty/Nifty* : S**[5]undry **O**[0]bjectives

"***Send My Bones*** [**S**[5]end **O**[0]ssicles] (25-26) *to Canaan when you*
move back!"

OT   Exodus   NT
[*ex* *ec* *es* *est* *akes* *egs*]
Exit Us From Egypt

[01] **Egypt Oppresses Israel : *Vex Sons*** *of God* (4:22) : l¹aborers
/ l¹ncatenated (chained)

[02] **Moses Found** (1-10) : ***Exhumed*** *from basket* **: n²ile** *baby*
n²ursed *by servant*

Moses Kills Egyptian (11-22) : ***Executes* : T²erminates**

Vexed Move *to Midian* **/ T²akes-off**

Takes Ewe*-shepherd Zipporah* **/ T²akes** *wife* **/ n²uptials**

[03] **Burning Bush at H³oreb : *Excretes*** *smoke* **: F³irebush //**
Checks leaves: *not consumed*

Next Speaks Angel of the Lord: *"I will* **F³ree** *Israel from Egypt!"*

[04] **God Gives Moses:**

Staff > Snake (3) ***Snake Forms*** *from staff* **: M⁴amba?**

Aaron To > (14) ***Express*** *for Moses* **: M⁴oses'** */* **M⁴outhpiece**

[05] **Pharaoh Decrees a >** (1-22) : ***"Bricks Drive*** *without straw!"* :
S⁵trawless *bricks*

[06] **Exodus Planned : *Exodus Fixed*** **: b⁶reak-out** *from* **// b⁶rick-**
production

God Sends Multiple Judgments on Egypt

[07] **Nile to Blood : *Decks Reddin'd*** *by blood* **: L⁷eukocyte // L⁷ake**

[08] **Frogs Overrun Land** (1-15) **: *Pests Take*** *over land* **: B⁸ullfrogs**

OT   Exodus   NT

[08] Gnats and Flies (16-32) **:** *Pests Ate everything* **: B**^{8}ugs

[09] Livestock Die (1-7) *Equines* **: g**^{9}razers *(all kinds)*

> **Boils** (8-12) **:** *Eczema Time // Infect Time* **: P**^{9}us / **P**^{9}uffy / **P**^{9}ain / **P**^{9}lague

> **Hail Pelts Egypt** (13-35) **:** *Wreck Time // "X" Time (everything in the field)* **: P**^{9}elted

[10] Locusts (1-20) **:** *Pest Trend* **: lo**^{10}custs / **l**^{1}ocusts **O**^{0}verun

> **Darkness "Felt"** (21-29) **:** *Ex/"X"-Lens* **: l**^{1}ights **O**^{0}ut!

[11] Passover : *"Ex/X Livin" firstborn* **: 1**^{1} **l**^{1}anced

[12] Passover : *Expel firstborns / "X" Lintels* with blood (7) **:** "**l**^{1}intels **T**^{2}ag!"

[13] Exodus : *Exodus: Stirring the Sea // Israel Treks The Sea // Red's The Sea* **: l**^{1}eave **N**^{3}ile *behind*

[14] God Drowns Pharaoh's Army : *Wrecks/X the Horse and rider in the sea* **: l**^{1}iquidates **M**^{4}ares/**M**^{4}en

[15] Moses/Israel Sing : *"Thanks!" Riffing* **: l**^{1}iberty **S**^{5}ong // "The **l**^{1}ord **S**^{5}trength/**S**^{5}ong!

[16] Manna: Israel > : *Collects Lunch Six* days **: l**^{1}unch **b**^{6}iscuit/ **b**^{6}read

[17] Water from rock : *Drinks From Heaven* **: l**^{1}odestone *L*^{7}iquid // **l**^{1}iquidate *T*^{7}hirst

> **Joshua defeats Ama<u>lek</u>** (16) **:** *-Leks Severing* **: l**^{1}ick's Ama*L*^{7}ek

OT   Exodus   ## NT

[18] Jethro's "Aid" Counsel: Moses > : *Selects Aiding/Some Aids* **:** l[1]itgation B[8]ench / l[1]itigation B[8]oys

[19] Israel Crosses Sinai Desert to Horeb : *Treks the Sinai* **:** to l[1]ord's P[9]resence *(Mountain of God)*

[20] Ten Commandments : *Lex Many/Plenty* **:** T[2]en 0[0]beys / T[2]o 0[0]bey

[21] Debt-Relief Laws : *Excuse Funds* **:** T[2]erminate l[1]oans *in 7th year* **/** T[2]erminate l[1]ordships *(masters free slaves)*

[22] Restitution for Stolen Property (1-15) **:** *2X To You in some cases* **/***Rest[u]tute* **:** V[2]alue 2[2]x *in some cases*

Justice to Rule (16-31) **:** *Lex To Rule* **:** T[2]rial n[2]orms / T[2]ruth V[2]iolations

[23] Don't Spread False Reports (1-2) **:** *Check Loose Speech* **:** T[2]erminate F[3]alsehoods / n[2]o F[3]alsehoods

Treat Enemy's Ox Nicely (4) **:** *Check Loose Beasts*: V[2]eal m[3]issing? > T[2]reat N[3]icely!

No Farming on Sabbath (10-13) **:** *"X" To Seed* **:** V[2]oid F[3]arming **//** *Instead* > *"Ecstasy to Lord on the Sabbath!"* = T[2]o ω[3]orship *on Sabbath!*

Three Festivals (14-19) *Fests To Keep* **:** T[2]hree F[3]easts / T[2]o K[3]eep!

Guardian Angel before you (20) **:** *Execute Lead* **:** V[2]ex F[3]oes

[24] "Confirm My Law!" : *Lex To Store in your heart* **:** V[2]ow M[4]osaic *Law!*

Exodus

[25] Tabernacle Donors : *Checks To Write* : T^{2}abernacle
S^{5}ponsors *to cover expenses*

[26] Tabernacle Designs : *Specs To Fix* : T^{2}abernacle b^{6}lueprints

[27] Bronze Altar (1-8) : *Necks To Severin* : V^{2}ictim *T^{7}able /
T^{2}hroats **L^7**anced

Court (9-19) : *Next To Heaven* : T^{2}abernacle **L^7**ayout

[28] Ephod (6-14) : *Vest To Lace on / "V^{2}est* B^{8}reast *person in
Israel!"*

Breastplate (15-30) : *Breast To Plate* : T^{2}o B^{8}reast, *a plate*

Thummim : *Vest To Rate* (judge) Israel : T^{2}hummim B^{8}ound

[29] Priests Sprinkled with Blood (1-46) : *Specks To Bind* them
to service : T^{2}o P^{9}riest's *ears*

[30] Altar of Incense (1-10; 22-37) : *Excretes Smoke* : F^{3}ragrant
O^{0}dor to *the Lord // Ex-Dirty > Next: Sweet Smoke*

Census Tax (11-16) : *T[a]x Worries* : F^{3}ees O^{0}wed

Bronze Basin (17-21) : *Ex-Dirty hands/feet (priests wash)* :
H^{3}and/F^{3}oot O^{0}rganisms/O^{0}ils/O^{0}dors *removed*

[31] OH^{3}ol^{1}iab and BeZ^{3}al^{1}el (1-11): *Techs: Weave-Ones* :
H^{3}em/H^{3}oly I^{1}oincloths *// Make* F^{3}ragrant I^{1}ncense

Sabbath (12-18) : *Rest: Working/Worry None/Rest Me Some!*
: N^{3}o I^{1}abor!

[32] Golden Calf : *Ex-Rings/Neck Rings Fused into golden calf* :
N^{3}eck T^{2}rinkets > H^{3}eifer T^{2}otem

OT   Exodus   NT

[33] **Leave Horeb!** (1-6) : *Exit th[e] Peak!* : **F³**lee **H³**oreb! **/** **m³**ount **H³**oreb

Moses Pitches Meeting Tent (7-11) : *Erects Teepee* : **F³**ace *[to]* **F³**ace *with Lord*

Moses Intercedes (12-24) : *Moses Pleading* : **m³**oses **N³**egotiating

[34] **New Tablets/Covenant Renewed** : *Lex Restored* : **N³**ew **W⁴**ritings/**M⁴**asonry

[35] **Artisans Work** : *Techs Devise art* : **H³**andicraft **S⁵**kills

[36] **Weavers Work** : *Techs Weave Six curtains* : **H³**em **6⁶** *curtains*

[37] **Ark, Table, Lampstand/Altar** : *Techs Seat Seven Lamps* : **F³**abricate **L⁷**ampstands *and other articles*

[38] **Altar for Burnt Offerings** (1-7) : *Decks We Make/Blaze/ Flame* **>** : **F³**or **B⁸**urnt *offerings* **/** **H³**eat/**F³**ire **B⁸**odies

Court/Tabernacle Design (9-31) : *Specs We Make/Take and adhere to* : **F³**abrication **B⁸**lueprints

[39] **Priests' Garments** : *Techs Weave Fine garments* : **H³**em **g⁹**arments

[40] **King's Glory Fills Tent** : *Rex Glory* : **M⁴**ajesty **O⁰**ccupies *the Tent*

OT   Leviticus   NT

[*e* eev* *eef* *ave*]

Levitic Offerings

[01] **Burnt :** *Levite Oven offerings* **:** I^{1}nflamed *offerings*

[02] **Grain :** *Levite N[u]t/Fruit offerings* **:** T^{2}hreshings

[03] **Peace :** *Levite Peace offerings* **:** H^{3}armony

[04] **Sin:** *Levite Immoral offerings* **:** M^{4}isbehavior

[05] **Guilt :** *Levite Hide offerings (hide in shame)* **:** S^{5}hame

[06] **Sin** (1-29) **:** *Levite Sin offerings*

Altar Fire (8-13) *Levite Bricks* **:** b^{6}urn *continuously*

[07] **Various Laws of Offerings :** *Levite's Several offerings* **:** *T^7*enderings *// L^7*aws

Levites Never to Eat Blood (26) **:** *Levites Never* **:** *L^7*ifeblood *of the flesh*

[08] **Moses Consecrates Aaron and Sons :** *Levites bathed* **:** B^{8}athed

[09] **Lord Accepts Aaron's Sacrifices :** *Levite's Shrine/Fine offerings* **:** g^{9}oat *for sin, then burnt and peace offerings*

[10] **Nadab and Abihu :** *Levite Xen (foreign/strange) offerings* **:** I^{1}evite O^{0}ffense

[11] **Clean Animals :** *Every L[a]vened one* **:** I^{1}aundered I^{1}ivestock

[12] **Unclean Time Periods :** *Leave Smells* **:** I^{1}aundering T^{2}imes

[13] **Leprosy Marks :** *Lep-r[o]-sy* **:** I^{1}eprosy H^{3}allmarks

[14] Leprosy Washings (1-32) : *Lave The Sores* : l^{1}eprosy W^{4}ashings

House Cleanings (33-57) : *Lave The Porch* : l^{2}odging W^{4}ashings

[15] DIS^{15}charges / IS^{15}sues : *Leaks Dripping* : l^{1}eaky S^{5}ores /S^{5}eed

[16] Day of Atonement : *Leave A Kid* to wander : l^{1}ive G^{6}oat *offering to Azazel*

[17] The Place of Sacrifice: Tabernacle (1-9) : *Levite Severing* (throats) place : l^{1}ocation T^{7}abernacle

Eating Blood (10-16) : *Levite Blood "Etin"?* : l^{1}ngest L^{7}eukocytes? *Never!*

[18] Sexual Sin : *Never Laying* with/*Raping* relatives : l^{1}ncest B^{8}ad

[19] Be Holy for I Am (1-8) : *Separate One I'm* : l^{1}ord's g^{9}ap

Kind of Love: Neighbor as Self (9-18) : *Love One Kind* : l^{1}ove q^{9}uality

Grape Gleanings (9-10) : *Leave B[e]hind / Leave "Findings"* : l^{1}eave g^{9}leanings *for poor*

Keep My Statutes (19-37) : *Levitic Ones Mine* : l^{1}aws P^{9}rescribe/P^{9}roscribe

[20] Capital Crimes : *Levites To Stone* : T^{2}o O^{0}re (stone) child sacrificers : T^{2}oddler O^{0}fferings, *sexual acts* / T^{2}o O^{0}bviate

[21] Levite Regulations/Prohibitions : *Levite Rules/Shuns* : n^{2}orms/T^{2}aboos l^{1}evites

[22] Levite Food Regulations (1-16) : *Levite Food Rules* :
V^{2}ictual n^{2}orms

No-Defect Offerings (17-33) : *Leave Bruised-Oozed out!* :
n^{2}o-n^{2}icks

[23] Lev^{2}ite F^{3}easts (1-44) : *Levites To Feast* : T^{2}o F^{3}east //
V^{2}acillate F^{3}irstfruits (Wave!) // T^{2}rumpet/T^{2}ent F^{3}east

[24] Lamps Burn Continually (1-4) : *Levites To Pour oil* : T^{2}orch
E^{4}ternal / n^{2}ever E^{4}xtinguish

Tabernacle Bread (5-9) : *Levites To Form loaves* :
T^{2}abernacle M^{4}atzo *bread*

Stone Blasphemers (10-16) : *Levites To Ore them* :
V^{2}illifiers E^{4}xecuted

Eye-for-eye (17-23) : *Left Due For right* : T^{2}ake E^{4}ye

[25] Sabbath Year Land Rest (1-7) : *Left To Thrive* : n^{2}o
S^{5}eeding / T^{2}urf S^{5}abbath

Jubilee: Free Slaves! (1-21) : *Left To Thrive* : T^{2}erminate
S^{5}lavery

<u>Sabbath Year</u>: Favor the Poor! (23-55) : *Left To Thrive* :
T^{2}erminate S^{5}tarvation/S^{5}qualor/S^{5}lums/S^{5}hortages

[26] Covenant Obedience (1-13) : *Levites To Bliss* : V^{2}irtue
b^{6}ehaviors

Covenant Disobedience (14-46) : *Levites To Miss out* :
V^{2}ice b^{6}ehaviors

[27] Vowed Things (1-34) : *Left To Heaven* : V^{2}owed [to] L^{7}ord

OT   Numbers   NT
[*um* *un*]

God Orders Israel to Count Things

[01] **Soldiers :** *Number Sons/Guns* **:** I^{1}nfantry/I^{1}evites *exempted from counts*

[02] **Tribes/Peoples and Camp Arrangement :** *Number Jews* **:** T^{2}welve/T^{2}ribes

[03] **Levite Priests** (1-39) **:** *Number Priests* **:** H^{3}oly/F^{3}athers.

Firstborn Males Redeemed (40-51) **:** *Number [1] Freed* **:** M^{4}ales: *firstborn*

[04] **Kohathite (Sons of Levi: Priests) Duties :** *Number Chores* W^{4}ork

Laws about Adultery and Nazarites

[05] **Adulteresses :** *Bum Wives* **:** S^{5}trays

[06] **Nazirite Vows** (alcohol +) **:** *Rum Nix!* **:** b^{6}ooze/b^{6}eer *No!*

Local Events at Sinai

[07] **Leader Offerings :** *Number Collections*: *animals/money* **:** L^{7}eader

[08] **Levites Consecrated:** *Sons Laved for Lord* **:** B^{8}athed

[09] **Passover Regulations:** *Come Dine at the proper time* **:** P^{9}assover

Cloud Signal When to Move: *Run Times (travel)* **:** g^{9}o *times*

OT   Numbers   NT

Moving On . . . Sinai to Paran

[10] **Leave Horeb :** *Trumpet Send-off* **:** l^{1}eave O^{0}rder **//** l^{1}eave HO^{0}reb!

[11] **Grumblers' Camp Burns** (1-15) **:** *Grumblers Leveled* **:** l^{1}odgings l^{1}ncinerate

70 Elders to Aid Moses (16-30) **:** *Numbers Level* work load **:** l^{1}ighten l^{1}oad **/** All^{11}eviate *Moses*

Quail^{11} from Sea (31-35) **:** *Num-Bir[d]s Come From* sea **:** l^{1}ight l^{1}unch

[12] **Aaron/Miriam vs. Moses :** *Trump The Truth / Grumblers Shelve* Moses' authority **:** l^{1}mpugn T^{2}ruth

On the Border to the Promised Land

[13] **Canaan: Honey and Milk :** *Runs Honey* and milk **:** l^{1}and's H^{3}oney/H^{3}olsteins *spies report*

Grasshoppers : *Numbers of Wings/Whirring—we appeared* l^{1}ike H^{3}oppers *to the giants in the land!*

[14] **People Grumble** (1-12) **:** *Grumbler-Swording* **:** l^{1}srael M^{4}assacred *as result*

Moses Intercedes (13-19) **:** *Plumbs The Lord* for mercy **:** l^{1}nterceding M^{4}oses

Forgiven but Death (20-45) **:** *Numbers "Mort"ing* **:** l^{1}srael **>** W^{4}ilderness *where this generation will die = not see promised land* **:** l^{1}and W^{4}ithdrawn

OT   Numbers   NT

[15] God **Numbers "Living** laws" *for His people when they enter land*

    I[1]aw S[5]acrifices
    I[1]aw S[5]ojourners
    I[1]aw S[5]ins

        I[1]gnorant S[5]ins
        I[1]ntentional S[5]ins

    I[1]aw S[5]abbath-breakers
    I[1]aw S[5]ashes *(tassels)*

[16] Korah Rebels : *Grumbler's "Picketing"* Moses : I[1]eads b[6]reak

    Korah's Family + 250 Sent Alive to Sheol (35). *Grumblers Missing :* Another 14,700 die (49) : I[1]ngrates b[6]uried *alive*

[17] Aaron's Staff Buds : *Lumber From Heaven :* I[1]ive T[7]wig

    Grumblings Lessen (5) : I[1]ess L[7]aments/I[1]ess L[7]oss of life (10)

[18] Priest/Levite Duties : *Some Blamings (they bear guilt 1) and Some Wagings (manage contributions: 8-32) :* I[1]evite B[8]urdens /B[8]usiness *(duties) and* I[1]evite B[8]ounty/B[8]onuses

[19] Purification by Red Heifer: *Dump The Grime :* I[1]avender g[9]uernsey // I[1]oosen g[9]rime.

[20] Moses Strikes Rock for Water (1-13) : *Rock Pumps Plenty* of water : T[2]eeming O[0]re / Moses told T[2]o O[0]rate, *not strike.*

    Edom Blocks Passage to Israel (14-21) : *Cumbers Entry* : T[2]ravel O[0]bstruction.

    Aaron Dies in Wilderness (22-29) : God *Cumbers Entry* = : n[2]ot O[0]ccupy *the land.*

OT   Numbers   NT

[21] Bronze Serpent (4-9) **:** *Grumblers To Come* *against Moses*

God sends **Stunners To Numb** *them* **:** V^2iper I^1njection.

Grumblers To Come *to bronze* V^2iper I^1mage *for healing*

Song of the Well (10-20) **:** *Hummers To Hum* **:** T^2o I^1ord's well

Israel *Plunders Two Chums* (21-35) —*kings* **Sihon** *(Amorites) and* **Og** *(Bashan)—who attack them* **:** "V^2ictory I^1srael!"

Facing Jericho across the Jordan River

[22] Balak Asks Balaam to Curse Israel (1-21) **:** *Summon-Curse To Bruise* **:** T^2o V^2illify *Israel. God tells him not to* (12)

*Ba***laam's Mule Stoops** (22-41) *to stop his approach to the Angel of the Lord about to kill him* **//** *Lord* **Un-mutes Mule** *to speak to Balaam* **:** T^2alking T^2ransport

[23] Balaam's First Refusal to Curse : *Mum To Speak* a curse **//** *None To Speak* **:** n^2o H^3exes

[24] Balaam's Second Refusal to Curse : *Mum To Word* a curse **:** n^2o M^4aledictions *to Israel, just* T^2hree M^4essages *(Blessings)*

[25] Intermarriage and Baal Worship (1-9) **:** *Some Took Wives* *from Moabites who invited them* > **:** T^2o S^5acrifice *to their gods. Moses commands leaders* T^2o S^5lay *them*

Headline "*Numbers Due Lives* to Phinehas!" (10-18) *who atones for the Idolatry* **:** n^2o S^5laughter *coming*

[26] Second Census : Moses *Numbers New Kids* **:** n^2ew b^6oys**/** b^6raves *able to fight*

OT   Numbers   NT

[27] **Moses Commissions Next Generation :** *Youngers To Servin* Israel after he's gone : ***Joshua**, the son of* n^{2}un L^{7}eads

[28] **No-Defect Offerings :** *None To Slay* > : n^{2}o-B^{8}lemishes

[29] **Animals Offered at the 3 Feasts :** *Come To Shrine* (altar) : n^{2}umerous g^{9}oats *and other animals*

[30] **Oaths :** *Some Sealed Oaths*—m^{3}arriage/H^{3}itch O^{0}aths *(permanent)*—and **Some "Cleave" Oaths** *(annullable)*—n^{2}ullify /n^{2}ullable O^{0}aths

[31] **Moses Attacks Midian :** *Plunders The Sons* of Midian : m^{3}oses'/m^{3}idian I^{1}nvasion

   Plunders Kings' Sons (5 of them) : K^{3}ings'/K^{3}ids I^{1}nvaded

[32] **Moses Settles Two Tribes :** *Bunkers Thē Reubs* and Gads : H^{3}omesteads T^{2}wo/T^{2}ribes—*Reuben and Gad in Gilead* (29)

[33] **Moses** *Numbers "Teepee"* campings of Israel > : N^{3}umbers H^{3}alts *(frequent stops in desert)*

The Land of Israel: **Moses' Numbers**

[34] *Metes 4*—Borders for Israel (west, north, east, south) : the N^{3}ation's M^{4}argins

[35] *Levite Cities :* *"Lev Sites"* which are > : H^{3}oly S^{5}ites

   Flee-Fight Cities of Refuge : K^{3}iller S^{5}anctuaries

[36] **Moses Specifies** *Some "She Gifts"* rules for >: F^{3}emale b^{6}eneficiaries

Deuteronomy
[*oo* *u*]
Deus and ***Deun'ts*,**

Sinai to Jordan

[01] **"Leave Horeb!** (1-18) : ***"Jews Done*** *at Horeb* : **I**[1]srael/**I**[1]eaves

Israel Refuses to Take Land of "Giants" (19-34) : *Huge Ones / Cruel Ones* : **I**[1]eviathans

Penalty: 40 Years of Wandering in Desert (34-46) : ***"Doom: Run*** *back and forth***/Stuck** *in desert!"* : **I**[1]ollygag! *(Wander)*

[02] **Wilderness** (1-25) : ***Doomed To*** > : **T**[2]rek *wilderness and die*

Defeat of Sihon and Og (26-37) : *Two Rules demolished (Sihon's and Og's)* : **T**[2]wo**/V**[2]ictories

[03] **Defeat of Og** (1-22) : ***Doomed King*** : **K**[3]ing *of Bashan*

God Tells Moses He will Not Enter the Land (23-29) : ***"Do See/Peek"*** **(N**[3]otice) *at the land but* ***"Deun't Seek"*** (26) *to cross* (**F**[3]ord) *the River* : ***Deun't Streak*** (**F**[3]lee) *across the Jordan and* ***Deun't Be*** *in the land* (**H**[3]abitat) : **F**[3]orbidden *entry*

Covenant Laws: Deus and Deun'ts

[04] **Moses Commands Israel to Obey** (1-14) : *Do Lord's commands* : **W**[4]orship *Him only*

Idolatry Forbidden (15-31) : ***Deun't Form*** *gods* : **M**[4]ake *none*

Lord Alone is God (32-40) : ***Do Lord's*** *commands only* : **W**[4]orship *Him alone*

Cities of Refuge (41-43) : ***Scoot Forts / Elude Sword*** : **M**[4]an-slayer *refuge***/**sanctuary // **M**[4]onasteries

[05] Moses Recounts Ten Commandments : *Do > Life! / Two Fives >* : **S⁵**um up **S⁵**ervice *to God and man*

[06] Greatest Commandment (Love) : *Do Big one!* : **G⁶**reatest/ **b⁶**enevolence

[07] Displace Peoples in Canaan! : *Boot Seven (7⁷) nations out* : "**L⁷**eave *[our]* **L⁷**and!"

[08] Remember the Lord : *"Do Wait on Him // Deun't Erase/ Raze* (**B⁸**lock *out*) *Him* : **B⁸**ear *Him in mind // Do Praise* (**B⁸**less) *Him after you have eaten and are full* (10)

[09] Not Chosen because Righteous (1-11) : *You Choose Crime* : **g⁹**loating/**g⁹**odless *but I choose you anyway!*

"**Golden Calf Destroy!**" (13-29) : *"Do Grind down to powder!"* : **g⁹**olden *calf/***g⁹**rind *it!*

[10] New Tablets (1-11) : *New Penned Commandments* : **10¹⁰** *re-written*

[11] Love/Serve the Lord > Prosperity : *Do L[o]ve the Lord To Live prosperously in the land* : **l¹**ove **l¹**ord *and* **l¹**ive **l¹**ucratively

[12] God to Tabernacle with People : *To Dwell with His people* : **l¹**ive **n²**ear *them* **l¹**n **T²**abernacle

[13] Kill False Prophets : *Shoot Errings* : **l¹**dol **F³**aiths/**F³**antasies *// Do Hurting! / Shoot The Dreamers* (1, 3, 5)

[14] Clean and Unclean Foods (1-21) : *Food Unpure/Purity* **l¹**mpure **M⁴**eats

Tithes (22-29) : *To The Store-house/To Storing every third year* : **l¹**evite **W⁴**ages

[15] **Sabbatical Year** : *Loose D[e]prived peoples (slaves, debtors)* : l[1]oose/l[1]ose S[5]laves *(persons)* and l[1]oose/l[1]ose S[5]ureties *(debts)* / l[1]oan S[5]crapping

[16] **Three Food Feasts:** *Do Picnic-ings/Fixings/Mixings*

1. **Passover** (1-8) : *Food Afflictings (Bread of Affliction: 3)* : l[1]eaven b[6]anned

2. **Weeks** (9-12) : *New Sicklings/Pickings (Sickle: 9)* : l[1]ater b[6]lade

3. **Booths** (13-17) : *New Sicklings/Pickings* : l[1]ive-in b[6]ooths *in desert*

   Justice (18-20) : *Do Justice* : l[1]ay-off b[6]ribes

[17] **Forbidden Worship Forms** (1-7) : *Shoo Reverencing idols* : l[1]llegal T[7]eraphim *(idols)*

   Just Administration (8-20) : *Rules From Heaven* : l[1]eader L[7]aws

[18] **Levite Food Provision** (1-8) : *Food Slating for Levites* : l[1]evite B[8]read *Portions: First Fruits*

   Mediums (9-14) : *Ghoul Fakings* : l[1]ose B[8]lack-arts

   God to Raise Up New Prophet like Moses (15-22) : *To Raising up a prophet* (18) > l[1]ike B[8]rothers (15)

[19] **Refuge City Laws** (1-13) : *Roosts From Crime* : l[1]odging g[9]uarded

   Neighbors' Landmarks (14) : *Move The Line is forbidden* : l[1]andmark g[9]uard

OT   Deuteronomy   NT

[19] 2-3 Witnesses (15-21) : *Prove/"Truth" The Crime* : l^1egal q^9uery/P^9roof

[20] First Offer Peace to Enemy : *Truce To Foe / Truce Enemy* : T^2ruce O^0ffer

[21] Atonement for Unsolved Murders (1-9) : *Due To Blood* : n^2o l^1nformants

Marrying Captives (10-14) : *Do Unions* : n^2abbed/V^2ictim l^1adies

Firstborn Inherits 2x (15-17) : *Two Due One* : 2^2 l^1ots *(portions) to firstborn*

Stone Rebel Sons (10-21) : *Do/Due Rude Son* : T^2o l^1ob *stones* / n^2on-l^1isteners / V^2iolent l^1ads

Hangees Cursed (22-23) : *Doomed Noosed Ones* : T^2ree l^1ynchees

[22] Assorted Prohibitions (1-12) : *Deun'ts To Do* : n^2umerous "n^2ots" / V^2arious V^2iolations

Sex Offenses (13-30) : *Deun't Do Lude behaviors* : V^2irgin V^2iolations

[23] Assembly Exclusions (1-8) : *Groups To Keep* out : T^2o F^3orbid *entry*

Cleaning the Camp to be Holy (9-14) : *Due To Clean the camp* : T^2o F^3reshen / T^2o H^3oliness

Assorted Prohibitions 15-25) : *Deun't Duties* : V^2arious N^3ots/N^3orms

Deuteronomy

[24] Divorce (1-4) : *To Lose Your* wife **:** **2**nd **M**[4]arriage *to same wife prohibited if she has married another and divorced again*

War and Newlyweds (5) : *"News" To War? No!* **:** **n**[2]ewlywed **W**[4]aivers

Fathers Die for Sons? (16) : *Shoot Good For* bad? No! **:** **n**[2]o **E**[4]xchanges

No Clothing for Collateral (17) : *Dues To Force* payments **:** **n**[2]o **M**[4]antles

Hoarding (19-22) : *Rules To Hoard/Store* **:** **n**[2]o **M**[4]isers **/ n**[2]ourish **W**[4]idows

[25] Deceased Brother's Wife (5-10) : *Rule/Due To Wife* **:** **T**[2]ake **S**[5]pouse!

Fair/Just Measures (13-16) : *Do True Size / Rules To Size* **:** **T**[2]rue **S**[5]tandards

[26] First Fruits / Tithes to Levites : *Due Fruit/Food Picks* **:** **n**[2]umber-one**/T**[2]op **b**[6]erries *go to Levites*

[27] Curses on Evils : *Dooms To Several* **:** **T**[2]ransgression **L**[7]ashings

[28] Covenant Blessings/Curses: *Dues To Take* **:** **T**[2]reaty **B**[8]lessings**/B**[8]anes

[29] Covenant Renewed : *Do New Bind / Two To Bind* **:** **T**[2]reaty **P**[9]rolonged

[30] Restoration (1-10) : *"Newed" Slurry/Dirty* **:** **F**[3]orgive**/F**[3]ix **O**[0]ffenders

OT   Deuteronomy   NT

[31] **Choose Life, not Death** (11-20) **:** *Choose: Freed[o]m/Devote* **: F**^{3}reedom **O**^{0}ptions **/ F**^{3}uture**/H**^{3}ealth **O**^{0}ptions

Historical Wrap-up

[31] **Moses Commissions Joshua to Lead:** *Choose/Rules the Nun* **: N**^{3}un **l**^{1}eads!

[32] **Moses' Victory Song :** *Do/Tune Review* **: Y**^{3}ahweh's **V**^{2}ictories!

[33] **Moses Blesses Israel :** *Good He Speaks* **: F**^{3}avors**/H**^{3}onors **N**^{3}ation

[34] **Moses Mourned :** *Do Thirty Mourn days!* **: m**^{3}ourn **M**^{4}oses **/ 3**^{3}0 **M**^{4}ourn *days* **/ F**^{3}arewell **M**^{4}oses!

<u>OT</u>   Joshua   <u>NT</u>
[Josh]

Conquering and Settling Canaan

[01] Joshua Leads: *Joshua Runs* the nation **:** J^{1}oshua/l^{1}eader

[02] Rahab Hides Spies in Jericho : *Joshua's Roof* spies **:** V^{2}eiled

[03] Joshua Crosses Jordan : *Joshua Streams* across Jordan River **:** F^{3}ords *it*

[04] Joshua's 12 me<u>mor</u>ial stones : *Joshua Memor*ial stones **:** M^{4}emorial *stones*

[05] Circumcising New Generation (1-9) **:** *Joshua Knifes* the kids **:** S^{5}kin/S^{5}nip

Commander of the Lord's Army (13-15) **:** *Joshua's Guide* **:** S^{5}pirit *(angel)*

[06] Jericho : *Joshua Rips* through walls **:** b^{6}urst/b^{6}reak/b^{6}ust

[07] Ai Setback (1-9) : *Joshua's Severe* loss at Ai (yi-yi)! **:** L^{7}oss

Joshua punishes Achan (10-26) **:** *Joshua Severs* him (cuts him off) from the people **:** L^{7}ooted *banned goods*

[08] Ai Victory (1-29) **:** *Joshua Raids/Takes Ai* (Ay) **:** B^{8}eats *them*

Renews Covenant (30-35) **:** *Josh States* the Covenant **:** B^{8}ook *of the Law*

[09] Gibeonites Punished : *Joshua Binds* them to be permanent Woodcutters because they lied to the people of God (**Fib**eonites really!) **:** g^{9}ibeonites

OT   Joshua   NT

[10] **Sun Stands Still** (1-28) : ***Joshua Ends*** *sun's motion to defeat 5 Amorite kings* : l^{1}ight O^{0}verhead **/** l^{1}ords O^{0}verthrown

[11] **Joshua Takes Northern Canaan** : ***Joshua Levels*** Canaan > : *now* l^{1}srael's l^{1}and

[12] **Conquests: 31** : ***Joshua Fells*** *31 kings* : l^{1}and T^{2}aken**/**n^{2}abs**/** V^{2}ictories **// *Joshua's Twelve*** *tribes now ready to settle* : **12^{12}**

Land Distribution and Settlements

[13] **East of the Jordan River** : ***Joshua Turning*** *land over to 12 tribes* : l^{1}and H^{3}andouts **// *Joshua "Dirting"*** *("land"ing people)*

[14] **West of Jordan River** : ***Joshua Portioning*** *lands* : J^{1}ordan's W^{4}est **// J**^{1}oshua M^{4}eting *out land including*

Hebron to Caleb *because he was the one spy who did not make the people's hearts melt at the sight of the Anakim (giants)* : l^{1}ord's W^{4}arrior (11); l^{1}and A^{4}nakim

For now ***Joshua Shuns*** *war* **/** *Land rests* ***From Warring*** : l^{1}ose W^{4}ar **/** l^{1}and E^{4}ase

[15] **Judah** : ***Joshua's Fittings*** > : J^{1}udah's**/**l^{1}and S^{5}ettlements

[16] **Ephraim** : ***Joshua's Sticking*** *Ephraim in the land* : l^{1}and's b^{6}oundaries **//** l^{1}ands: b^{6}ethel**/**b^{6}eth-horon**/**b^{6}ashan

[17] **Manasseh's Ten Portions** (5) : ***Joshua's Settling*** *Manasseh in the land* : l^{1}nherit's L^{7}and **//** l^{1}and T^{7}en *portions including* T^{7}appuah

[18] **Remaining Land** (1-10) ***Joshua's [E]statings*** : l^{1}and B^{8}roken *up***/**B^{8}orders

OT   Joshua   NT

[19] Inheritances for 5 tribes : *Joshua's Assignings* to 6 tribes— *Simeon*, *Zebulun*, *Issachar*, *Asher*, *Naphtali*, and *Dan* (**SiZ**es **IAND**) : **l^1**ands **g^9**ath-heffer, **g^9**reat *Sidon*, **g^9**ibbethon, **g^9**ath-rimmon

[20] Refuge Cities (6) : *Joshua's "Fuge Zones"/Many* Cities of *Refuge (6)* : **T^2**o **O^0**utrun *Avenger of Blood* **//** **T^2**emporary **O^0**ases *for killers*

[21] Levites : *Joshua Roots Monks* : Lev^{2}i^{1}tes **//** -**V^2**ite **T^2**ribe

[22] Reubenites : *Joshua Roots "Reubs* east of the Jordan* : Reuben^{2}i**T^2**es **//** -n^{2}ite **T^2**ribe

[23] Joshua Retires (1-5) : *Josh To Leave* his post : **T^2**o **F^3**orfeit *leadership* **/** **T^2**o **H^3**ang *it up!*

Joshua Charges Leaders to be Firm (6-16) : *Joshua Schools Team* : **T^2**eaches **F^3**irmness

[24] Covenant Renewed at Shechem (1-13) : *Joshua To Forge* new commitment **/** *Joshua To Force* Covenant

T^{2}o **M^4**ake *new commitment* **T^2**o **A^4**brahamic *Covenant*

Choose Whom You will Serve! (14-28) : *Joshua: "Choose Lord!"* **//** "**T^2**ake **E^4**lohim**/M^4**oses' *God!"* **//** **V^2**ote **W^4**hom *you will!*

Israel Mourns Joshua (29-33) : *Joshua, To Mourn* : **T^2**o **M^4**ourn *Joshua*

OT   Judges   NT
[*uh* *ud* *uch*; capital "Judge" is the Lord]

[01] Israel's Military Victories : *Bludgeoned "Guns"* : "I¹icked" *enemies, not all*

[02] Disobedient so Partial Deliverance (1-15) : *Judged Few Enemies, so the rest will be >* : "T²horns *in your sides*" (3)

God Appoints Judges (16-23) : *Judges Rule* : V²aluators/ T²rial *judges*

[03] God Tests Israel with Remaining Enemies : *The Judge Leaves* 5 *Philistine lords among Canaanites, Sidonians, and Hivites to test Israel's loyalty* (3)

Three Notable Judges [Your H³onors] : *Judges Three* : "Your H³onors": OtH³niel, EH³ud, Sha**m³**gar *Free Israel respectively from* **m³**esopotamia, **m³**oab, *and* PH³ilistia

[04] Deborah and Barak fight Sisera/Canaanites : *Judge De**bor**ah and Judge B[a]rak* : W⁴ar *against* // W⁴icked // DE⁴borah// // SisE⁴ra

JA⁴el Pegs SisE⁴ra : *Studs/Plugs Toward ground with tent peg* : A⁴ttaches *to ground*

[05] Deborah's Victory Song : *The Judge's Fights on behalf of His people* : S⁵ong / S⁵alute: *God's* S⁵uperlative *faithfulness from* S⁵eir/S⁵inai *to* S⁵isera

[06] Midian Oppresses Israel (1-7) : *Judge Mids oppress* Israel : **b⁶**ullies *Israel who hides in caves* (**b⁶**ear-dens *are their* **b⁶**urdens) // Mi**d⁶**ia

Gideon Called to Save Them (11-27) : *Judge Gideon to save them* : **G⁶**ideon. *This Judge Kicks* **b⁶**aal *out of Israel*

OT   Judges   NT

[06] Gideon's Fleece : *Judge Gid / Judge's Kid/Knits/Skins* **:**
b⁶lanket *to check that* **The Judge is** *behind his next battle*

[07] God: "Reduce the Size of Your Army!" (1-18) **:** *Nudges*
Several *out* **:** **L⁷**essens *it to 300*

Gideon Defeats Midian (19-25) **:** *Judge Severs* *threat* **:**
L⁷ord's *sword* (20)

[08] Gideon Kills Kings Zebah and Zalmunna (1-21) **:** *Judge*
Slays *two kings* **:** **b⁶**uries *them*

Israel Tells Gideon to Rule (22-28) **:** *"Judge, Rule* *us!"* (22) **:**
B⁸e *over us!*

Gideon Makes Ephod (22-28)**:** *Judge Makes/Plate* **:**
B⁸reastplate—*cover, becomes snare [***B⁸***ait] to the people*

Gideon Dies (29-32) **:** *Judge Fate* **:** **B⁸**reathes *his last* **/** **B⁸**uried

People Return to Baal (33-35) **:** *Clutches Baal* **:** **B⁸**aal *[is]*
B⁸ack

[09] Abimelech Kills 70 brothers (1-6) **:** *Grudge Crime* **:**
g⁹rudge: *"I rule over you better than 70!"* (2)

Jotham's Curse (7-21) **:** *"Judge Crime!"* **:** **g⁹**rill *Shechem and*
Abimelech

Woman Kills Abimelech (22-57) **:** *Judge Crime* **:** **g⁹**rinding-
stone **/** **g⁹**al **//** **g⁹**aal *from Shechem first entices him to war*

[10] Israel Returns to Idolatry (6-18) **:** *"Crutchin" / "Clutchin"*
again idols **//** *The* **Judge Ends** *prosperity* **:** **I¹**dols **O⁰**wned >
I¹srael **O⁰**verthrown **:** *Philistines afflict them18 years after they*
serve 7 gods from the nations around them

[11] Jephthah (1-28) : *Judge Jelephthah :* the Gill**11**eadite *(<msp)* // l**1**iberates l**1**srael

Jephthah's Foolish Vow (29-40): *Judge Pledgin to sacrifice first thing to enter door:* J**1**ephthah l**1**aments *but carries it out*

[12] Jephthah Beats Ephraim : *Judge Jelphthah (<msp) :* l**1**srael's T**2**wo/T**2**ribes *battle.* The Gileadites' l**1**etter-T**2**est *fugitives— the first "***h***" in* Shibbol**1**eT**2**h

[13] Samson Born : *Judge Conceived :* l**1**ad N**3**azirite *from birth—* l**1**eave H**3**air *alone! This* **Judge Stirring** *up the Philistines*

[14] Samson Marries (1-4) : *Judge Courting Delilah /* ***Judge Forming/Forging*** *contract with Delilah :* DelilA**14**h / l**1**ady M**4**arries

Sampson Kills a Lion (5-9) : *Judge Goring it!* (6) **:** l**1**ion M**4**auled

The Riddle (10-20) : *Judge Sporting :* l**1**ion M**4**ystery

[15] Samson Jawbones Philistines : *Judge Biffing City of Lehi :* l**1**ehi S**5**laughter / J**1**awbone S**5**lashes

[16] Delilah Betrays Samson (1-22) : *Grudge Snitchings* **:** "l**1**ong b**6**raids *will weaken him!"*

Samson's Vengeance (23-31) : *Judges Philistines :* l**1**oosens b**6**races *of their temple* (29) / l**1**ords b**6**eaten *down* (30)

[17] Micah's Levite and Idol : *Clutches A Graven idol :* and a l**1**iquid-silver **L**7ikeness *(molten image) of something* (3-5) *but later hires a* l**1**ive-in-**L**7evite *priest* (10-12) *believing the* **Judge From Heaven** *will prosper him* (13)

OT   Judges   NT

[18] Dan Attacks Laish : *Bludgeonings : "Laishings"* **:** l[1]aish B[8]eating—*Dan* **Clutches The Graved** *idol of Micah and takes away his priest*

[19] Levite's Concubine (1-21) **:** *Thugs Malign a Levite's concubine* l[1]evite's g[9]irl **//** l[1]n g[9]ibeah. *After she dies the Levite* l[1]acerates g[9]irl *into 12 pieces and sends them to the 12 tribes*

[20] Civil War : *Israel* **Punishes/Judges/Bludgeons Benjy** *for this ruthless sin* **:** T[2]ribe O[0]bliterated? *21:6 and 15 say "Yes!"*

[21] Benjamin's New Wives : *Much New Mums* **:** n[2]ew l[1]adies *needed*

OT   Ruth   NT

A Short Story of Redemption

[01] **Ruth Bonds with Naomi : *Ruth Clung* to Naomi / *Ruth One*** *with her* (14) **:** I¹inks **/** *"Where you* I¹*odge, I'll lodge"*

[02] **Ruth Gleans Boaz' Field : *Ruth's Food**—gleanings* **:** T²idbits

[03] **Ruth Sheltered by Boaz : *Ruth Sleeps* at Boaz' F³eet //** N³aps**/**F³orty-**/**ω³inks

He Promises to Redeem Her : *Ruth F³ree* from her *poverty*

[04] **He Redeems Her : *Ruth Poor* no more : *Ruth Moored* to debt** *no more* **:** M⁴anumits**/**E⁴mancipates *her*

He Marries Her (13-17) **: *Ruth Swore** "to death do us part"* **: *Ruth Moored* to Boaz :** M⁴arried**/**W⁴ed

David's Genealogy (18-22) **: *Youth Born* to Perez :** A⁴ncestry

OT   1 Samuel   NT
[*am* *an*]

[01] Samuel Born (1-20) : *Hannah's **Son/Handsome*** : I^{1}nfant

Vowed to Lord (21-28) : ***Sam One*** *with Lord* : I^{1}ord's **/** I^{1}ad

[02] Hanna's Praise Song (1-11) : ***Han's Tunes*** : V^{2}ocal/V^{2}oices *praise* **//** T^{2}outs**/**V^{2}aunts**/**T^{2}hanks *God*

Eli's Bad Sons *gorge themselves* (1-26) : ***Lamb Stew/Scandals Too*** *(women)* all *for themselves* : **V^2**ulgar, **n^2**o-good

Lord Rejects Eli and kills his sons (27-36) : ***Tramples Two*** *sons on same day* : **T^2**oppled *(Hophni and Phineas)*

[03] God Calls Samuel 3x : ***"Samuel!" Three*** *times* : **3^3**-time *call*

[04] Philistines Capture Ark (1-11) : ***"Hand [A]rk*** *over!"* : **A^4**rk**/** **W^4**ooden *chest*

Eli Dies (12-22) : ***Man Corpse*** : **E^4**li **/** E^{4}xpires **/** M^{4}ortal

[05] Ark Plagues Philistines with Tumors : ***Hand Hives*** : **S^5**ores

[06] Tortured Philistines Return Ark > : ***Mangles Phlists*** *so badly they send it* **>** : **b^6**ack *to Israel*

[07] Samuel Judges Israel : ***Samuel Savin*** *Israel from enemies* : **J^7**udging *enemies*

[08] Israel Craves a King (1-9) : ***Clans Crave*** : **B^8**eg *for king!*

Samuel Warns (10-18) : ***Samuel Hates*** *idea of king* **/** *He'll* ***Trample Slaves*** : **"B^8**ully *you he will! Take your things!"*

Lord Gives Israel a King (19-22) : ***"Samuel Makes*** *one for them!"* (22) : <u>to</u> **"B^8**e *like other nations!"* (20)

OT   1 Samuel   NT

[09] Saul Chosen King : *Samuel Finds* him : **P⁹**rince (16) of Israel
// Clan's Crime is *"rejecting Me as their King!"*

[10] Samuel Anoints Saul : *Samuel Scents* him : **lo¹⁰**tion

[11] Saul Saves Gilead from Ammonites : *Ammon Leveled :*
Gil¹¹ead (or msp > **Gill¹¹ead**) *rescued from Nahash's threats
to gouge out their eyes*

[12] Samuel Retires: *Samuel Shelves* himself : **I¹**eader **V²**acates

Recounts Israel's History : *Samuel Tells* their history :
I¹srael's **n²**arrative/**T²**raditions

Tells People to *"Stand Selves* for the Lord!" (7, 16) : **I¹**isten
V²oice *of the Lord* (14)

[13] Saul Fights Philistines (1-7) : *Tramples -Stines (or singular
like "Frankensteen")* : **-I¹**istines **F³**ight

Saul's Illegal Burnt Offering (8-22) : *Lamb/Mammal
Burning illegally* : **I¹**llegal **F³**ire/**K³**illing

[14] Jonathan's Wars (1-23) : *Jonathan's Warring* : **I¹-M⁴**an/
W⁴ar : *Jonathan and his armor carrier attack Philistines*

Saul's Immoral Vow (24-46) : *Man "Sworing"/***I¹**mmoral
E⁴dict/ **W⁴**ish : *"Curse man who eats before my vengeance."*

[15] Samuel Dethrones Saul (1-34) : *Samuel Deprives Saul of his
kingdom // Samuel Lifting Saul off throne* : **I¹**oses **S⁵**eat /
I¹oses **S⁵**pirit *of God too*

Samuel Hacks Agag into Pieces (32-35) : *Samuel Deprives
Agag of life / "Samuel The Knife"* : **I¹**imbs **S⁵**lashed

OT   1 Samuel   NT

[16] Samuel Grieving over Saul (1-5) : *Samuel's Afflicting* :
I^{1}asting **G**^{6}rief (1)

Samuel Anoints David (6-13) : *Samuel's Slicking* new king :
I^{1}avers/I^{1}otions **d**^{6}avid *with oil*

Saul Tormented by Evil Spirit David Relieves him (14-23) :
Man's Afflicting from "evil spirit from God" : I^{1}asting **G**^{6}rief

[17] Goliath Taunts Israel (1-11) : *Rants On Heaven* : I^{1}ampoons
L^{7}ord **/** I^{1}ord **T**^{7}aunts

David Beheads Him (12-58) : *Man Severing* head with sword
after > : I^1 **L**^{7}ob *from his slingshot*

[18] Jonathan and David's Love (1-5 : *Man "Mateys"* (Mates)
: I^{1}oving **B**^{8}rothers

Saul's Jealousy (6-16) : *Man Craving* David's superior skills
: I^{1}oftier **B**^{8}attles

Man's Ragings from his I^{1}ncorporeal **B**^{8}ad spirit causes him to
try *Man-Staking* : I^{1}obs **B**^{8}arb (11); *fortunately, he misses*

David Marries Michal (17-30) : *Ma'am Craving* David—Saul's
daughter : I^{1}ntriguing **B**^{8}ride

[19] Saul Plans to Find/Kill David (1-22) : *Plans Finding/Grinding*
David : "I^1'll **g**^{9}ore/**g**^{9}rind him!"

Saul Prophesies by Hand to Sam (23-24) : *Man "Signing"* to
people : Saul^1 **P**^{9}rophesies : "I^{1}s **P**^{9}rophet?" (24)

[20] Jonathan Vows to Protect David : *Plan New Oath* : **V**^{2}**O**^{0}w
/ n^{2}ew **O**^{0}ath based on **T**^{2}hree **O**^{0}vershot arrows (22)

OT   1 Samuel   NT

[21] **David Flees to Nob** (1) : *Camels To Nob* : n²ob I¹am/I¹and

He and his men **Eat the Bread of the Presence** (2-9) : *Sample Two Buns / Banned To Some* (5) : **T²**abernacle **l¹**oaf

David Fakes Insanity to King Achish at Gath (10-15): *Rambles to one / Man To Dumb* down : **V²**eiled **l¹**nsanity

[22] **Saul Slashes Priests at Nob (6-23)** : *Plans To Hew* them, *thinking* they will ***Am-b[u]sh To*** kill him (8) : **n²**ob **V²**aticide

[23] **David Flees To Keilah** (1-12) : *Scrambles To Keilah / To "Keil"* *Philistines :* **T²**o **K³**eilah—**T²**o "**K³**eil" *Philistines*

David Flees To Ziph (13-29) : *Scrambles To Zeeph* (13-29) > : **T²**o **Z³**iph *where Saul sends men **To Seek*** (25)/***Seize*** (26) him

[24] **David Spares Saul #1** : *"Lance To Lord's* Anointed? No!" : "**T²**ouch **A⁴**nointed? No!" but ***Man's Suit Torn!***—**T²**ore **E⁴**dge *(5) off robe to prove to Saul he "had a shot"!*

[25] **Samuel Dies** (1) : *Samuel To Die; Samuel Lose Life* today : **n²**o **S⁵**amuel

Abigail Saves Worthless Husband Nabal (1-43) : *N[a]bal To Die / David **Grants to Wife*** Abigail his life : **n²**abal's **S⁵**aved

David Marries Abigail : *Plans To "Wife"* Abigail : n²ew **S⁵**pouse. *This **Man's Two Wives*** listed in vv. 43 and 27:3

[26] **David Spares Saul #2** : *Second **Chance To Stick*** Saul : 2²ⁿᵈ **b⁶**reak; *takes Saul's jug and spear—**V²**essel [and] **b⁶**ayonet to prove "2ⁿᵈ shot at" him*

[27] **David Flees Back to Gath** : *Scrambles To Savin* his neck again : **T²**o **L⁷**and *of Philistines*

[28] **Loots Negev** (10) : *Camels To Negev / Man Loots Neg* : n^{2}egev l^{1}ooted

Samuel "Fates" Saul through Medium : *Samuel To Fate* *Saul >* : "T^{2}omorrow B^{8}e *with me," he says, "you and your sons"* (***Samuel's Spook/Ghoul To Fate****? (Usually malevolent spirits)*

[29] **Philistines Reject David's Marching with Them Against Israel** : *"Man To Hind of us!" / "Man To Line's end!"* : T^{2}rustless P^{9}hilistines/g^{9}athians (Gath)

[30] **Amalekites Capture David's Wives (1-15)** : *Amalekite's Herding Dave's wives* : ω^{3}ives O^{0}f *David* / F^{3}emales O^{0}btained / ω^{3}ives O^{0}vertaken/O^{0}verpowered

David Beats Ziklag/Amalekites (16-30) : *Amalekites He Smote / Am's Hurting* : Z^{3}iklag/-K^{3}ites O^{0}verthrown/Am^{3}s O^{0}verthrown

[31] **Defeated Saul Asks Armor-bearer to Stab Him** : *"Lance Me, Son!"* : *He refuses* "N^{2}o l^{1}ance, *sir!*"

Saul Falls on His Sword (4) : *Lance He Runs through himself* / F^{3}alls *[on]* l^{1}ance

OT   2 Samuel   NT
[oo + am or an]

Civil War

[01] **David Laments Saul's Death** : *To Lament One* : l¹ament

[02] **Kingdom Conflict** (1-7) : *To Champion Two to be king* / *Two-Clan Feud* starts // *Two Champs To* rule > Judah crowns David, Abner crowns Ishbosheth, Saul's son : **T²**ribal *feud*

[03] **Abner Makes Peace with David** (1-25) : *Two-man Peace* : **Y³**oked // but the *Two-Clan Siege* continues : **K³**illing

  Joab Stabs Abner (26-39) : *To Stab/Trample Chief* : **K³**ills/**H³**omicide

[04] **Two Men Murder IshboshE⁴th** : *Two-Man Sword* : **M⁴**urder

[05] **David Anointed King/Shepherd** > *To Lamb Drive* his people (1-24) : **S⁵**hepherd *[his]* **S⁵**heep (2)

  To Trample -St[i]nes (17-25) : **S⁵**lays/**S⁵**trikes/-**S⁵**tines

[06] **David Moves Ark to City** (1-4) : *To Plan Ship* of Ark to Jerusalem : **b⁶**ring to city from **b⁶**aale-judah (2)

  Uzzah Touches it and Dies (5-15) : *To Handle/Angle it* : **b⁶**udged it / **d⁶**ied

  David Dances; Michal Despises (16-23) : *To Dance Jig/To "Wrangle" Mich* who considers this a *Lewd-Dance Jig* : **b⁶**elittles/**d⁶**espises David

[07] **God Promises David his Son will Build God's House** (1-17: *To Plant/Camp Heaven* in a permanent house on earth : **T⁷**abernacle/**L⁷**ord's dwelling // *To Plant Ever* David's family *[To "Fam" Ever]* on the > **T⁷**hrone

OT   2 Samuel   NT

[07] David Praises/Thanks/ God (18-29) **: *To Thank Heaven*** *for this* **: L⁷**auds**/T⁷**hanks *Lord*

[08] David's Victories (1-14) **: *Troops Trample/Trammel/Mangle "Greats"*** *all around Israel* **: B⁸**attles *won*

Appoints Staff (15-18) **: *Hu-man Aids / To "Man"*** *[his]* ***Aids*** **: B⁸**ureacrats**/ B⁸**rass

[09] David Looks for Men from Saul's Family > ***To Man Find Act"*** (9) **:** *Saul's* **g⁹**randson**/**Me**p⁹**hibosheth > *restores land to him and lets him eat at his table*

[10] David Slays Ammonites/Aramites : *Slew Ams'/Rams' Men* **: I¹**srael **O⁰**ver-powers *Ammon and Aram*

[11] David and Bathsheba : *Roof-Man Lovin* **: I¹**ust **I¹**ures ***To Scandal-Lovin***

[12] Nathan Confronts David (1-15) **: *"You-man!" Tell // You "Lambed" Self*** *with another's lamb* **: I¹**amb **n²**abbed

David/Bathsheba Baby Dies (15-23) **: *New Man Felled*** *by God* **: I¹**nfant **T²**erminated (14, 15)

Solomon Born/Vowed to God (24-15) **: *New Man Held*** *by God* (24) **: I¹**nfant **V²**owed

Joab Takes Ammonite City of Rabbah (26-31) **: *Took Am****monite-****held*** *city* ***/***

Tooled "Ams" Held **: >** **I¹**mposed **T²**oil *(saws, picks, axes, kilns)* **/ I¹**abor **n²**on-union

[13] Amnon Rapes Tamar (1-22) **: *Lewd Am****non* ***Hurting*** *sister Tamar* **: I¹**ncest **F³**orced

OT   2 Samuel   NT

[13] Absalom Kills Amnon (23-33) : *To Amnon Murdering* :
I[1]ncester K[3]illed

[14] David Restricts Absalom (1-27) : *To Annual Scoring/
ig]noring* : I[1]gnores A[4]bsalom *two years* / I[1]imits A[4]bsalom's
movements

Absalom Burns Joab's Field (28-33) : *To Land Scorching* :
I[1]and A[4]rson

[15] Absalom's Revolt Conspiracy (1-11) : *To Plan/Gamble
Shifting* David's subjects' loyalty to himself (6) : I[1]nstalls S[5]pies
to blow trumpets and announce that he's king (10)

David to Flee (12-37) : *To Scramble Alive* : I[1]eaves S[5]alem,
the city of God

David *To Plant A Spy* in Jerusalem named Hushai ("Hush-
eye!") : I[1] S[5]py *in Jerusalem*

**[16] Mephibosheth's Servant Ziba Gives David Donkeys, Food
and Wine** (1-4) : *Two Mammals From Zib / To Plan Fixing
David up with provisions* : I[1]oads-up d[6]avid

Shimei Curses/Stones David (5-14) : *To Land/Scramble
Some Bricks* on him : I[1]aunches b[6]ad *words too!*

[17] Two Plans: Hushai's *To Plan A Saving*—David; and Ahithophel
To Plan A Severin—David's head : I[1]nitiatives T[7]wo /
AhI[1]T[7]hophel

When his Plan Fails, Ahithophel Hangs Himself : *Doomed
/Cruel Man Severing* Head : I[1]oser L[7]ynches *himself* (23)

[18] J[1]oaB[8] Plans to Kill Absalom (1-18) : *To Plan Slaying
Absalom* : J[1]oab B[8]arbs *(javelins) him* / -I[1]om B[8]arbed

OT 2 Samuel NT

[18] **David Grieves his Son Absalom** (19-33) : *To Sample Aching* (33) : l¹aments B⁸oy

[19] **Joab Criticizes David** (1-8) : *Too-Ample Whining* demoralizes troops : -l¹om g⁹rieved / J¹oab B⁸erates/B⁸lames *David*

David Returns to Jerusalem (8-43) : *To HomeLand Timing* : J¹erusalem g⁹o-back

[20] **Sheba Plans to Overthrow 10 Tribes** : *To Trample Many* tribes : V²entures O⁰verthrow

Abel Inhabitants Toss Sheba's Head to Joab: *To Plan To Throw* his head over the wall of the City : T²oss O⁰ver

[21] **The 3-year Famine is Due to Saul's >** : *Cruel Plan To Gun/ Run* the Gibeonites out of their land : V²acate l¹and

David Turns Seven of Saul's Descendants Over to the Gibeonites > : *To Plan Noosed Sons* : n²oose l¹ads!—T²oken/ T²ribal l¹ynching / T²urn l¹ads *over*

[22] **David Sings Praises God for Deliverance from Enemies** : *To Chant New Tune* : n²ew n²umber

[23] **List of David's Soldier-Heroes** : *Troop Champs To Read* about : n²oteworthy H³eroes / V²alor H³onored

[24] **David's Evil Census** : *To Plan To Score/Sort* people by nation-soldiers (Israel: 800,000; Judah: 500,000: 9) : n²umber M⁴en / W⁴arriors. *Prophet Gad tells David he can choose one of three judgments from God:*

T²o M⁴alnutrition *(3-year famine)*
T²o M⁴auling by *enemies (3-month chase)*
T²o M⁴alaria *(3-day pestilence)*

<u>OT</u>   **1 Kings**   <u>NT</u>
[*ing*]

Solomon's Kingdom

[01] **Civil War :** *Kings Drum* up war*/King's* David's **Sons** >
: **Sol¹omon** *and* **Adoni¹jah/l¹**ock *horns*

*Joab and Abiathar support Adonijah but Nathan and
Bathsheba make sure David has Solomon anointed by
Zadok. Adonijah flees to the temple to take hold of the
horns of the altar for mercy. Solomon lets him l¹ive.*

[02] **David Instructs Solomon** (1-9) : *King Clues/Cues/Tutors
Son*: **T²**eaches **/ T²**utors

Solomon Slays David's Enemies : *King Slew* enemies > :
n²emeses *Joab and Shimei*

[03] **Solomon Prays for Wisdom :** *King Seeks* wisdom :
ω³isdom/**K³**nowledge *to govern God's people*

[04] **Solomon Forms His Court** (1-19) : *King's Court* > :
M⁴agistrates/**A⁴**uthorities

Solomon's Wealth and Wisdom (20-34) : *King's Ore (gold) /
Hoard / Lore* : **W⁴**ealth **/ W⁴**isdom

[05] **Solomon Orders Materials for Temple** (1-12) : *King Hires/
King Hir*am *to supply cedar and cypress for temple*

Imposes labor (13-18) : *King Drives* many > : **S⁵**laves *to build*

[06] **Solomon Builds Temple :** *King Fits* stones together from a
quarry (7) > : **b⁶**ricks **/ b⁶**uilding

[07] **Solomon Builds/Furnishes Palace :** *King's Heaven*ly
House : **L⁷**avish **/ L⁷**odge

OT   1 Kings   NT

[08] Solomon Takes Ark to Temple (1-11) : *King Takes* ark to temple : **B⁸**ox to **B⁸**uilding

Solomon Blesses Lord (12-21) : *King's Praise* to God : **B⁸**lessing

King Prays (22-53) *for the new Temple* : **B⁸**lesses/**B⁸**uilding

King Prays (54-61) *for the congregation* : **B⁸**enediction/**B⁸**lessing

King Slays (62-66) *animals for sacrifice* : **B⁸**urnt/**B⁸**arley *[grain] offerings*

[09] Lord Appears to Solomon (1-9) *The **KING Finds** the new king* : **g⁹**lory

Solomon's Enslaves Gentiles to Build Temple and Ships (10-28) : *King Binds* > : **g⁹**entiles *to build temple and a fleet of* **g⁹**alleys

[10] Queen of Sheba Visits : *Brings Gems* to add to *King's Gems* : **l¹**eaves **O⁰**pals/**O⁰**nyx maybe? *"Opal" may be derived from Sanskrit upala meaning "precious stone"* // *King Spends* a lot on **l¹**uxurious **O⁰**pulence

Kingdom Dividing

[11] Solomon's Idolatry (1-8) : *King [God] Left In* space in temple for idols of his foreign wives **l¹**dol **l¹**overs

Adversaries (9-43) : *Kingdom Levelers* : cha**ll¹¹**engers (Hadad, Rezon, Jeroboam

*Ah**ij¹¹**ah predicts **King**dom **Left In** two pieces* : **l¹**eft **l¹**n two

OT   1 Kings   NT

[12] Rehoboam Toughens his Father's Policies (1-15) : *"King's Belt will be tightened!"* (10-11) : **I¹**ntensifies **T²**oil/**T²**asks / **I¹**abor **T²**oughened

Israel Splits in Two (16-24) : *King[dom]* **Felled** : **I¹**srael **T²**orn—***Rehoboam*** *gets two tribes in the south,* ***Jeroboam*** *ten in the north*

Jeroboam's Golden Calves (25-33) : ***King Melts*** *gold to make idols*: **I¹**dols **T²**hermoformed. *He also establishes non-Levite priests and feasts* : **I¹**evite-**n²**ot *priests and feasts*

[13] Man of God Prophesies that Josiah will Sacrifice Priests on Jeroboam's Altar (1-3) : ***King Burning*** *priests* : **I¹**eaders **F³**ried

Jeroboam Attacks but Hand Dries Up (4-10) : ***King's Hurting*** *but the prophet heals his >* : **I¹**anguished **H³**and

Old Prophet Tells Man of God (11-23) > *"****Bring Thirsting-****hungering man of God to your house to drink and eat" (a lie)* : **I¹**ying **F³**atiloquent/**F²**orecaster

Lion Kills Man of God for Disavowal (24-34) : ***King Purring*** *(king of the beasts)* : **I¹**ion **K³**ills *him*

[14] Prophet Ahijah Tells Jeroboam's Wife Her Husband's (1-18) > : ***Kingdom Torn*** *away due to >* : **I¹**dols: **M⁴**etal *images* (9)

Jeroboam Dies (19-20) : ***King "Morting"*** : **J¹**eroboam *[is]* **M⁴**ort *(French)*

Rehoboam in Jerusalem—

   Idol Worship (1-24) : ***King Forming*** *idols* : **I¹**dol **W⁴**orship

1 Kings

[14] **Rehoboam in Jerusalem**—

Egyptian King Shi¹shA⁴k Raids Temple (25-32) : *King Storming* Temple : I¹nvades A⁴bode *of Lord*

Rehoboam Fights Jeroboam Continually (29:30) : *Kings Warring* continually (29-30) : J¹eroboam's W⁴ars

[15] **Abijah ["Bye Yah!"] Rules Judah** (1-8) : *King Abijah / King Drifting* toward idolatry : I¹dol S⁵ins *of his father* (3)

Asa (Grace-a) Rules Judah (924) : *King Shifting Judah toward good* : J¹udah S⁵hifts *to the Lord*

Nadab (Nabad) and **Baasha (Bash Ya) Take Israel Against Judah** (25-34) : *Kings Lifting* swords against *Asa* "all their days" (32) : I¹dol S⁵ins *of fathers*

[16] **Baasha Bashes Israel** (1-7) > : *King Afflicting* Israel : I¹srael b⁶ash *// then a series of bad kings* (8-34) : **Elah** (Cruelah), **Zimri** (Flinty; Whimsy), **Omri** (Ornery), *and* **Ahab** (A bad)

[17] **God Feeds Elijah** (1-7) > : *Things From Ravens* at Cherith and *Drinks From Heaven* at Cherith Brook (4) : I¹oaves/ L⁷amb (6) > *brook dries up under a 3-½ year drought in Israel* (7) : *Israel* I¹acks L⁷iquid

Zarephath Widow > Elijah

Multiplies Oil and Flour (8-16) : *Things From Heaven* : I¹ady Z⁷arephath

Raises Her son from Death (17-24) : *Springs From Heaven*—his Life "returns" when Elijah calls on God (21) : I¹ifts L⁷ad *from death*

[18] **OB⁸adi¹ah Hides (Oba-hide-a) Prophets** (1-19) : *Brings From Cave* 100 prophets : **l¹**ike **B⁸**ears *in hibernation*

Elijah Confronts Priests of Baal (20-40) : *"Bring The Baal!"* —*suggests he's sleeping or vacationing (27)* : **l¹**azy **B⁸**aal!

Elijah Prays and the Lord Sends Fire : *Brings Blazing* on *offering* (38) : **l¹**ord **B⁸**urns/**B⁸**lazes/**B⁸**ull (23). *False prophets executed*

Elijah Prays For Rain (41-46) *"Bring Raining!"* *and God does, ending The 3-½ year drought* : **l¹**ord **B⁸**athes *Israel*

[19] **Ahab and Jezebel Hunt Elijah** (1-8) : *King Finding Elijah* : **J¹**ezebel **g⁹**unning *for Elijah*

Elijah Hears Lord at Horeb (9-14) > : *The King's Divine "still small voice"* : **l¹**ow **g⁹**utterals?/**l¹**owing **g⁹**od?

God Tells Him to Anoint Kings (15-18) : *King Anointings/ Appointings to be done!* : **l¹**aver **g⁹**overnors: *Elijah anoints* k**l¹**n**g⁹**s *Hazael of Aram and Jehu of Israel* : **J¹**ehu **g⁹**reased

Elijah Cloaks Elisha (19-21) : *Thing [cloak] Binding him to service* : **l¹**ays **g⁹**arment *on him*

[20] **Syria's King Ben-hadad Threatens Ahab's Possessions** (1-12) : *"The King's 'Plenty' is mine!"* (3) : **T²**akes **O⁰**wnership

Ahab Defeats -Ha-Bad (13-25) : *King Empties his stuff / King Shoots Foe* : **V²**ictory **O⁰**ver *Syria*

Ben-hadad Rejects God's Sovereignty > (26-34) : *The King's Many Powers are "***n²**ot **O⁰**ver *valleys /* **V²**alleys **0⁰**, *just mountains." He's beaten again*

[20]   Prophet Condemns Ahab for Sparing -Ha-bad (35-43) **:**
*bad **King To Roam** free whom God had "devoted to destruction"*
(42) **: T^2**o **O^0**bliteration

[21] Ahab Takes Naboth's Vineyard : *King Loots One vineyard*
belonging to Naboth **: V^2**ineyard **l^1**ooting *of* **n^2**aboth's **l^1**awn

Ahab's Sons Doomed (29) **:** *King's Doomed Sons* **:**
T^{2}hreatened **l^1**ads *inherit father's "disaster"*

[22] Micaiah Predicts Ahab's Fall : *King's Doomed To be defeated*
by Aram and lose Ramoth-gilead.

King's Spooked To believe this won't happen by a lying spirit in
the mouth of his prophets. Micaiah alone tells him the truth **:**
T^{2}ruth **T^2**old *by one only*

Two New Kings Rule Judah and Israel : *Kings Two New* **:**
T^{2}wo **n^2**ew**: Jehoshaphat (good)** and **Ahaziah (bad)**

2 Kings
[*to* + *ing* or *oo*-ing]

[01] Elijah Indicts Ahaziah (1-8) : *Ruined Kingdom / To King: "Done!"* *Won't recover because you sought healing from Baal-zebub* : I^{1}ndicted *for* I^{1}dolatry

Elijah "Fires" 3 sets of 50 Soldiers (9-18) : *Cooking Guns* : I^{1}gnites *troops*

[02] Elijah Ascends to Heaven in a Chariot of Fire (1-14) : *"Hoofings" [horses]/Zooming To Heaven* : V^{2}ertical / T^{2}akeoff!

Elisha Asks Elijah for Double Spirit/Power : *"Boosting 2x* please!"* (9) : 2^{2}x

Elisha Curses Kids who Call Him "Baldy!" (23-25) : *Looking Smooth/Nude-headed!"* . . . *"He needs a Toupee!"* : T^{2}aunt/ T^{2}wo *Female Bears (not T^{2}eddies!) rip 42 of them to pieces*

[03] Israel/Jehoram Taxes Meesha/Moab's Fleece: *To King Meesha—"To Bring fleece"*: F^{3}leece H^{3}ikes/deF^{3}aults/ F^{3}ailures. *Time for* **Looting Meesha's/Fleece-a**

Elisha Predicts Valley Filled with Water without Rain (13-20) : *To Bring Teems of water* / *To bring Teams of thirsty horses drink* / *"Hoofings" Drink* : V^{3}alley filled / H^{3}orses *drink*

Moabite King's Foolish Plea to his god (21-27) : *Fool king's Plea* : F^{3}orfeits *son to win a battle* (27) /m^{3}oab / F^{3}ights, *Israel* ω^{3}ithdraws

[04] Elisha Produces Oil for Widow (1-7) : *Booking/Cooking Stores (inventory) for her / To Bring Poor help* : W^{4}idow/ W^{4}anting

Elisha Raises a Shunamite Widow's Son from Death (16-37) : *To Bring Corpse to life* : M^{4}obilized *him!*

OT   2 Kings   NT

[04] Elisha Purifies a Poisoned Stew (38-44) **:** *Stewing's Pure* **:**
A⁴rsenic *stew purified*

**[05] Elisha Tells Naaman to Dive into River Jordan to Cure
Leprosy** (1-14) **:** *Booking Dives* (7 *of them*) **: S⁵**oak **/ S⁵**kin

Elisha Catches Gehazi Demanding Money from Captain
(15-27) **:** *Looting/"Crooking" Life* **: S⁵**windler**/S²**neak-thief

Elisha Curses Gehazi with Life-long Leprosy (27) **:** *To Cling
Tight* to him and his descendants forever (27) **: S⁵**tick *to them*

[06] Elisha's Stick Toss to Recover an Ax Head (1-7) **:** *Looking/
Hooking Stick* to float it to surface **: b⁶**uoy *it*

Elisha's Chariots of Fire against the Arameans (1-17) **:**
Cooking Rigs/Ships **: b⁶**urning *rigs*

**Elisha Prays; Lord Blinds then Restores Sight to Aramean
Army** (18-23) **: "***Lookings" Nixed/Fixed* **: b⁶**linded**/b⁶**rought
*to Samaria***/b⁶**almed *(healed)***/**then **b⁶**anished *from Israel* (23)

**b⁶en-hadad b⁶esieges Samaria, Creates Famine: Children
Eaten** (24-33) **:** *Cooking Kids* **: b⁶**oys *eaten* (28-29)

[07] Elisha Promises Food Price Deflation (1-2) **:** *Cooking
Lessens* ($) **: L⁷**ess *shekels for flour, barley, cooking lessons.*

Lord Scares Aramaeans off with Horse/Chariot Sounds
(3-20) **:** *Hoofings Heavy* **: T⁷**remolos

[08] King Restores Shunammite Widow's Land (1-6) **:** *Good
King Takes* land **B⁸**ack *for her*

Hazael Murders Ben-hadad (7-15) **:** *Slew King Hadad* **: B⁸**en-
hadad *killed*

<u>**OT**</u>   **2 Kings**   <u>**NT**</u>

[08] Two Bad Kings in Judah (16-29) : *Two Kings Hate* God :
Jehoram a-whorin after other gods then **Ahaziah "Ah**
Hates Zion!" : **B**^{8}ad *kings worship* **/ B**^{8}aals

[09] Jehu Anointed King of Israel (1-13) : *JeHu/Good King Slimed*
*An*oin*ted with oil* : **g**^{9}reased *by a prophet Elisha sends; told to*
g^{9}ore *Ahab's house until it perishes* (7-8) (14-29)

JeHu King Finds and kills *Jehoram, Ahaziah, and Jezebel* :
g^{9}ores *both*

[10] Jehu Kills Ahab's Descendants (1-17) : *JeHu King Ends*
Ahab's line : **l**^{1}ine **O**^{0}verthrown.

Jehu Kills Baal Prophets (18-27) : *JeHu King Ends idolatry,*
Baal worship : **l**^{1}dols/**l**^{1}dolators **O**^{0}verthrown

Jehu Inconsistently Permits Golden Calves in Dan (28-31)
: *JeHu King Bends rules* : **l**^{1}dols **O**^{0}wned *in Dan*

The Lord Cuts Land Off from Israel (32-36) : *JeHu Kings'*
Fence (borders) smaller : **l**^{1}oses **O**^{0}utlands *to Hazael*

[11] Athaliah (Wrathaliah) Rules Judah, Kills Competitors (1-
3) : *Slew King's Young Sons* : **l**^{1}iquidates **l**^{1}nheritors

Joash Hidden (4-20) : *True King Livin in hiding* : **J**^{1}oash **l**^{1}ivin
in hiding **/ l**^{1}ivin **l**^{1}ncognito *6 years thanks to Jehosheba*

Joash Begins Rule (21) : *True King Elevated to rule Judah at*
7 : **J**^{1}oash **l**^{1}naugurated **/** Athal**l**^{11}iah *is* ki**ll**^{11}ed

[12] Joash Loots Temple to Make Repairs (1-16) : *Loot King*
Welds Temple : *Jo Cash* **l**^{1}oots **T**^{2}emple

Joash Buys off Hazael who Threatens Jerusalem (17-18) :

[12] *Loot King Sells* out to Hazael : l¹oots T²emple *(Jo Cash) again* —*sacred treasury items former kings had dedicated*

[13] Jehoahaz and Jehoash Hurt Israel (1-13) : *Two kings Hurting* Israel with idols : l¹srael H³urting / l¹dol H³urts : *JehoAdz* and *JehoAsh Bash* enemies

   Elisha's Bones Raise Man to Life (14-25) : *To Bring Stirring* to dead body : l¹ife-giving H³ipbone/F³emur (21) : *E-Life-a*

[14] Good King Amaziah Rules Judah but Loves War (1-22) : *Good King Warring* : l¹oves W⁴ar : *Amazing* warrior but sacrificed in high places and warred with Joash of Israel

   Jeroboam Restores Israel's Borders and Idolatry (23-29) : *Good King "Bordering"/ Restoring* borders but *Fool King Restoring* idols : l¹and M⁴ultiplied / l¹dols M⁴ultiplied

[15] Five Bad Kings Ruin Israel : *Doom/Fool Kings Shifting* Israel to idols / l¹dol-worshipping S⁵overeigns:

   Zechariah : *Wreckariah*
   Shallum : *Shall dump* God and babies (16)
   Menahem : *Mayhem*
   Pekahiah : *Pick-a-Fight-a*
   Pekah : *Peak of Evil*

   Two Good Kings Rule Judah : *Two kings Shifting Israel to God* : l¹ord-worshipping S⁵overeigns

   Azariah : *As a right as* you can get 'um
   Jotham : *Jobbed 'em* (got them jobs building upper gate: 35)

[16] Ahaz Rules Judah : *Jūd King/Fool King "Litting"/Whipping* son : *made his son pass through the fire* (3) : l¹ad b⁶urned : *A hazard* to Israel and his own family

OT # 2 Kings

[17] Hoshea (No-Shame-a) Takes Down Israel (1-23) : *Doomed King Severing Israel from land* : I^{1}srael T^{7}aken *to Assyria*

Assyrian King Shalmaneser (Shall Men Raise Their Idols? Yes!) Resettles Samaria (24-41) : *Doom King Settlin five new peoples in Samaria who bring seven gods with them* : I^{1}dols 7^7

[18] Hezekiah (He's a Kinda Guy!) Rules Judah (1-12) : *Good King Razing idols* : I^{1}dols B^{8}roken *to pieces* (4)

Assyrian King SennacherIB^{18} (Send a Syrian) Attacks Judah (13-28) : *Doom King Raiding Judah* : J^{1}udah B^{8}ash

Chief Officer Rabshakeh (Rob & Shake Ya) *says Lord sent us and you should trust no god of any nation* (29-35) : *Doom King berating Judah's God* : "I^{1}ord B^{8}id *us to do this!*" (27) *I* I^{1}dols B^{8}eaten *by us* (33-35)

[19] Hezekiah Trusts Isaiah's Prophecy : *Good King "Minding" his prophet* : I^{1}saiah P^{9}redicts */ I^{1}ord g^{9}uards city, sending an angel who strikes down 185,000 Assyrian soldiers (35)*

[20] Hezekiah Recovers from Disease (1-11) : *Good King's Many / Plenty years* (15) *more* : T^{2}o O^{0}ld *age*

Hezekiah Shows Off his Wealth to Babylonian Envoy (12-21) : *Good King's "Plenty" / Looking To Show off* : T^{2}oo O^{0}stentatious

[21] Manasseh (Manasty) of Judah Burns Son (1-9) : *Fool King Cooks Son* : T^{2}orches/T^{2}ortures I^{1}ad // V^{2}enerates I^{1}dols. *Son Amon same bahd-mahn Manasty is.*

[22] Josiah Rules Judah, Renews Temple: *Good King To "New" the temple* : n^{2}ew T^{2}emple. *Joe Sides With Yahweh, Joe Sides*

OT   2 Kings   NT

[22] *The temple, and **Joe Cites The** book of the Law Hilkiah fin*

[23] **Josiah's (Jo-Wise-a's) Reforms** (1-27) : *Good King To Lead* : n^2ew F^3orms.

Joe Dies-a at Megiddo in a Battle with Pharaoh Neco : *Good King To Cease in battle* : T^2o F^3ight/F^3ail/F^3ate / n^2eco K^3ills *him*

[24] **Jehoiakim and Jehoiachin Fight Nebuchadnezzar** (1-9) *Two Kings To War against Babylon* : n^2eb W^4ars *against—He Destroyed-Akim and Destroyed-Achin*

Jehoiachin and People Deported (10-17) : *Doomed King Too Forced to Babylon* : n^2eb E^4xiles/E^4xpels/E^4xports/E^4xtradites *Jehoiachin and others; only poor left in Jerusalem*

Zedekiah Rules Judah under Babylon but Rebels (18-20) : *Doomed King To Scorn Nebuchadnezzar (rebel)* : T^2o M^4utiny / "T^2raitor ZE^4d!"

[25] **Nebuchadnezzar Installs Two Puppet Rulers** : *Two Kings To Drive things for him in Jerusalem* : T^2wo S^5ock-puppets / n^2eb's S^5laves, *but Zedekiah and Gedaliah rebel*

Zedekiah *blinded (**Deadened Eye-a**) and* **Gedaliah** *killed (**Deadened Life-a**)*

1 Chronicles
[Recaps: Action Verbs]

Genealogies: 1—9

[01] **Adam to Israel** : *One > Son(s)* : 1^1 > I^{1}srael

[02] **Jacob's Sons to Saul** : *Jews > Rule* : T^{2}welve/T^{2}ribes > T^{2}hrone *(1st king)*

[03] **David** to **Captivity** : *King > King / Free > Flee* : K^{3}ingdom > K^{3}aptivity/N^{3}ebuchadnezzar

[04-08] **Twelve Tribes/Sons** : *Born > Jācob* : TW^{4}elve/M^{4}en B^{8}orn *[Chapters 4 + 8 = 12]*

[09] **Exiled Families Rebuild:** *Shrine rebuilders* : g^{9}o-backs

[10-13] **David Commands Army and Staff)** : *Men > Decrees* : I^{1}ssues O^{0}rders

Events: Saul to David

[10] **Saul's Line Overthrown** : *Ends* : I^{1}ine O^{0}verthrown *(sons)*

[11] **David Elevated / Lavered** (1-9) : *Elevated/Lavered king* : I^{1}avered I^{1}ord

   David's Leaders (10-46) : *Elevated* : I^{1}mpressive I^{1}eaders

[12] **David's Troops** : *The Troops* : I^{1}srael's T^{2}roops

[13] **Uzza Killed for Touching Ark** : *Burning anger of the Lord* : I^{1}ord K^{3}indled / I^{1}ocker K^{3}illing / I^{1}ost Uz^{3}za

[14] **David's Wives and Kids** (1-7) : *Sons More* : I^{1}ads/W^{4}ives

OT   1 Chronicles   NT

[14] David Wars with Philistines (8-17) : *David's **Warrings*** :
-l¹istine **W⁴**ars

[15] Levites Take Ark to Jerusalem : *Levite **Lifting/Trunk Drive*** :
l¹ocker **S⁵**hipped / l¹evites **S⁵**hip *it*

Michal Hates David's Dance (29) : ***Shifting / Despised*** :
l¹ndecent **S⁵**how?

[16] Praise Song for Ark's Return : *"Licks"ing* : l¹ocker **b⁶**ack!

[17] Solomon to Build Temple (1-15) : ***A Haven/Havening*** *for
God* : l¹ord's ***L*⁷**air

David's Prayer (16-27) : ***"From Heaven*** *rule!"* : l¹mperial
***L*⁷**ord

[18] David Attacks/Defeats Enemies : ***Raiding/Slaying/Fating***
bad guys : l¹icks **B⁸**ad *guys*

[19] Ammonites Shave David's Men / Cut Clothes (1-9) :
*Ma**ligning*** : l¹acerate **g⁹**arments

David Defeats Hadadezer / Ammon (10-19) : *Ma**ligning***
back : l¹srael **g⁹**athers/**g⁹**ores *Ammonites*

[20] Joab Enslaves Rabbah (1-3) : ***To Blows/Strokes/Lodes*** *(ax,
pick, saw)* : **T²**o **O⁰**perations *with axes and picks (mining
lodes) and saws*

Philistine Giants Killed (4-8) : ***Huge Foes*** : **T²**itans
O⁰verthrown

[21] David Numbers Israel (1-17) : ***To Sum*** : n²umbers l¹srael

3 choices for Judgment : *"**Choose One!**"* : 2² + 1¹ (3)

OT   1 Chronicles   NT

[21] Pestilence Kills 70,000 : *Flu Bug?* : T²hreatens J¹erusalem

David's Altar Checks Plague (18-30) : *To Blunt plague* : T²o l¹imit *deaths*

[22] Solomon Tasked with Building Temple : *New room for God to dwell in* : T²emple T²asked

[23] Levite Duties : *Dūt Lēvs* : -V²ite F³unctions

[24] Levite Divisions/Groups by Lot : *Groups Formed by lot* : -V²ite M⁴ultiples

[25] Musician Divisions : *"Group Fifes!"* (1) : T²eam-up S⁵ingers /S⁵axophones (7)

[26] Gatekeepers (1-19) : *To City / To "Sit" [as in babysit]* : T²o b⁶lock *entry*

Treasurers (22-32) : *To List accounts* : T²reasury b⁶usiness

[27] Troop Leaders (1-15) : *Troop Supervisors* : T²roop L⁷eaders

Tribe Leaders (16-34) : *Group Supervisors* : T²ribe L⁷eaders

[28] David's Temple Plans : *To Make temple* : T²emple B⁸lueprint

[29] Temple Finance (1-9) : *To Buyin temple furnishings* : T²emple g⁹old (2, 7)

From Your Hand We Gave (1-22) : *Moved Thine into temple* : T²emple g⁹old

Solomon Anointed (22-25) : *To Slime/Anoint* : T²o g⁹rease

David Dies (26-30) : *To Dyin* : T²o g⁹rave *of fathers*

["To" + action verb]

Solomon to Civil War

[1-9] I^{1}srael's > g^{9}overnor: **Solomon**

[01] **Solomon Sacrifices at Gibeon** (1-6) **:** *To One!* **:** I^{1}auds *the One God*

Solomon Asks for Wisdom to Govern (7-13) **:** *To Run people (10)* **:** I^{1}ead/I^{1}earning

Solomon Gets Wealth (14-17) **:** *To Fund projects* **:** I^{1}nvests

[02] **Temple Trees :** *Huram (king of Tyre) To Hue trees* **:** T^{2}emple/T^{2}yre/T^{2}rees

[03] **Temple Built :** *To Beam Temple* **:** F^{3}oundation/m^{3}ount/m^{3}oriah) **//** *To "Leaf" parts with gold leaf* **:** Y^{3}ellow/N^{3}uggets *originally*

[04] **Temple F[o]urnishings :** *To Form articles/To F[o]urnish/F[o]urniture for inside* **:** A^{4}rticles

[05] **Solomon Brings Ark to Temple :** *To Drive Ark to temple* **/** *To Hide it there* **:** S^{5}anctuary/S^{5}torage

[06] **Solomon Blesses People** (1-11) **:** *To Bid God* **/** *To Wish God's best for them* **:** b^{6}eseech/b^{6}est/b^{6}lessing

Solomon Commits Temple to Lord (12-42) **:** *To Give to God* **:** b^{6}estow

[07] **People See Fire and Glory Descend from Heaven on the Temple** (1-3) **:** *View heaven* **:** L^{7}ord *descends upon it* **//** *Lord To Settlin on it* **/** L^7*it it up*

OT   2 Chronicles   NT

[07 Solomon Sacrifices to God (4-10) **: *To Sever*** *throats of oxen and sheep/**To 7** days of feasting* (9) **: 7^7** *days/**T^7**emple sacrifice*

If My people Pray and Repent (11-22**) : *To Bendin*** *knees //* ***To* Re*pentin*** *: **T^7**alk and **T^7**ransform / **T^7**urn from sin*

[08] Solomon Builds Cities : *To Frame* *new cities : **B^8**uildings including **B^8**eth-horon and **B^8**aalath*

[09] Queen of Sheba (1-12) : *To Wine/Dine* *her :* **q^9**ueen *of Sheba brings him **g^9**ifts of **g^9**old and other **g^9**ems (v. **9^9**)*

Solomon's Wealth (13-28)**: *To Find/Mine*** *gold himself :* **g^9**old *mined* <u>and</u> *imported >* 666 *talents per year* (13)*, bad number!*

Solomon Dies (29-31) **: *To Shrine*** *of fathers :* **g^9**rave *of fathers*

> ## The Kingdom Splits

---

[10] Civil War Splits Kingdom : *Two kings to Rend* *the kingdom :* **10^{10}** *tribes in the north versus 2 in the south*

Solomon's Son Rehoboam *drives people : **To Bend*** *their backs with hard labor* (11) **: l^1**abor **O^0**ppression **/ l^1**srael's **O^0**verlord **: (10^{10}**) *in north*

Jeroboam : *To End* *his hiding in Egypt from Solomon :* **l^1**eaves **O^0**ases */ becomes* **J^1**udah's **O^0**verload *(and Benjamin's)*

[11] Rehoboam Fortifies Cities (1-12) **: *To Lever*** *for war > sends spears and shields to cities* (12) **: l^1**evers **l^1**ocals with **l^1**ances

Priests and Levites Move to Jerusalem (13-17) **: *To Leavin*** *their lands* (14) *in order **To Leaven** [fill] Jerusalem with **Lev**ites* **: l^1**eavin **l^1**ands **/ J^1**oin in **J^1**erusalem

2 Chronicles

[11] Rehoboam's Family (18-23) : *To leaven* [fill] *land with kids* : l^{1}eaven l^{1}and

[12] Shi^{1}shak of EgypT^2 Raids Jerusalem (1-5) : *To Belt/Pelt* Judah : l^{1}ord [of] n^{2}ile/T^{2}hebes) *// To Sell* treasures from temple : l^{1}oots T^{2}emple/T^{2}reasury) (9)

[13] Rehoboam's Son Abijah Rules Judah Defeats Israel : *To Hurting/Defeat* Israel : l^{1}srael F^{3}lees!

[14] Asa Rules/Reforms Judah : *To Reform* Judah's idolatry : l^{1}egislator A^{4}sa

[15] Asa to Revive Judah : *To Revive* faith in the Lord : l^{1}dols S^{5}mashed

[16] Asa joins Aram's Ben-hadad to Fight Baasha (1-6) : *To Mixing* with Ben-hadad : l^{1}oyalty b^{6}en against l^{1}srael's b^{6}aasha who's coming *To Afflicting* Judah : J^{1}udah b^{6}eating

Hanani the Prophet (7-14) : *To Predictings* of future wars : l^{1}ong-term b^{6}attles because of Asa's reliance on Aram instead of the Lord. Asa *To Sticking* him in prison */ To prisoning* him : l^{1}mprisons d^{6}iviner

[17] Jehoshaphat Reforms Judah : *To Severing* Judah from idols : l^{1}dols L^{7}iquidated *// To Sending* Levites to Judah to teach God's Ways (8-9) : J^{1}ehosaphat's L^{7}evites

[18] Jehoshaphat (Judah) Joins Ahab (Israel) to Get Ramoth-gilead Back from Syrians : *To Raiding* / l^{1}and B^{8}ack plan

The Lord Sends a Lying Spirit : *To Placing* lie in 400 prophets who tell Ahab he will prevail l^{1}n B^{8}attle. Ahab is accustomed *To Hating* Micaiah who tells him he will die in battle, which he does, struck by a "random" shot (33: l^{1}ucky B^{8}ow

OT   2 Chronicles   NT

[19] **Jehoshaphat Reforms Judah** : *To Refining Judah* : **J**[1]**udah g**[9]**odly** *again*

Jehu Rebukes Him for Loving those who Hate Lord : *To Minding godless* : **l**[1]**oving g**[9]**odless** / **J**[1]**ehu's g**[9]**ibe**

[20] **Jehoshaphat Prays: Three Armies Attack Each Other** : *Two New Foes* (Ammon and Moab) *attack the third (Seir) then each other* : **T**[2]**urn O**[0]**n** *each other*

[21] **Jehoram Rules Judah, Kills brothers** : *To Shoot/Doom Sons of Father* : **n**[2]**o l**[1]**nheritance** *for them* : **Je-Swords-'Em!**

God Stirs up Philistines and Arabians to Attack Judah (12-17) : *To Shoot Sons of Judah* : **T**[2]**rample J**[1]**udah**

God Causes Jehoram's Bowels *To Move from* the inside to the outside : **V**[2]**acating l**[1]**ntestines** (19)

[22] **Ahaziah Rules Judah at 22**[22] (1-9) : *To Choose Views* of Ahab (3-4)—**V**[2]**ile V**[2]**iews** / *A Hazard* to Judah with a bad mother named—**WrAthalia** (10)—*To Shoot Jews* from the house of Judah (8-10) after Jehu kills her son : **V**[2]**indictive V**[2]**illainess**

Jehoshabeath Hides Joash from Athaliah (11-12) : *To Snooze/Sloom-Room* (11) : **T**[2]**oddler T**[2]**ucked** *away in bedroom for the six years Athaliah rules* (12)

[23] **Joash Rules Judah, Kills Athaliah** (1-15) : *To Shoot Queen Athaliah*—**V**[2]**illainess K**[3]**illed** / **Jo-Bash**

Priest Jehoiada's Reforms (16-21) : *Due To Clean* temple and people : **T**[2]**emple F**[3]**reshened/H**[3]**oly/F**[3]**lush** *out evil* (19)

[24] **Joash Funds Temple Repair** (1-19) : *To Support* temple repair : **T**[2]**emple M**[4]**ending** / **Jo-Cash**

OT   2 Chronicles   NT

[24] Joash Stones Jehoiada's Son Zechariah (20-22) **:** *To Shoot Ores* at him in the court of Temple **:** T^{2}emple M^{4}urder

Syrians Attack Judah, Kill Joash (23-27) **:** *To Pūsh Sword* Into Joash in bed **:** T^{2}rundle M^{4}urder **/** *Joashashinated*

[25] Amaziah Rules Judah, Kills Edomites (1-13) **:** *To Doom -Mites* **:** T^{2}ook S^{5}eir **:** *Amazing* victories *Amassed*

Amaziah Sets Up Edomite Idols (14-16) **:** *To Loot/Choose Ids* of Edom **:** T^{2}ook S^{5}eir's *gods* T^{2}o S^{5}et *them up* **:** *Amazing* idols *Amassed*

Joash Defeats Amaziah (17-28) **:** *To Doom Lives* of Judah **:** T^{2}ribes S^{5}lay *each other* > T^{2}en "S^{5}core" (Israel), T^{2}wo S^{5}coreless (Judah *To Lose Fight*) **:** *Jobash*

[26] Uzziah Rules Judah, Defeats Philistines (1-15) **:** *To Shoot* ("Uzzi'd") *Ph'lists* **:** V^{2}ictory b^{6}attles **:** *"Uzzit or Lose it!"*

Uzziah illegally Burns Incense (16-23) **:** *To Fuel Sticks/ Wicks* **:** T^{2}hurible b^{6}ad *(Terrible Thurible)* so God strikes him with leprous sores (*Ooziah* **:** 19ff)

[27] Jotham Rules Judah, Seeks Lord (1-4) **:** *To Choose Heaven* for help **:** V^{2}enerated L^{7}ord **:** *Jotham: God's Chum*

Taxed Ammonites (5-6) **:** *To Put Several* taxes on them**/***Dues To Send In* **:** T^{2}ribute L^{7}oot

[28] Ahaz Rules Judah, Burns Sons (1-5) **:** *To Fuel Babes* **:** T^{2}ots B^{8}urned/T^{2}o B^{8}en-Hinnom *with them*/V^{2}ictim B^{8}abies/ V^{2}enerates B^{8}aal **/** *Ahazard* to Judah

Syria Attacks/Defeats Judah (1-21) **:** *To Jud To Raid* **:** T^{2}o B^{8}eat *up Judah/Ahaz*

[28] Ahaz Builds High Places for Idols (22-27) : *To Ruin Faith* in God (23) : **T²o B⁸**uild *high places for idols* (25)

[29] Hezekiah Rules Judah Righteously, Cleanses Temple (1-19) : *To Do Fine/To "New" Shrine* : **T²**o **g⁹**reatness**/g⁹**lory

Hezekiah Restores Worship (20-36) : *To New Shrine* : **T²**emple **g⁹**ifts**/g⁹**oats**/g⁹**lory

[30] Hezekiah Restores Passover : *To Priest Mode / To Feast Mode* : **ω³**orship **O⁰**nly *the Lord***/F³**east **O⁰**nly *to Lord*

[31] Hezekiah Organizes Priests into Divisions : *To Priest "Sums"* (groups) : **F³**orms **l¹**evite *divisions/groups*

[32] Sennacherib Plans to Attack Judah's Fortified Cities (1) : *To Beat Jud*ah : **F³**ortified **T²**owns

Hezekiah Asks God to Fight for People (2-8) : *To Plea To Lord* : **H³**ezekiah **T²**alks *God* : *Heze-cries "Yah!"* : **F³**ighter **T²**heos (< *Greek: God*) **/ Y²**ahweh **V²**ictory

Sennacherib Blasphemes (9-19) : *To Speak Rude* of God : **H³**orrible **V²**ocalizations : *Sennacherib's Debaucheries*

Lord's Angel Cuts Off Assyrian Army (20-23) : *To Reduce/ To Rebuke Army* : **K³**ills **V²**eterans

[33] Manasseh Rules Judah, Restores Idols (1-9) *To Retreat* to idolatry : **H³**eaven's **H³**osts (5) **// *To Lead Breed*** (sons) *through Valley of Ben-Hinnom* : **H³**innom **H³**ollow **/ H³**innom **F³**ires (6) / *One* **m³**anasty **K³**ing

Manasseh Captured, Repents, Freed (10-20) : *Assyria **To Free King*** : **F³**ree **K³**ing **//** *Returns to Jerusalem **To Dēlete*** idols : **F³**ell **F³**igurines **/ K³**ill **N³**ergal (2 Kings 17:30; *Burgle Nergal*)

OT   2 Chronicles   NT

[33] Amon Rules Judah (21-24) **:** *To Retreat to idolatry* **:** **H³**eaven's **H³**osts **/** **F³**ollowed **m³**anasseh, his father (22) **:** *Bad Mahn*

[34] Josiah Rules Judah (1-21) **:** *To Reform Judah* **/** *To Restore Temple* **/** *To Re-Torah the people*: Hilkiah **F³**inds **M⁴**oses' **Law** in **Y³**ahweh's **M⁴**ansion **/** **H³**ouse **E⁴**lohim**/A⁴**donai

Based on Covenant Curses Huldah Warns Judah > (22-33) **:** *To Be Warned from the Lord* **:** **H³**uldah **W⁴**arns *of God's* **H³**oly **W⁴**rath *recorded in the Law* (**H³**orrors **W⁴**ritten) *when people* **F³**orsake **A⁴**donai (24ff.; *Huldah's Fulla the anger of the Lord*)

[35] Josiah Celebrates Passover (1-19) **:** *To Revive Passover* **:** **F³**estal **S⁵**upper

Pharaoh Neco Kills Josiah in Battle (20-27) **:** *To Demise when Pharaoh Neco Fights him* **:** **N³**eco **S⁵**lays *him*

[36] Egypt and Babylon Evict Judah's Last Kings: (1-16) **:** *To Evict Kings* **/** *To Egypt for some people* **:** **T²**o **b⁶**abylon **/** **Z³**edekiah **b⁶**linded **//** *Kings: Jehoahaz, Jehoiakim, Jehoiachin, and Zedekiah*

Nebuchadnezzar Burns Jerusalem (17-21) **:** *Jeru He Lit* **:** *God's* **H³**ouse **b⁶**urned (19; 2 Kings 25**:**9)

Persian King Cyrus of Persia (22-23) **:** *To "Edict" rebuilding of God's house in Jerusalem* **:** **K³**ing's **b⁶**ehest**/d⁶**ecree**/H³**ouse **b⁶**uilding

OT   Ezra   NT
[*ė* *ess* *ez* *uh*]

Bless or Test/Stress the People

[01] Cyrus's Decree : *Says [Cy]rus, "Run home!" to the Jews :* "l¹eave *Persia!"*

[02] Happy Exiles Return : *Blessed Jews returning :* V²acate *Persia* / V²oyage *home*

[03] Priests Revive Worship (1-7) **:** *Blessed Priests / Kept Feast of Booths :* H³oly F³east

Rebuilt Temple (8-13) **:** *Blessed Priests / Blessed Trees/* Cēdars *for Temple* F³oundation

[04] Adversaries Oppose Rebuildings (1-6) **:** *"Test"/Stress Force* **:** A⁴dversaries/E⁴nemies *test determination of workers*

Pests W⁴arn/A⁴rtaxerxes that the people are planning to rebel

Ezra Forced to stop work : W⁴ork/E⁴nds

[05] Rebuilding Re-starts (1-5) **:** *Fresh Drive :* S⁵tarts *up again*

Tattenai Writes > (6-17) **:** *Says [Tatte]nai" / "Press Cy's Decree!" :* S⁵tatute/S⁵tick *with it!*

[06] Darius Decrees the Work (1-12) **:** *Says "Dig!" :* b⁶uild *temple!*

Temple Finished (13-18) **:** *Ezra Bricks/Rigs it :* b⁶uilt /6⁶ᵗʰ *year of Darius*

Passover Celebrated (19-22) **:** *Ezra Fixes Feast :*b⁶anquet

[07] Ezra Sent to Teach God's Ways : *Ezra's Sent In to :* T⁷each

<u>OT</u>   **Ezra**   <u>NT</u>

[08] Ezra Lists Exiles' Genealogies: *Ezra Makes* lists **: B**[8]loodlines

[09] Ezra Tells Men to Confess Marriage to Foreign Wives :
"Fess Up Crime of **: g**[9]entile *wives!"*

[10] Ezra Commands Separation : *Ezra Sends* away gentile brides
: I[1]ntermarriage **O**[0]ver **: I**[1]nfidels **O**[0]usted/**O**[0]stracized

<u>OT</u>   Nehemiah   <u>NT</u>
[*ee*]

[01] Nehemiah Asks God to Help Distressed Exiles in City of Jerusalem : *Nehemiah Summons* God **: I**^{1}mplores *Him for help*

[02] Artaxerxes Sends Nehemiah to Judah (1-8) **:** *Nehemiah To/Jud*ah **: T**^{2}ravel **T**^{2}o *Judah*

Nehemiah Inspects City Walls (9-20) **:** *Nehemiah Views* walls of city and suggests they repair them **: V**^{2}iews**/ T**^{2}roubleshoots **/ T**^{2}ouches *up*

[03] Priests Rebuild Wall : *Need Priests* to fix wall **: F**^{3}ix wall

[04] Sanballat "Sanbaggets" the Work (1-14) **:** *Nehemiah Wars* against Sanballat **: A**^{4}dversary**/E**^{4}nemy**/M**^{4}ocks**/W**^{4}ork on **W**^{4}all **:** *Sanballat the Man Mallet*

Work Resumes (15-23) **:** *Restored* work **: W**^{4}ork resumes

[05] Nehemiah Stops Oppression of Poor (1-13) *Nehemiah Strives* against usury **: S**^{5}tops this injustice **/** *Revives* debtors

Nehemiah Shares Food (14-19) **:** *Nehemiah Divides* food **: S**^{5}hares his own

[06] Nehemiah Deceived (1-14) **:** *Nehemiah Tricked* by Sanballat into believing rumors are flying that he's planning to rebel against the king **: d**^{6}eceived **/ b**^{6}uzz flying to stop wall production

But He Completes the Wall (15-19) *Nehemiah Fix*es the wall **/ b**^{6}uilt

[07] Nehemiah Lists Returning Exiles : *Nehemiah's Census* **: L**^{7}ists

OT   Nehemiah   NT

[08] Ezra Reads Book of the Law (1-8) : *Reads Ways of God* **/ Nehemiah States** *Law* : **B**^{8}ook *of Law*

Nehemiah Declares the Day Holy (9-12) : *Nehemiah States/Dates/Day* : **B**^{8}lessed *date/day*

Feast of Booths Celebrated (13-18) : *Feast Day* : **B**^{8}ooths

[09] People Confess Sins (1-31) : *Knee Time for the people* **/ Need Time** *to confess* **/ Need Crime** *confessing* **/ need Pine** *for sin* : **g**^{9}uilt/**g**^{9}rieving

People Renew Covenant (32-38) : *Rebind to God's covenant* : **g**^{9}uarantee **//**

Need Sign *it* (38b) : **P**^{9}rint *names?*

[10] The People who Sign the Covenant (1-27) *"We Men Sign!"* : **I**^{1}nitiate **O**^{0}ath

The Oath—A Pledge to (28-39) > *Keep Ten commandments and all in Moses' Law* : **10**^{10} *commandments*

[11] Leaders Live in Jerusalem (1-24) : *Leaders Live In City of Jerusalem* : **J**^{1}erusalem **I**^{1}eaders **//** *Jerusalem = leaders + 10% of rest chosen by lot* > **I**^{1}ot **I**^{1}ucky!

Rest in Other Cities (25-35) : *90%* **Need Livin** *in other cities* : **I**^{1}eftovers **I**^{1}ive *in other cities*

[12] Levitical Priests Return to Jerusalem (1-26) : *Priests Dwell in Jerusalem* : **I**^{1}evites **n**^{2}est *in Jerusalem* **/ I**^{1}evite **n**^{2}ames *listed*

Levites Celebrate Wall (27-47) : *Levites Bells/Yells in two choirs* : **I**^{1}evites **V**^{2}enerate *God*

OT   Nehemiah   **NT**

[13] **Nehemiah's Last Reforms** : *Nehemiah's Decrees* noted :
l^{1}ast F^{3}ixes:

Nehemiah Turning *away Ammonites and Moabites from Israel and Tobiah from the temple*

Nehemiah Turning *away foreign wives*

Need Earnings *of people for Levites (Tithes)*

Nehemiah Returning *Sabbath to people*

Esther
[*es*]

[01] King Ahasuerus to Parade Queen Vashti (1-9)**:** *"Dress Her Up!"* **:** I[1]dolizes *her*

Vashti Refuses (10-22) **:** *Stress Up the king* **:** I[1]gnores *request* **:** *Vashti "Quashtis" the request*

[02] Ahasuerus Makes Esther Queen (1-4) **:** *Esther Rules* **:** V[2]irtuous **/** n[2]oble

Mordecai Warns Esther to Not Reveal Her People (5-18)**:** *Esther's Jews* **:** V[2]eil *them* **:** *Mordecai Warn a Guy*

Mordecai Uncovers Plot to Kill King (19-23) **:** *Rescues king from* **:** T[2]reachery **/** T[2]reason

[03] Haman (Hate-Man) Plots to Kill Jews : *"Let's Seize/Beat Jews!"* **:** H[3]aman**/**K[3]ill *plot*

[04] Esther Fasts and Plans to Save Them : *Esther Swore off food* **/** *Esther Forms a masterplan* **:** M[4]eals**/**M[4]asterplan

[05] Esther Prepares a Banquet (1-8) **:** *Esther Drives the "Prep"* —*Esther's Site and Esther's Pies* **:** S[5]upper**/**S[5]oiree

Haman Hates Mordecai, Plans to Hang Him (9-14) **:** *Despise Mordecai* **/** *Press Life out of him* **:** S[5]corn *him* **/** S[5]tring *him up*

[06] King to Honor Guest Mordecai at Banquet : *Guest Picked to* **:** b[6]estow *honor on*

[07] Esther Tells King Haman's Plot (1-6) **:** *Esther Threatens Haman* **:** T[7]ells**/**T[7]estifies**/**L[7]ets on**/**L[7]eaks *it out*

OT   Esther   NT

[07] **Hamon Hanged on Gallows He Prepared for Mordecai** (7-10) : *Breaths Severed* : *L*⁷ynched

[08] **Esther Saves the Jews** : *Esther Saves* Jews : **B**⁸ails out *//* King says Jews can **Es-cape** oppressors—defend themselves against all enemies

[09] **The Jews Kill Their Enemies** (1-19) : *Assign* enemies to death : **g**⁹ore them (swords: 5)

Feast of Purim Designed (20-32) : *Design* the Feast of Purim—a feast of : **g**⁹ladness (22)

[10] **Mordecai Promoted Second in Rank to Ahasuerus** : *Ascends* in rank : **l**¹ord #2 over all people

OT   Job   NT
[*obe* *ode* *ope* *o*]

[01] **Job's Integrity and Wealth** (1-5) **:** *Job Shuns* evil **:** I^{1}ntegrity
/ *Job's Funds* vast **:** I^{1}ivestock/I^{1}and

   God Tests Job through Satan (6-22) *Probe/"Strobe" One*
   : I^{1}nquiry/ I^{1}nvestigate/I^{1}nspect. *Satan attacks* **Job's Sons/
   Funds/Trunk** *(body)* = I^{1}ads/I^{1}oot/I^{1}imbs

[02] **Satan Attacks Job's Health** (1-10) **Job's Wounds** *are deep* **:**
V^{2}ictim/T^{2}ested/T^{2}rampled/T^{2}raumatized

   Job's Three Friends (11-13) **:** **Job's Few** *friends* **:** T^{2}hree /V^{2}isit

[03] **Job Curses his Birth : Job Treats** *his birth as a bad thing* **:**
N^{3}ativity / H^{3}exes *(curses) it* / m^{3}alediction

[04] **Eliphaz: The Innocent Prosper! :** *If* **Job's Pure** *he'll prosper* **:**
M^{4}eek / M^{4}oral *do well* **:** E^{4}liphas **:** **Well/Swell if Fast** *(food)*

[05] **Eliphaz: The Guilty Don't Prosper :** *If* **Job Strives** *with God,
he won't* **:** S^{5}trivers **:** **Hell if bads**

[06] **Job Argues Innocence : Job Sticks** *to his innocence* **:**
"b^{6}lameless *I tell you!*"

[07] **Job: "Life is Labor!" : Job Slavin** *is normal* **:** *L^{7}ife is L^{7}abor*

[08] **Bildad: God Hates Only Enemies :** *"**Foes Hates**," that's it!*
B^{8}ad *only killed* // B^{8}ildad: **Kills Bad!**

[09] **Job: External Righteousness** (1-32) *"**Shows Fine**" but no
base for debate* / **No Mind** *can argue with* God **:** g^{9}roundless

   Job: There's No Mediator Between > : Job's Mind *and God's*
   : g^{9}oel *(mediator), someone* g^{9}uiltless *like himself—since "**No-
   Crime**" (innocent) people are in fact punished*

[10] Job: God Oppresses men : *Job Probed/"Strobed"* like all men only for the purpose of oppression : l^{1}ord O^{0}verwhelms *men*

[11] Zophar Zo Good! : Job Deserves Worse : *Job's Level* of punishment *Zo Phar* lower than he deserves because God l^{1}essens l^{1}iability

[12] Job: I'm Not Inferior to You (1-6) : *Job's "Well"* (goodness) not inferior to Zophar's : "l^{1}nferior n^{2}ot!

God Probes Nations and Men : *Probes Selfs* (subjects) of all kinds : l^{1}ifts n^{2}ations *up then* T^{2}akes n^{2}ations *away; so too men*

[13] Job: I will Still Hope in God : *Job's Serene/Stirring* himself up : "l^{1}ord K^{3}ills, l^1 K^{3}eep/F^{3}aith (*"Yet will I trust Him!"* 15)

[14] Job: Everyone Born of Woman Dies : *Job's One Born* of woman so headed for death like everyone else : "l^1'm M^{4}ortal"; there are no l^{1}mmortal M^{4}en

Job's Mourning for death but also for God's vindication (13-17) : "l^1 W^{4}ant *to die but also to be vindicated*"

[15] Eliphaz: "You're Impure, Smelly Pants!" : *Job's Living* an impure life : l^{1}mpure S^{5}oul *because no-one's pure*

Job's Ignorant : *Job's "iffing"* (speculating). His knowledge does not go back to God's secret counsel so he's an : l^{1}gnorant S^{5}pirit/S^{5}oul *like the rest of us* (7-13)

[16] Job: God Afflicts (7-18) : *Job's Kicks-ings/Afflictsings/ Fixings* are from God : "God l^{1}ays b^{6}urdens *on me!"*

But *Job's "Witnessing"* is Heaven (19) : l^{1}ord b^{6}ears *witness*

OT   Job   NT

[17] **Job: Considers Afterlife as Hopeless :** *Hope Of Heaven* does *not descend into Sheol* (15-16) **:** "I[1]'m *L*[7]ost!"

[18] **Bildad: God Punishes Bad only :** *Job's Fating* himself to *death* **:** I[1]nflicts **B**[8]ad *only* / *"Job-Hating"* legitimate I[1]f **B**[8]ad

[19] **Job: My Redeemer will Save Me :** *Job-Finding/Timing* in the future **:** "I know My redeemer lives [I[1]iving **g**[9]oel] and will stand on the earth at the last!" (The Shepherd finds His lost sheep)

[20] **Zophar: The Wicked Suffer so :** *Job's Plenty* evil / *Job's Many* afflictions are consistent with God's attacking His enemies **:** *Job's Due Probe* as an enemy **:** **V**[2]engeance **O**[0]nly on wicked

[21] **Job: The Wicked Prosper :** *Foes' Plenty Funds* **:** **V**[2]ile/ **n**[2]efarious I[1]uxuriate (8-16)

[22] **Eliphaz: Job's Plenty Wicked (No End to it) :** *Job's Plenty "Cruel"* to the poor **:** "**n**[2]o **n**[2]umber" to *Job's Cruel Pool* of sins

[23] **Job Will Plea to God :** *Job To Plead* his case to God (3-4) **:** **T**[2]ribunal **H**[3]ope

   Job To Be gold before God after testing—**T**[2]ested **N**[3]ugget (10)

[24] **Job: Injustice Prevails :** *Justice Owed To Poor* but the wicked continue to exploit them **:** **n**[2]eedy/**V**[2]ulnerable **E**[4]xploited

[25] **Bildad: Nothing Created is Pure before God :** *No True/ Good Lives* **:** **n**[2]o **S**[5]ouls/**S**[5]pirits pure; even **V**[2]ile **S**[5]tars (5)

[26] **Job: God is Inscrutable :** *Shows You Fringe/Rim* of His ways (14)—**n**[2]o **b**[6]ig revelations—so your counsel can't be very deep

[27] **Job: My integrity's Intact :** *Job To Savin* his integrity **:** **n**[2]o *T*[7]ales, **n**[2]o *L*[7]ies

OT   Job   NT

[28] Job Asks Where Wisdom Is : *Probe To Sage* : n^{2}o B^{8}asis *for*
/B^{8}acking/B^{8}rain[s] on earth (13)

[29] Job Reviews Good Behavior—Helping the Blind : *Job To*
Blind was "Eyes" : *Strobelight To Blind*: V^{2}ision g^{9}uide (15ff.)

[30] Job's Humiliated : *Job's Deemed Low* : H^{3}umiliated O^{0}ften

[31] Job Lists Internal Evils He has Not Done: *Job's Free From*
these—adultery (9), idolatry (26-27), pride (25) : H^{3}e's
I^{1}nnocent *of secret sins* : *Job's Secret? Job's Dirty None!*

[32] Elihu ("My God [is] He") Rebukes Job—*Job Rebuke—and the*
three who have been probing him **/ *Probe Rebuke*** : 3^3 V^{2}etted

[33] Elihu Speaks for God : *Boasts He Speaks for God* : F^{3}or
Y^{3}ahweh *// God's **Probes/Goads Decreed** to make men return*
to Him (17-18; 29-30)

[34] Elihu: God is Just : *Probes The Morals* > : Y^{3}ahweh M^{4}oral
(just)

[35] Elihu: Job is Bad : *Job Speaks Jive, vanity* : F^{3}utile S^{5}peech

[36] Elihu: God Probes For Good : *Probes > Re-Fits/Equips* : F^{3}ix-
me b^{6}rowsings

[37] Elihu: God Rules All : *Probes The Heavens with lightning,*
snow, thunder and rain storms : H^{3}eavens' L^{7}ord **/** H^{3}igh L^{7}ord,
high above our understanding

[38] The Lord is Creator of All : *Globe Creates/He makes and*
everything else in the universe : H^{3}e B^{8}uilt *all things*

Job Debates/Derates/Berates/Deflates God in vain because
his knowledge is limited

OT   Job   NT

[39] The Lord is Sovereign Over All : *Globe He Minds/Binds* :
H^{3}e g^{9}rips *all things*

[40] The Lord Controls Behemōth on Land : *Holds Force -mōth*
in his hand : Behe**M^{4}O^0**th /**M^4**onster **O^0**nshore/**M^4**anipulates
O^{0}x *or bigger*/**M^4**oth **O^0**versees/**O^0**verpowers *land animals*

[41] The Lord Controls Leviathan in the Sea : *Holds Force -than*
in His hand : **M^4**anipulates **l^1**eviatian / **M^4**onster **l^1**eviathan

[42] Job Repents: *Job Forms New* thoughts : **M^4**ind **N^2**ew/**V^2**aries
/ **M^4**odifies **T^2**houghts

Job's Fortunes restored by the Lord : **W^4**ealth **n^2**ewed/**v^2**ivified
(10-17)

OT   Psalms   NT

[*om* *on* Gods', I'm, Ma(h)n's]

[01] Righteous Tree, Wicked Chaff : *God's Son* delights in the
Law and prospers *// **God's Dust*** blows away* : **l**[1]ifestyles (two)

[02] Lord's Anointed Inherits the Nations : *God Rules* nations
through His Anointed One (2)* : **n**[2]ations *His inheritance* (8-9)

[03] Surrounded by Foes! : *I'm Seiged/Seized* on all sides* : **F**[3]oes

[04] God Calms Me : *Calm Lord* calms me* / ***God's Lord*** of my*
M[4]oods *// **M**[4]ellows me* (1)

[05] Lead Me in Your righteousness : *God Drives* me in His*
righteousness : **S**[5]teers *me*

[06] God Saves Me from Enemies! : *God Rids* me of enemies* :
b[6]eats *my* **b**[6]eaters

[07] God Saves Me from Tearing Lions (2) : *I'm Severed* by **L**[7]ions
unless ***God Severs*** them with His sword (12)*

[08] God's Name Majestic : *God's Name/Great* : **B**[8]rilliant

God's Babes Speak His Strength (2) : B[8]abies/**B**[8]oast

God Made Man to Rule All Things (5-8) *including* : **B**[8]easts

[09] I Will Recount Your Deeds : *God-Mind* : **g**[9]od-thoughts

Consigns the* **g**[9]uilty *to Sheol* (17)

God Minds the* **g**[9]hetto (18: *poor*)

[10] Why do You Hide in Times of Trouble? : *God "Dens"* Himself*
when evil's around?* : **l**[1]ord **O**[0]ff?—*elsewhere when I need Him?*

[10] Wicked Prosper Over the Poor : *The **Strong Bend** the backs of the weak until God judges them :* l[1]ords O[0]ppress

[11] God Calls All Men into Account : ***God Summons*** *both the righteous and the wicked :* l[1]ord l[1]nvestigates *all* (5)

[12] Man's Lies and God's Truths : ***Some Tell*** lies (1-5) ***/ God Tells*** *pure words* (6-7) : l[1]ying T[2]ongues *vs.* l[1]ord's T[2]ongue

[13] How Long, Lord? : ***I'm Worried / God Hurry!*** : l[1]'m ω[3]orried / l[1]ord H[3]urry *to answer me* (3)!

[14] Fool Says There's No God Running the World: ***God Story*** *False!* : l[1]ord M[4]issing *from universe*

[15] Who Dwells on God's Holy Hill? : ***Some Living*** there : l[1]ord's S[5]anctified S[5]lope**) /** *the* l[1]nnocent S[5]tay there (2-5)

[16] Lord will Not Abandon My Soul to Sheol (the Pit) : *I'm* ***Missing*** *in action but not for long because the* l[1]ord's b[6]y *my side* (8, 11). *The* l[1]ord b[6]rings *up from Sheol* (1 Samuel 2**:**6)

[17] Hide Me in the Shadow of Your Wings : ***God's A Haven/ "Havening"*** : l[1]ark L[7]ord**/**L[7]odge (8)

[18] Lord is My Rock and Fortress Against Enemies : ***God's Slating*** *me* : l[1]ord B[8]edrock**/** B[8]oulder

[19] Heavens Declare God's Glory : ***God's Shining*** *seen in the heavens :* l[1]ord's g[9]lory **/** l[1]uminary g[9]lory (1-6) *in His heavens and also in His Law :* l[1]aw's g[9]lory (7-14)

[20] God Saves From Zion : ***God's Sending*** *help from Zion His* sanctuary (2) : l[1]ord's O[0]rigin *of help*

God's Enemies *Conquered :* V[2]ictories O[0]ver *enemies*

[20] Who Do Men Trust? : *Some* T^{2}rust O^{0}ats *(horses) but we* T^{2}rust O^{0}mnipotence (7)

[21] God Prolongs Life and Reign of the King : *"I'm To Run* the *Kingdom with "length of days forever and ever" :* T^{2}hrone I^{1}ength (4)

God To Stun *the King's Enemies* (7-13) **:** V^{2}ictory l^{1}ord

[22] Why Have You Forsaken Me? : *God To Loose/Lose* me? **:** T^{2}o T^{2}erminate *my relationship with You? /* T^{2}erminate T^{2}ies?

[23] The Lord Shepherds His Sheep To Green Pastures : Some/ *'m To Green* pastures **:** V^{2}erdant F^{3}armland

[24] Who Ascends the Hill of the Lord? (1-6) **:** *Some/I'm To Soar* there**:** V^{2}irtue M^{4}ountain—*those with Pure Hearts* = V^{2}irtuous M^{4}yocardiums *and Clean Hands* = V^{2}irtuous M^{4}itts

King of Glory Enters the Everlasting Doors : *God Through Doors / God Moves Glory* **:** T^{2}hrough E^{4}ntrance *to Inside* T^{2}o E^{4}nlighten *the Place*

[25] Teach Me Your Paths! : *Prom To Life* **:** T^{2}each S^{5}traight *and narrow paths /* n^{2}arrow/T^{2}ight/T^{2}hin—S^{5}traight *path*s

[26] I Mix with God, Not Sinners. Vindicate Me! : *I'm To Mix* with God */ God To Fix* my parking tickets (4, 8: *the right way*) **:** V^{2}indicate *[my]* b^{6}enevolence! (1, 9)

[27] God is My Light and Salvation in the Temple : *God To "Heaven"* me with Light and the Beauty of the Lord in His Temple**:** T^{2}emple L^{7}ight */* V^{2}ision L^{7}ord

[28] God is My Strength and Shield : *God's To Brace* me **:** T^{2}ough B^{8}uckler

OT   Psalms   NT

[29] **Ascribe Glory to God :** *I'm To Shine* God in my thought and speech **:** T^2hink/V^2oice g^9lory

[30] **Weeping For the Night, Joy In the Morning :** God *Calms Hurting* **:** N^3ight O^0utcries but m^3orning O^0verjoyed

God's Hurting for a moment **/** *God's Mercy* runs for life **:** F^3lash O^0utrage **/** F^3or l^1ife (5).

[31] **Into Your Hands I Commit My Spirit :** *I'm Serving You* my spirit **:** H^3andles l^1ife **/** H^3ands T^2rusted

[32] **Does Not Impute Sin :** God *[I]mputes* no sin **:** F^3aults n^2one

[33] **Lord's Steadfast Love Fills Earth** (5) **:** *God's "Repletes"* earth with love **:** F^3ills F^3avor/F^3riendship

Lord Frustrates Wicked (10) **:** *God Keeps Mean* from success in evil **/** *Stops Meanies* **:** F^3rustrates m^3eanness **/** F^3oils F^3iends/$ω^3$icked

Lord Preserves Kings (16) **:** *God Keeps Kings* **:** K^3eeps K^3ings

[34] **God's Saving the Brokenhearted :** *God's Curing/Heals Torn* hearts **:** H^3eart M^4ends

[35] **God Fights Our Foes:** *God—He Fights* **:** F^3ights S^5atan/S^5trikers/S^5trivers

[36] **Flatterers Deceive :** *Cons' Dirty Tricks* **:** F^3latterers b^6eguile us but God Steadfastly Loves Us **:** F^3ixed b^6eloved

[37] **Delight in the Lord and He will Give You Desires of Your Heart :** *Some "Glee" Heaven!* **:** T^2hrill L^7ord and He will give you **:** H^3eart L^7ongings/L^7ikings **//** **Enemies of the Lord Perish :** *Some Leave Heaven* (20) **:** $ω^3$icked L^7ose everything

OT   **Psalms**   ## NT

[37] Righteous Inherit the Land Forever (29) : *Some Reap Heaven* : **F**[3]orever/**H**[3]eritage **L**[7]and / **I**[1]nheri**T**[7]

[38] Discipline Without Wrath! : *God, Deflate* my pride lightly! : **N**[3]o-**B**[8]eatings *discipline please!*

[39] Make Us Know the Measure of our Days : *M[a]n's Fleet Time* (4-5) : **F**[3]leeting **P**[9]eriod

[40] Out of Pit, Onto Rock! *God Forcing* me out of pit and onto rock : **F**[3]orced **O**[0]ut / **A**[4]byss/**W**[4]ell **O**[0]ut / **M**[4]ountain **O**[0]nto

Inner Obedience : *Alms For Show? No!* : **W**[4]ithin **O**[0]bedience

[41] Blessed are Those who Help the Poor : *Calm Poor Ones/ Alms For Some* : **A**[4]ssist **I**[1]mpoverished

[42] Desiring God as the Deer Pants for Water : *P[a]nts for You* —**M**[4]yocardial **T**[2]hrobbing; **M**[4]y/**M**[4]itral **V**[2]alve/**T**[2]hrobbing *as the deer pants for water* : **E**[4]lk **T**[2]hirsting/**T**[2]hrobs

[43] Light and Truth Lead us to God's Holy Hill : *I'm For Peak*—*heading to God's Holy Hill* : **M**[4]ount **H**[3]oly / **W**[4]orship **H**[3]ill / **E**[4]lohim's/**E**[4]ternal **H**[3]ill/**H**[3]abitation

[44] You Scattered your People among the Nations : *God's Scorned World* : **M**[4]oved **M**[4]en *out to heathen nations* (11)

[45] King's Eternal Throne : *God: Your Might/Right* are eternal : **E**[4]ternal/**E**[4]verlasting **S**[5]eat *(Throne)*

[46] God is Our Fortress : *God-Fortress*—*our refuge* : **A**[4]lamo/ **W**[4]all/**M**[4]ight/**W**[4]atchtower **G**[6]od

[47] God is King Over All the Earth : *God Lords Events* : **E**[4]arth/ **E**[4]vent **L**[7]ord

OT   Psalms   NT

[48] **Zion, the Beautiful City of God** : *God's Ornate* City (2) :
M^{4}ount B^{8}eautiful

[49] **Faith and Wealth Hoarding** : *Some Hoard Dimes/Wines* :
W^{4}ealth g^{9}ains / W^{4}ealth g^{9}athered/g^{9}arnered *then*
W^{4}ealth g^{9}uarded/g^{9}loated *over*

Death Ends Ownership : *M[a]n's Hoard-Time is Short-Time*
: M^{4}oney g^{9}one *before you know it*

[50] **God does not Want External Sacrifice** : *M[a]n's Shifty*
(hypocritical) offerings : S^{5}hifty O^{0}fferings/"O^{0}uties" (7-15)

[51] **Create in Me a Clean Heart** (inside) : *God's "Innie" Ones* :
S^{5}acrifice I^{1}nner *things* : S^{5}crub I^{1}nsides / S^{5}potless I^{1}nsides

[52] **Man's Pride Judged** : *Man's Pride Doomed* to God's
judgment : S^{5}elf V^{2}anity/T^{2}erminated

God's Life-long Steadfast Love (1, 8) : *God's Life Lūv* :
S^{5}teadfast T^{2}enderness

[53] **God looks Down to See if Any Seek God** : *God Sights*
Seekers but : S^{5}ees N^{3}one (2) / S^{5}eekers N^{3}one! (2-3)

[54] **Lord Preserves My Life** : *God's [a] Life Lord* : S^{5}ustains M^{4}e/
M^{4}y *life* (4)

Vindicate Me! : *God "Rights" Poor* (oppressed) : S^{5}ave M^{4}e
from oppressors by Your Power (1)

[55] **God Overthrows Enemies, Betrayers** : *God Fights/Smites*
Strife (9, 12) : S^{5}mites S^{5}trife

[56] **God Overthrows Ambushers** : *God Fights "Hids"* lurking in
shadows to pounce on us (5-7) : S^{5}trikes b^{6}ushwhackers

OT   Psalms   NT

[56] God Hides Tears in His Bottle : *M[a]n's Cries Hid* in His bottle and book **:** **S⁵**orrow/**S⁵**adness ... **b⁶**ottled/**b⁶**ooked (8)

[57] God's Glory is Above the Earth : *God's High Heavens* **:** **S⁵**ky/**S⁵**overeign/**S⁵**uperior/**S⁵**upreme ... **L⁷**ord

[58] Wicked From Birth : *Mom's Drifting Babes* sin from birth **:** **S⁵**in **B⁸**orn/**B⁸**egotten (3)

Break Teeth! : *God's Bite Breaks* Wicked's Fangs **:** **S⁵**in **B⁸**ites!

[59] Save Me from Strife! *Some Strife Crimes* I need saving from **:** **S⁵**trife **g⁹**uerrilas

God is My Stronghold Against Enemies : *God's Might Mine* **:** **S⁵**tronghold **g⁹**od (9, 16)

[60] God Beats Foes : *God's Licking Foes* **:** **b⁶**reaks **O⁰**pressors

[61] Lead/Lift Me to the Rock Higher than I : *God Picks-Me Up* **:** **b⁶**oulder **l¹**ead/**l¹**ift (2)

[62] God Alone is My Rock and Salvation (2)**:** *God's Bricks To* me **:** **b⁶**ricks **T²**o me **/** **b⁶**ricks-**T²**ethered

[63] God is Water to Me in a Dry, Thirsty Land : *God Dips Me* in water **/** *God Drips Me* **:** **b⁶**e **ω³**ater to me! **/** **b⁶**lessed/**d⁶**ivine **ω³**ater **/** in **b⁶**aked **F³**ield **/** **d⁶**ry **m³**esa

[64] God Overthrows Ambushers : *Man's Hid/Trick Wars* (1-6) God catches in the act (7-8) **:** **b⁶**esieges **A⁴**mbushers

[65] God Chooses a Wife : *God Picks Wife* **:** **b⁶**rings **S⁵**aints to dwell in his courts (4)

God Drips Life to earth with water (9-13) **:** **b⁶**irth **S⁵**howers

OT Psalms NT

[66] God's Awesome Deeds : *God's Big Gigs/Dids* **: b**^{6}ig d^{6}ids— *awesome actions, deeds, works*

[67] Make All Nations Know Your Saving power : *"God, Give Savin* to every nation **/** let them all **b**^{6}less **L**^{7}ord!"

[68] God Scatters and Melts His Enemies : *God Displaces / Dissipates* the wicked **: b**^{6}reaks-up/**b**^{6}oils **B**^{8}ad *people* (2)

God Fathers the Fatherless : God "Kids" Waifs : b^{6}egets **B**^{8}egottenless (5)

Scatters Kings: *God Sifts Greats* **: b**^{6}reaks-up **B**^{8}osses (12, 14),

Captures Captives : *God Sics Prey* **: b**^{6}etraps **B**^{8}etrappeds (18), *and* **b**^{6}ears **B**^{8}urdens (19.

[69] Saves Me from this Deep Mire! : *God Rids Slime!* **: b**^{6}og g^{9}oodbye! **/ b**^{6}ye g^{9}unk!

[70] Don't Delay Saving Me! : *God's Savin-Me* quickly **: L**^{7}ag 0^0 *Not* S**LO**^{70}w!

[71] Save the Old/Weak : *God/Calms Seventy-One-year-olds* **: L**^{7}ord's l^{1}egacies/l^{1}ongstanding-saints

Saving From Wicked : *God Savin From* wicked **: L**^{7}ucifer l^{1}iberating

[72] Makes Just Kings : *God's Savin Truth* kings (1; cf. Ps. 103:19) **:** *who exercise* **L**^{7}ord's **V**^{2}erdicts

[73] Prosperity of the Wicked Ends : *God Severs Ease* of the wicked **:** They increase wealth (1-15) but then **L**^{7}ose **F**^{3}unds/**F**^{3}inances (16-28)

OT   Psalms   NT

[73] **Whom Have I in heaven but Thee?** (25) : *God's Heavenly* : *L*[7]ord's **H**[3]eavenly *Himself*

[74] **Is God Forever Angry?** : *God's Ever Sore?* : *L*[7]ivid **E**[4]ternally?

[75] **God Demotes/Promotes** : *God Severs Pride* and *God Levers Mild*—*He puts down one and exalts another* : *L*[7]ord **S**[5]cales *(ranks) peoples* : *L*[7]ord **S**[5]upplants/**S**[5]poils/**S**[5]trengthens

[76] **God Breaks Pride** : *God Severs Big/Whigs of the world)* : *L*[7]ofty **b**[6]roken 5-9)

 Man's Wrath will Praise Him (10): *L*[7]auding **b**[6]etrayals

[77] **Has God's Love Ceased Forever?** : *God Severing Ever?* (7-9) : *L*[7]ove *L*[7]ost? (8)

[78] **History of Israel** : *God's Savin Tale*: *L*[7]ord's **B**[8]iography *of His people* : *grace, rebellion, judgment* / *L*[7]ofties & **B**[8]elowlies

[79] **Gentiles Oppress Jerusalem:** *God's Severed Vine / Man's Heaven Crime*—*Gentiles ruling over God's people in Jerusalem* (1-3): *T*[7]yrannical **g**[9]entiles

[80] **Break Our Enemies!** : *"God, Break Foes we have had since Egypt!"* : **B**[8]reak **O**[0]pponents / **B**[8]reak **O**[0]ur *Enemies!*

[81] **God Gave Up on Idolaters** : *God Gave Up His people to stubbornness* (12) *when they* : **B**[8]locked **I**[1]istening *and obeying* (11) / A**B**[8]andoned **I**[1]dolators

[82] **God Rules/Judges the Congregation of gods** : *God Takes Rule in the congregation of gods/rulers* : **B**[8]enevolent **V**[2]indication

 God Breaks Cruel: **B**[8]reaks **n**[2]efarious/**V**[2]illainous (4)

OT Psalms NT

[82] God Saves the Weak and Needy : *God Saves "Used"/ Abused*—*the afflicted, weak, needy* **: B⁸**roken **V²**indicated**/ V²**ictorious**/T²**urned around *by good rulers* (3-4)

God Slays Cruel sons (judges/gods) (6-8) **: B⁸**ad **T²**erminated

[83] God Shames His Enemies! : *God Shames These! / God Shames Fiends* **: B⁸**eats-down **F³**oes **/** *The* **B⁸**ad **H³**umiliated (17)

[84] I Long For Your Courts : *I'm Ached For Your courts / God's Safe Courts* **: B⁸**uilding **W⁴**orship

[85] Revive Us! : *God, Make Life again!* **: R⁸**estore **S⁵**alvation (4-7)

[86] God's Steadfast Love : *God's Patience* (3-15) **: B⁸**elated **b⁶**acklash

[87] Zion—City of God : *God's Gates: Heaven* **: B⁸**uilding **L⁷**ord's

[88] God Puts in the Pit : *God Slays, Graves* **: B⁸**uried **B⁸**odies (5)

God's Great Waves **: B⁸**ig **B⁸**illows *pass over me* (7)

Some Grave Praises? **:** *Do the* **B⁸**uried **B⁸**less *You?* (11-12)

[89] David's Seed on Throne (3-37) **:** *God's Dave Line* **: B⁸**irthed **g⁹**overnors**/P⁹**rinces

M[a]n Breaks Line (38-52:) **: B⁸**roke **g⁹**uarantee (*covenant: 39*)

[90] God From Everlasting To Everlasting : *God's Timing/God's Time Old* **: g⁹**od **O⁰**lam (Hebrew**:** 2)

Teach Us to Number Our Days (12) **:** *God's Time Zone* **: go⁹⁰** *count your days (limit)!*

OT   Psalms   NT

[91] **God's Tight Love Grip** : *God Binds Us* to Him : **g**[9]uardian **l**[1]ord/**l**[1]ove

Angels Guard Our Ways so We Tread on Enemies: *God's Shine Ones* **g**[9]uard **l**[1]anes so we **g**[9]rind **l**[1]ions *and cobras* (13)

[92] **God's Lovingkindness** (2) : *God's Kind "Lūve"* : **g**[9]reat **T**[2]houghtfulness *makes me* **g**[9]lad **n**[2]ight *and day*

God's Great Works (5) : *God's Prime/Fine "Do"s* : **g**[9]od's/**g**[9]reat ... **T**[2]asks/**V**[2]entures

God's Great Thoughts (5) : *God's Mind Huge* : **g**[9]od's/**g**[9]reat ... **T**[2]hought

The Righteous Root and Flourish (12-15) : *God's Kind Root/Grew* : **g**[9]row **V**[2]irtues

[93] **Seas and Floods Praise God** : *God Mind[ed] Seas and floods* : **g**[9]lorifying/**P**[9]raising ... **F**[3]loods/**ω**[3]aters

[94] **God Does Not Forget the Poor** : *God Minds Poor* of His *people who are oppressed* : **g**[9]od **M**[4]inds; *He will not forsake them to the wicked*

[95] **Psalmist Sings Songs of Praise to God** : *Psalmist Chimes Lively when entering His presence with thanksgiving* (1-6)

We're the Sheep of His Pasture (7) : *God's Ovine Līves* : **g**[9]od's **S**[5]heep / **g**[9]razing **S**[5]heep

The Stray Generation (8-11) : *God's Ovine Dive* : *A 40-year* **g**[9]eneration **S**[5]trayed/**g**[9]od-**S**[5]trayers

They will Not Enter Rest : *Some Whine Lives* : **g**[9]oodbye **S**[5]leep

OT — Psalms — NT

[096] Sing of God's Splendor : *God's Shining "Hits" (Songs)* : g^{9}lory b^{6}allads

[097] Lord Reigns Forever : *God's Prime Ever* : g^{9}od's *L^{7}ord forever* : g^{9}lobal *L^{7}ord—judges idolatry, delivers saints*

[098] Joyful Noise to Lord: *God-Chime Make* : g^{9}lad B^{8}lare!

[099] The Lord is Great in Zion : *God's Zion Shines justice and righteousness* (2-4) : g^{9}od g^{9}reat *in Zion/Jacob*

[100] Lord Made us His People/Sheep : *God's Sons—Own Folks, the sheep of His pasture* : l^{1}amb's O^{0}wner O^{0}versees *them*

[101] Walk With Integrity : *God's Sons: Roam None!* : l^{1}ntegrity O^{0}n l^{1}ntegrity

[102] God's Immutable : *God's "One," No "Two"—Immutable* : l^{1}ord C^{0}hanges n^{2}ot / l^{1}ord's O^0 V^{2}ariance

[103] God Removes Our Sins Far as East is from West (12) : *God Flung Those East!* : l^{1}iniquities O^{0}ut F^{3}ar

[104] God Purposes the Sun : *God's Sun-Mold For purpose* (19) : l^{1}ight O^{0}f M^{4}eaning (24)

[105] Israel's History: Abraham > Exodus : *God's Son Grows Life God's Son Throws Life (of slavery)* : l^{1}srael O^{0}ut S^{5}arah > l^{1}srael O^{0}ut S^{5}lavery

[106] Israel's History: Exodus > Captivity : *God's Son Roams Sticks (wanders in wilderness) > God's Son Homesick* : l^{1}srael's O^{0}ppressor: b^{6}abylon

Moses Intercedes (23) : *God's Son Moses intercedes* : l^{1}ord O^{0}f b^{6}reach

OT   **Psalms**   NT

[107] **God Attacks Israel's Enemies:** *God's A Foe-Saver* : I^{1}srael's
O^{0}ppressors *T^{7}erminated/L^{7}iquidated*

[108] **God's Love Above Heavens** : *God's Love So Great* : I^{1}ove
O^{0}ver B^{8}lue-sky (4)

[109] **Judge Enemies!** *God, Judge Foes Mine* : I^{1}ord O^{0}f g^{9}odless

[110] **God "Footstools" King's Enemies** : *God's Son On Throne* :
I^{1}ord I^{1}ords O^{0}pponents *of His Son/King* (1, 5-7)

[111] **God's Works Just** (7) : *God's Just Just Just!* : I^{1}aw I^{1}aw I^{1}aw

[112] **Righteous Never Shaken** (6-8) : *God's Just Unmoved* :
I^{1}awful I^{1}ack V^{2}olatility/T^{2}urbulence

[113] **God Exalts Humble/Poor** (7-9): *God Funds The Need*(y) :
I^{1}ifts I^{1}owly F^{3}rom *dust*

[114] **Tremble At Lord of the Exodus** : *Qualms From The Lord* :
I^{1}ord I^{1}nitiates A^{4}gitation *(trembling)*

[115] **Idols Dead/Speechless** : *God-Shunned From Life* : I^{1}dol's
I^{1}ifeless S^{5}peechless

[116] **God Saves From Death** (8) : *Some Come From Crypts* : I^{1}ord
I^{1}ooses d^{6}eath

[117] **God's Truth/Faithfulness Forever** : *God Of Trust Ever* :
I^{1}ord I^{1}ords *T^{7}ruth/T^{7}rust*

[118] **Lord Cuts Off Enemies:** *God Blunts Hating/The Hate* :
1^{1}ord I^{1}ords B^{8}ad

God's Cornerstone Rejected : *God's Son Hating/Some
Hate* : I^{1}ord I^{1}ays B^{8}edrock

OT   Psalms   NT

[119] Word Lamp to Feet : *God Of Shining* **:** l¹ord's l¹amp g⁹uides

I Love God's Laws : *Psalmist Loves The Binds* *(laws)* **:** l¹ove l¹aw g⁹od's

[120] Save Me From Lying Tongues : *Some Tongues To Close* **:** l¹ying T²ongues O⁰cclude!

[121] Israel's Keeper Never Sleeps (4) **:** *God's None To Slum* **:** l¹ord n²ever l¹nactive/l¹nsomniac/l¹apses//l¹ord n²ot l¹azy

[122] "**To Temple!**" (1) **:** *Mobs Run To You* **:** "l¹et's T²o T²emple!"

[123] Look to God Until Mercy Comes : *God, Come To Me!* **:** l¹ook T²ill F³orgiven

[124] Lord Fights on my Side (1) **:** *God Comes To War* against my enemies **:** l¹ord's V²ictory-W⁴ar / l¹ord's V²ictory M⁴ine

[125] God Surrounds Us : *God's Love "Loops" Lives* **:** l¹ord T²otally S⁵urrounds *us*

[126] Restore Us From Captivity: "*God, Undo Kicks* we've received from enemies **:** l¹ord V²italizes b⁶rutalized

Sow Tears, Reap Joy : *S[o]me Glum To Grins* **:** l¹ord V²oids /T²erminates b⁶lues

[127] Lord Builds or Labor Vain : *God's "None!" To Sweatin* **:** l¹ord *or* V²ain *L*⁷abor

Lord Guards or Guarding Vain : *God's "None!" To Hedgin* risk **:** l¹ord *or* V²ain *L*⁷ookouts

[128] God-Fearers Blessed : *God's Sons To Quake/Shake* **:** l¹or'd's T²remblers B⁸lessed

OT　　　　　　　Psalms　　　　　　　NT

[129] "Overthrow Zion's Enemies!" : *"God, Come To Zion's aid!"* : "l^{1}ord, T^{2}erminate g^{9}uerillas!"

[130] My Soul Waits for God! : *I'm A Needy Soul Lord, don't take too long!* : I^1'm H^{3}olding O^{0}n/O^{0}ut / I^1'm ω^{3}aiting O^{0}n You!

[131] I Calmed My Soul : *Calmed A Needy One* : I^1 H^{3}ushed I^{1}t

[132] Zion, God's Resting Place : *God's One Ease Roost* : l^{1}ord's Z^{3}ion n^{2}est/T^{2}ranquility/l^{1}ord's Z^{3}ion^2

[133] Brethren Unity Pleasant : *God "Ones" We Three* : 1^1 H^{3}armonious F^{3}raternity/1^1 ω^{3}e 3^3 *(or more)*

[134] Lift Hands to Bless Lord : *Palms Up, Thee, Lord* : l^{1}ift H^{3}ands W^{4}ay *up!*

[135] The Lord Does His Pleasure (6) : *God's Fun He Drives* : l^{1}ord's ω^{3}ill S^{5}atisfied

[136] God's Love Forever: *God's Love Ceaseless* : l^{1}ord's F^{3}avor b^{6}oundless

[137] God's People Grieve for Zion in Babylon : *God's Sons Grieve Heaven (Zion)* : l^{1}ament Z^{3}ion's L^{7}oss

[138] God Exalted His Word (2) : *God's Son (Word)* ***He Raised!*** l^{1}ord H^{3}onors B^{8}ible *(Word of God)*

　　　He Fulfills His Purposes for Us (8) : *God's Sons Pre-Made/Shaped/Framed* : L^{1}ord F^{3}ullfills B^{8}lueprints *for me*

[139] God Hems Us In (5) : *God Front Behind* : l^1 F^{3}ront P^{9}osterior

　　　If I Ascend to Heaven, You Are There! (8) : *I'm Up, Thee Find* : l^1 H^{3}eaven g^{9}o

OT   Psalms   NT

[139] **If I Descend into Sheol, You are There!** (8) : *I'm Sunk, Thee Find* : I^1 H^{3}ell g^{9}o

God Frames Us before Birth (15): *God's Sons Designed* : I^1 F^{3}rame P^{9}eople

[140] **Save Me from Evil People** (9-10) : *"God, Abort/Cut Short Foes!"* : "I^{1}ord, M^{4}assacre O^{0}pressors!"

[141] **Guard My Lips!** (3) : *"God, Blunt Forked Tongue!"* : "I^{1}ord, M^{4}anage/W^{4}atch I^{1}ips!"

[142] **My Refuge** (5) : *God's A Fort To* me : I^{1}ord's M^{4}y T^{2}ower

[143] **God Restores My Soul** (11) : *God R[e]stores Me* : I^{1}ord M^{4}ends H^{3}earts

[144] **God's My Fortress** : *God's A Fort Force* : I^{1}ord's M^{4}y W^{4}all

[145] **God's Might is Right** : *God's Punch For Right* : I^{1}ord's M^{4}oral S^{5}trength

[146] **Trust God's Strength** : *God's The Fortress* : I^{1}ord M^{4}anages b^{6}ehaviors/b^{6}usiness // I^{1}ord M^{4}ends b^{6}roken/b^{6}eggarly

[147] **God Heals Broken Hearts** : *God R[e]stores Severed* hearts : I^{1}ord M^{4}ends T^{7}ears (3)

[148] **All Creation Praises God!** : *Psalm: Tongues For Praise* : I^{1}ord A^{4}ll B^{8}elaud

[149] **Sing (Psalm) A New (Born) Song (Psalm)** *to the Lord* : *Psalm A Formed Chime* : I^{1}ark/I^{1}yric A^{4}dditional P^{9}salm

[150] **All With Breath Praise the Lord!** (6) : *Psalms—A Life Owes* : I^{1}iving S^{5}ouls/S^{5}pirits O^{0}we *praise!*

God

[06] **Hates 6 Things** (16-19) : *Six* : 6^6 b^{6}ads *hated*

[16] **Directs Things** (1, 2, 9, 24) : *God Picks* : l^{1}ord d^{6}irects

[17] **Tests Hearts** (3) : *God Testin* : l^{1}nvestigative *L^{7}ord*

[21] **Lord Turns Kings' Hearts like Streams** (1) : *To Run* where *He wants* : l^{1}ord's B^{8}rooks

   Weighs Hearts (2) : *Views Judged* : V^{2}aluates l^{1}ntentions

[25] **Conceals Things** (2) : *To Hide* : T^{2}hings S^{5}ealed *up*

[30] **Shields Trusters** (5) : *Shields Hope* : F^{3}ences O^{0}ptimism

Truth

[15] **No-Counsel Plans** (22) : *Dumb Life* : l^{1}acks S^{5}trategy

[19] **No-Knowledge Zeal** (2) : *Run Blind* : l^{1}gnorant g^{9}usto

[21] **No Counsel Against Lord** (30) : *Truth/Rule None* : n^{2}o l^{1}aws

   Lord Conquered, Not our Horses (31) : *Truth Won* : V^{2}ictory l^{1}ord's / n^{2}ag-l^{1}ess *victory*

[23] **No-Cost Truth** (23) : *Truth Free* (cf. Rev. 22:17) : T^{2}ruth F^{3}ree

[24] **Truth Wins Wars** (6) : *Truth War* : T^{2}ruth W^{4}ins/W^{4}ar

[28] **Relativism > Unstable** (5) : *Truth Gray* : V^{2}alue B^{8}reakdown

[29] **Relativism > Immoral** (18) : *Truth Blind* : V^{2}alue P^{9}leasure

Proverbs

Truth

[30] Don't Add to God's Word (6) : *Read Zero in* : **N³**o **O⁰**thers

Thoughts

Attitudes

[10] Hope / Fear Future (24, 28) : *One Hope/One Phobe* : **I¹**ove/**I¹**oathe **O⁰**utlook

[12] Love Disciplines (1) : *Love Rules* : **I¹**ove **T²**rains

[13] Wise/Scoffer Son (1) : *One/None Heeds* : **I¹**oves/**I¹**oathes **H³**eeding/**F³**ather

    Good/Evil Bequeathers (12) : *Bequeathe/Bereave* : **I¹**nheritance **F³**urnished/**F³**leeced

[14] Anger > Foolishness (16-17) : *Dumb War* : **I¹**ivid > **A⁴**bsurd

Planning

[14] Prudent/Imprudent (15) : *One Formed/One Tore* plan : **I¹**ong-run **W⁴**ise/**E⁴**mpty

    Way Seems Right > Death (12) : *Fun > Morte* : **I¹**ethal **W⁴**ay

    Right/Wrong Nations (34) : *Reformed/Deformed* ones : **I¹**ove/ **I¹**oathe **M⁴**orals

[16] Wink > Dishonest (30) : *One Winks* : **I¹**mmoral **b⁶**links

[22] Prudent are Cautious (3) : *Prudes Muse* future : **V²**irtuous **T²**hink *ahead*

OT   Proverbs   NT

Planning

[24] Schemers Plan Evil (8, 9) : *Loose "Forces"* : V^2ice M^4andates/A^4gendas

[27] Don't Boast "Tomorrow!" (1) : *Shoo Bettin* on tomorrow : n^2o T^7outing

Lust

[14] Envy/Passion Rots Bones (30) : *Lust Sores* : l^1ust > W^4eak/ W^4orn *bones*

[23] Don't Crave King's Food (1-3) : *Food King's* : V^2itals K^3ing's

[27] Jealousy is Cruel (4) : *Cruel Envyin* : T^2yrannical J^7ealousy

Integrity

[10] Paths Walked (9, 17) : *One Trends (straight)/One Bends* : I^1ntegrity O^0ptions

[11] Integrity/Duplicity (3, 20) : *One/None* : I^1ntegrity/ I^1nsincerity

[12] Truthing/Lying (17, 22) : *One Truth/None Truth* : l^1ying / T^2ruthing

[21] Wicked are Bold-Faced (29) : *Cruel's Front* : n^2asty l^1ofty

[26] Joke Digs (18-19) : *Cruel Digs* : n^2asty d^6igs

Lips Disguise Heart Hatred (24) : *"Fool" Lips* : T^2ongue b^6eautiful / T^2hinking/V^2iewpoint b^6ad

OT **Proverbs** NT

Behavior

General

[11] Righteous are a Tree of Life (30) : *Trunk Young : Won some* souls : I[1]ife I[1]otus

[15] Sacrifice by Wicked is Loathsome (8) : *Sac-r[i]-Vice* : I[1]oathsome S[5]acrifice

Associations

[22] Avoid Mockers (10, 24) : *Shoo Rudes* : V[2]oid T[2]aunters

[27] Iron Sharpens Iron (17) : *Do Whettin* : T[2]aper L[7]ance

Justice

[11] Just/Unjust Scales (1) : *One Just/Unjust* : I[1]mpartial/ I[1]nequitous

[14] Bless/Oppress Poor (31) : *Fund Poor /Shun Poor* : I[1]nvest/I[1]end/I[1]gnore M[4]isfortunate

[16] Just Scales (11) : *Just Sticks* (measuring) : I[1]egitimate b[6]enchmarks

[17] Justify Wicked (15) : *Just Theftin* : I[1]egitimize L[7]awbreakers

Condemn Righteous (15) : *Judge Heaven* : I[1]mprison T[2]ruth

[20] Unequal Measures (10, 23) : *Skewed Stones* : V[2]ariances 0[0]

The Just King (8, 26) : *Truth throne* : V[2]irtuous O[0]verlord

OT   Proverbs   NT

[22] Don't Move Boundaries (28) : *Move Rule* > : n^2o n^2udging

[24] Acquit Wicked (24) : *Rule Tort* favorably : V^2indicate W^4icked

  Condemn Righteous (28) : *Rule "Moral"* unfavorably : V^2ictimize *[the]* M^4oral

[26] Fools Dishonored (1, 8) : *Fools Fit* for dishonor (1) : T^2omfools b^6esmirched

[28] Right/Wrong Rulers (12) : *Rule Cases* : V^2irtuous/B^8ad *rulers*

[29] Right/Wrong Rulers (1-4) : *Rule Kinds* : V^2irtuous/g^9reedy

Endurance

[10] Good/Bad in Storms (25) : *One Copes/One Folds* : 1^1 O^0ver /1^1 U^0nder

[15] Good/Bad Finance (6) : *One Thrives / One Dives* : 1^1 S^5ucceeds / 1^1 S^5inks

[26] Dog To > Vomit, Fool To > Folly (11) : *Pooch/Fool Trips* : V^2omit/V^2anity b^6ack *To*

[28] Wicked Flee Not Chased (1) : *Who Chased?* No one! : n^2o B^8loodhounds

Reputation

[10] Good/Bad Legacies (7) : *One Gold/One Scold* : l^1egacy O^0ptions

[11] Win Souls > Tree of Life (30) : *Won Some* : l^1ife l^1imbs

OT   Proverbs   NT

Reputation

[12] **Good/Bad Wife** (4) : *Repute* : l^1ady V^2irtuous/V^2icious

[22] **Good Name Legacy** (1) : *Proved Good* : V^2irtuous/n^2oble n^2ame

Discipline

[13] **Love Disciplines with Rod** (24) : *Love Beats* : l^1ove K^3nock /K^3nuckle/F^3orms/N^3urtures

[20] **Stripes/Wounds Cleanse Evil** (30) : *Wound Soap* : T^2hrash C^0leansings

[22] **Train Up a Child!** (6) : *Youth Truth/Rule* : T^2rain T^2oddlers

   Folly in Children (15) : *Youth Fools* : T^2oddler n^2onsense

   Rod Drives it Out (15) : *Move Tool* : T^2oddler T^2ool

[23] **Discipline Rod** (13-14) : *Youth Reed* : T^2oddler F^3ormer

[27] **Faithful Wounds of a Friend** (6) : *Wounds Savin* : T^2hrash L^7oyal

Manners

[25] **Take Low Seat before Kings** (6-7) : *Shoo Heights* : T^2ake S^5eat *in back*

   Familiarity > Contempt (17) : *Used [to] > Strife* : T^2ight > S^5trife

   Feed your Enemy (21-22) : *Food > Strife* : n^2ourish S^5trikers/S^5trivers

OT   Proverbs   NT

Response to Provocation

[10] Love Covers All Sins (12) : *Love Cloaks* sins : I^1ids O^0ffenses

[12] Rash Tongue > Sword (18) : *Tongue Wounds* : I^1njury T^2ongue

Wise Tongue > Heals (18) : *Tongue Soothes* : I^1mprove T^2ongue

[13] Critique the Wise/the Fool (1) : *One Heeds/One Steams* : I^1nstruct ω^3ise/I^1ncite F^3ools

[26] Fool Meddles in Quarrels (17) : *Fool Sticks* nose in : n^2osy b^6uffoon

[27] Fools Provoke (3) : *Fools Severin* relationships : n^2innies /n^2incompoops/n^2itwits ...T^7empt/T^2ease/L^7ure

Gluttony

[20] Wine Deceives (1) : *Booze Coax/"Dopes"* people : V^2odka/ T^2equila ... D^0eceive/O^0bfuscate

[21] Wise Save Precious Oil (20) : *"Cūms"* (accumulates) *Some* : V^2alues I^1t

Fool Devours Precious Oil (20) : *"Cūms"* (accumulates) *None* : V^2oids I^1t

[23] Drink/Meat Gluttony (20, 21-35) : *Booze/Meats* : V^2oracious H^3ooch/m^3eat consumers

[31] Kings Don't Get Drunk (4, 5) : *Beer None?* : K^3ings I^1eave it

Proverbs

Speech

[10] **Few/Many Words** (19) : *Blunt Quotes / Run[-on] Quotes* : I[1]ittle/I[1]ong O[0]ration

[12] **Conceal/Blurt Out** : (23) : *One Cooped / One Loose* tongue : I[1]aconic/I[1]oose T[2]ongued

[13] **Guarded/Talkative** (3) : *One Mum /One Speaks* : I[1]aconic/ Y[3]akkity

[15] **Soft/Harsh Words** (1) : *One Life / One Strife* : I[1]nhibit/ I[1]nstigate S[5]trife

Tongue is Tree of Life/Strife (4, 18) : *Tongue Life / Tongue Strife* : I[1]ingual S[5]pirit/S[5]trife

[17] **Wicked Love Libel** (4, 9) : *Meddling/Spreading* lies : I[1]oves L[7]ibel

Guarded/Open-mouthed (27) : *Hemming/Spreading* : I[1]nfo L[7]ock/L[7]oose

[18] **Fools Opinions** (2) : *Dumb Prates* : I[1]unatic B[8]eliefs

Answer Before Hearing (13) : *Tongue Haste* : I[1]mmediate B[8]acktalk

Death/Life in Tongue (21) : *Fating/Saving* : I[1]ingual B[8]ury/B[8]irth

[20] **Fools Quarrel** (3) : *Fools Scold* : n[2]itwits/n[2]incompoops ... O[0]ppose/C[0]ontend

[21] **Control Tongue** (23) : *Rule Tongue* : T[2]ongue I[1]eash

OT Proverbs NT

Speech

[25] **Good News > Life** (13, 25) : *News Life* : n^{2}ews > S^{5}pirit

[26] **Gossip** (22) : *News Bits* : n^{2}ews b^{6}its/b^{6}ytes/b^{6}itter

[28] **Flatter/Rebuke** (23) : *To Praise / To Blame* : T^{2}o B^{8}utter-up/B^{8}lame

Confess/Conceal Sin (13) : *To Make/To Drape* confession : T^{2}o B^{8}lurt-out/n^{2}ame // T^{2}o B^{8}ury // V^{2}eil ... B^{8}ad *(sin)*

[29] **Fools Vent Anger** (11, 22) : *Fools Whine* : n^{2}itwits g^{9}ripe

[30] **"Gimme Now!" Leeches** (15) : *Leech Crows* > "N^{3}ow O^{0}ffer!" *(not later)*

Labor/Sloth

[06] **Ant/Sloth** (6-11) : *Quick/Drifts* : b^{6}risk/b^{6}um

[10] **Worker/Slacker** (5) : *One Loads / One Loafs* : l^{1}aborer/lO^{10}afer

[13] **Worker/Sluggard** (4) : *One Speeds / One Dreams* : 1^1 F^{3}armworker / 1^1 F^{3}reeloader

[14] **Worker/Talker** (23): *One Works / One Words* : 1^1 W^{4}orker/ 1^1 W^{4}indbag

Profit/Poverty (23) : *One Worth/One Poor* : 1^1 W^{4}indfall / 1^1 W^{4}retched/W^{4}elfare

[20] **Don't Love Sleep!** (13) : *Snooze No! / Shoo Doze!* : n^{2}o O^{0}versleeping

Labor/Sloth

[24] **Sleep Impoverishes** (33-34) : *Snooze > Poor* : n^2aps > W^4retched

[28] **Producer/Dreamer** (19) : *To Make / To Chase* : T^2o B^8uild/ T^2o B^8rood

Possessions

[06] **Debts** (1-5) : *Chits* : b^6ad-loans/b^6onds/d^6ebts

[11] **Givers/Hoarders** (25-26) : *One Funds / One "Trunks"* : 1^1 l^1ends / 1^1 l^1ays-up

[15] **Hate Bribes!** (27) : *Shun Bribes* : l^1oathe S^5ubornations/ S^5ops/S^5olicitations

[19] **Wealthy Loved** (4) : *Lush Dined!* : l^1ove P^9rosperous

     Poor Despised (4) : *None Dined!* : l^1oathe P^9oor

     Give Poor > Lend Lord (17) : *Consign* : l^1end g^9od

[21] **Bribe Propitiates Anger** (14) : *Soothe Funds* : T^2ranquilize l^1oot

[22] **Rich Oppress Poor** (16, 22) : *Loot Rules* : T^2ycoon T^2yrants

     Don't Add Debt (26-27) : *Shoo Dues* : n^2o n^2otes

[23] **Money Flies Away** (5) : *Loot Flees* : n^2ickles/T^2reasures F^3ly

[27] **Secure Loans** (13) : *Shrewd Pledgin* : T^2actful/n^2egotiated L^7oans

OT   Proverbs   NT

[28] Usury: Excess Interest (8) : *Cruel Pay/Wage* : n^{2}efarious B^{8}onus/B^{8}enefit

Women

[05] Adulterer (1-6) : *Wife Killer* : S^{2}winger/S^{5}leeps *around*

[07] Adultery/Adulterer (6-27) : *Beddin* : L^{7}overs

[31] Virtuous Woman (10-31) : *Deemed One* : N^{3}oble l^{1}ady

<u>OT</u> Ecclesiastes <u>NT</u>
[Philosophy without God]

[01] Nothing New Under Sun (1-10) : *None* new */ Sun* :
I^{1}terations *(cycles, repeats)*

[02] I Tried . . .

Laughter/Mirth (2) **:** *Hoots* **:** T^{2}ee-hees

Wealth (4-11) **:** *Loot* **:** V^{2}aluables

Work (4-6, 17-22) **:** *Tools* **:** V^{2}ocations/T^{2}rades/T^{2}ools

Wisdom (12-17) **:** *Schools* **:** T^{2}ruths/T^{2}eachings/V^{2}irtues

[03] Every Purpose is Timed (1-8) **:** *Mete* **:** F^{3}oreordained/
m^{3}eted/"H^{3}eavened"

Eternity in Man's Heart (11) **:** *Eons* **:** F^{3}orever/H^{3}eart

Eat, Drink, Be Merry (12-13) **:** *Meats / Drinks / Treats* **:**
m^{3}eats/F^{3}easts

Men Die like Beasts (18-22) : *Beasts/Cease* **:** F^{3}erals/
F^{3}inish/F^{3}ate

[04] Oppressors (1-3) **:** *Lords* **:** M^{4}anipulators/M^{4}altreators/
M^{4}aligners

All Labor is Competition/Rivalry (4) **:** *Sport / Score* **:**
M^{4}atches/W^{4}inners

No Dependents, Labor for Naught (8) **:** *Lorn* **:** 4^4-lorn/
A^{4}lone/M^{4}arooned

Promotion: Prison/Poor > King (13-15) **:** *"Scored!"* **:**
M^{4}oved-up/A^{4}dvanced

OT   Ecclesiastes   NT

[05] Rash Words before God (2-3) : *Jive/Hype* : S^5pout *off*

Pay Vows to God on Time (4-7) : *Ripe/Right time* : S^5peedily/S^5wiftly

Many Dreams > Empty Words (7) : *Sky thinking* : S^5targazing

Futility of Wealth (8-20) : *Strive / Drive / Buy* : S^5ecuritizing *(worldly)*

[06] Rich and Dissatisfied (1-12) : *Rich / Wish life* : b^6ourgeoisie *and* b^6ored/d^6issatisfied

[07] Wisdom and Folly (1-29) : *Heaven/Bettin* : L^7earning/ L^7unacy

[08] Obey Kings (1-9) : *Wait on them / Obey* : B^8ow/OB^8ey

[09] Fate (3-11) : *Blind Chance?* : g^9amble/g^9ripped/P^9redoomed /P^9ortion/P^9redicament

[10] Assorted Proverbs : *Tenets* : l^1ife O^{0}rdinances

Boss Gets Mad > Stay Composed! (4) : *Bend!* : l^1asting O^{0}ptimism

Dull Ax > Harder Work (10) : *Bend more* : l^1abor O^{0}utput *greater*

Indolence > House Leaks/Sags (18) : *Vents water* : l^1azy/ l^1ndolent O^{0}verlook *things that need repair*

Little Birds Do Tell Secrets (20) : *Wren/Hen?* : l^1ittle O^{0}wls?

[11] Cast Bread on Water (1-2): *Leaven toss* : l^1oaf l^1ob

OT   Ecclesiastes   NT

[12] Remember Creator from Youth (1) **:** *From Youth* **:** I^{1}ad T^{2}houghts

Spirit Returns to God (7) **:** *Unto* *God* **:** I^{1}ife V^{2}acates/I^{1}ord-V^{2}isit

No End to Books (12) **:** *Done books?* *Never!* **:** I^{1}nfinite T^{2}exts/n^{2}ovels

Conclusion (13) **:** *Conclude:* *God will judge secrets* (14) *I Judge Truth/Nooks* **:** I^{1}ocates n^{2}ooks—*Selves* *(inner) and* *With***helds** *(hiddens)*

OT Song of Solomon NT
[*ong*]

[01] **Love better than > Wine** (2) : *Strong Love* >> *Strong Rum!* : l^{1}ove >>> l^{1}iquor

Mutual Attraction : *Strong "Stun"* : l^{1}ovely / l^{1}ooker

[02] **My Lover is Finally Coming** (8) : *Long Due* : T^{2}ardy

[03] **Longing For My Lover in Dreams** (1, 5) : *Long Seek/Dream* : F^{3}antasy

Solomon's Wedding Day (6-11) : *Song Feast* : N^{3}uptial/ H^{3}itched/ω^{3}edding

[04] **Solomon Describes Flawless Bride** (1-16) : *Strong Form* : M^{4}atchless/W^{4}ork *of art*

[05] **Lovesick Separation** : *Strong Drive* : S^{5}ick/S^{5}eparation

My Strong, Sweet Man (10-16) : *Strong Guy* : S^{5}trong/ S^{5}weet/S^{5}uperior

[06] **Mutual Delight** : *Strong Fix* *on each other* : b^{6}liss/b^{6}eloved/ d^{6}elight

[07] **Your Figure (Form)** : *A Strong Seven?/Heaven*ly? : L^{7}ovely

[08] **Love is a Fire** (6-7) : *Strong Flame* : B^{8}onfire

OT Isaiah NT

[*ise* *ice* *ites* *ides* *i*]

[01] Judah's Wickedness (1-20) : *Dies One* : J[1]udah / I[1]niquitous

The Unfaithful City (21-31) : *Dies One* : J[1]erusalem/ I[1]niquitous

[02] Mountain of the Lord (1-5) : *Rise To* Highest (2) : T[2]all / n[2]ations *will flow to it*

Day of the Lord on Pride (17-21) : *Pride's Duel/"Through"* : V[2]anity *finished*

[03] Children Replace Leaders (4-7) : *Die Leads > Rise Teens* : K[3]ings > K[3]ids

[04] Branch of the Lord Glorious (2-3) : *Rise Lord/"Glor!"* : A[4]rm / M[4]agificent / M[4]ajestic

Spirit of Burning Cleanses (3-4) : *Fries Pure/Cure* : W[4]ildfire W[4]ashes *away filth*

[05] Lord's Vineyard Ruined (1-7) : *Dies Ivy* : S[5]auvignon / S[5]hortage

Call Evil Good and VV. (8-30, 20) : *Nice Vice / Vice Nice* : S[5]waps *bad*

[06] Isaiah's Vision of the Lord (5-7) : *Is' Vision/ Fries Lips* (6-7) : b[6]ehold! / b[6]urning *coal*

Preach Till Cities Desolated (11) : *Fries "Cits"* (13) : b[6]arren / b[6]urning

[07] Rezin/Pekah Threats (1-9) : *Rise Rezin/Threatins* : L[7]ooms

God With Us (10-25) : *Guise Heaven's* : L[7]ord *with us*

OT   Isaiah   NT

[08] **Assyria Invades** (1-10) : *S[y]riah's Raid* : **B⁸**attles *Israel*

Fear God and Wait for Him (11-22) : *Eyes Wait!* : **B⁸**elieve / **B⁸**ide *your time waiting*

[09] **To Us a Son is Given** (5-7) : *Tike's Sign* : **g⁹**overnment / **g⁹**iven *on shoulder* / *Mighty* **g⁹**od / **P⁹**rince *of* / **P⁹**eace

Pride Judged (8-21) : *Pride's Time to fall again* : **g⁹**loating/ **g⁹**lory/**P⁹**ride/**P⁹**ut *down*

[10] **My Rod Assyria Brags** (5-11) : *My Club Boasts / Rises A Boast* : "**I¹**m **O⁰**verconfident!"

Remnant Returns (20-34) : *My "Rem"* : **l¹**ord's **O⁰**utliers/ **O⁰**nly *survivors*

[11] **Stem of Jesse Sprouts** (1, 4) : *Rise of Son/Judge // Righteous One* : **J¹**esse's **l¹**imb/**l¹**eaves

Lion & Lamb Lie Together (6-9) : *Lion's Left Some meat* : **l¹**ion **l¹**amb

[12] **Lord My Strength/Song** (1-6) : *My Tough Tune* : **l¹**ord *[my]* **V²**igor/**V²**ocal

[13] **Medes to Take Babylon** (17) : *Rise Of Medes* : **l¹**ord's **m³**edes

[14] **Jacob Restored** (1-11) : *Zi's Restored* : **l¹**srael **M⁴**ended

Lucifer Falls (12-20) : *Rise-s North* (13) / *Dies From Sword* (19) : **l¹**ucifer **E⁴**xits *heaven*

AssyriA¹⁴/PhilistIA¹⁴ Struck (24-32) : *Dies The Lords* : **l¹**ose **E⁴**mpires

[15] **Moabi¹tes⁵ Waterless** (6, 9): *Dies The "-Bites"* (4) : I¹and S⁵corched

[16] **Pri¹de Moab⁶ judged** : *Pride Prickings* : I¹uster b⁶elittled/d⁶egraded (14)

[17] **Damascus Ruined Financially** : *Dies: Funds Severed* : I¹nvestments SyrI¹a / J¹udged > *L⁷anguises*

[18] **Cush: Tributes To Lord** (7) : *Rise Payings* to Zion : I¹ands' B⁸ounty *to God* / I¹and B⁸uzzing *wings* (1)

[19] **Egypt: Judged Then Saved** (18-24) : *Rise From Slime* : I¹dolatry > g⁹odliness

Israel, Egypt, Assyria "My people" (16-24) : *Rise Of Shines* *(each 1/3 the blessing)* : I¹ands g⁹lorious/g⁹odly

[20] **Isaiah's Naked Sign to Egypt/Cush** (2, 4) : *Is' Nude Stroll / Eyes Plenty* on him : n²aked/n²ude O⁰pen-footed (3)

[21] **Babylon "Fallen, Fallen"** (9) : *"Dies" To -Lon* : T²wo I¹ament / T²erminated I¹dols/I¹mages (9) / BabyI¹on²

[22] **Valley of Vision** (1, 10-11) : *Eyes To Tools* instead of the Lord : V²alley V²ision / V²ain T²rust

[23] **Fall of Tyre/Sidon** : *Sīd's Ruined Sea* trade : T²yre/T²rade F³alls *for 70 years* (14-15)

Rise of Tyre/Sidon : *Sīd's New Sea* trade : T²yre H³eightens / T²rade H³ealed/H³oly (17-18)

[24] **Lord Judges Earth's Pride** : *Pride's To Mourn* : V²anity > M⁴ourning

<u>**OT**</u>   **Isaiah**   <u>**NT**</u>

[24] Angels/Kings > Imprisoned > Visited (21-22) : ***"Highs" To Fort*** : T^2ie-up/V^2isit A^4ngels/A^4ristocrats

[25] God To Swallow up Death (7-8) : ***Rise To Life*** : n^2ecro-S^5wallow / V^2oid S^5lain

[26] Perfect-Peace Mindset (3) : ***Minds To Fix*** *on God* : T^2heos-b^6rained

Dead Will Rise (19) : ***Rise To Live*** : V^2ivified b^6odies

[27] Redeemed Settle Zion (2) : ***Zi's To Settlin*** *people* : T^2o L^7evant / T^2orah/T^2el-Aviv L^7iving

Leviathan Slain (1) : ***I Slew Leviathan*** : V^2anquished L^7eviathan / "V^2i" L^7iquiditated

[28] Ephraim's Prophets/Priests Drunk (7) : ***Wise Too Dazed*** : n^2obles B^8oozed

Zion's Cornerstone (16) : ***Zi's New Base*** : n^2ew B^8ase

[29] God Compasses Zion with Enemy (2-3) : ***I Hoop Zion / Zi's Hoop Time*** : n^2ation g^9irdled

Lip Honor, No Heart (13) : ***Guise To Shrine*** : n^2o-g^9ut *worship* / V^2ain g^9ums

[30] Don't Ally with Egypt! ***Ties Ēg No/0*** : N^3o O^0utsourcing *them!*

Prophet Lies to Us (10) : ***Lies He Spoke*** : F^3alse O^0rator

Lord To Heal People (26) : ***Zi's Hurty/Cure-ied*** : H^3eals O^0ccupants / H^3urting O^0bviated

OT　　　　　Isaiah　　　　　NT

[30] Lord Will Burn Kings (33) : *Rise Burning / Fries Th[e] Thrones* : **K**^{3}ings **O**^{0}vened *(Topheth!)*

[31] Woe to Egyptian Alliances! (1) : *Ties Ēg None!* : **N**^{3}o **l**^{1}eagues/**l**^{1}ink-ups

[32] Righteous King Rules (1) : *Nice King Rules* : **K**^{3}ing **V**^{2}irtue

Complacent Women Warned (9) : *Rise Ease-Fools!* : **F**^{3}emales/**ω**^{3}omen **T**^{2}ranquil

[33] Zion Will Be Freed (20) : *Zi's Seen Freed!* : **F**^{3}reed **Z**^{3}ion!

[34] God Swords/Burns Nations : *I Bring Sword / I Heat Floors* :

F^{3}ire & **M**^{4}achete

[35] Zion Restored : *Zi's Revived* : **Z**^{3}ion **S**^{5}eeded

Ransomed Return/Sing (10) : *Zi's Revived* : **Z**^{3}ion **S**^{5}ings

[36] Syria/Sennacherib Invades Judah : *Rise Syria "Stick"* : **Z**^{3}ion "**b**^{6}ranched"/**b**^{6}ludgeoned/**b**^{6}eaten *up*

[37] Hezekiah Prays to Win (20) : *HezeKiah's Seek-Heaven* : **H**^{3}ezekiah **L**^{7}ifts *voice to God*

Sennacherib's 185,000 Men Killed (36) : *Sights The Deadened* : **K**^{3}ing **L**^{7}oses *men* / **K**^{3}illed **L**^{7}ieutenants

[38] God Gives Hezekiah 15 More Years from Deathbed : *"Rise, Be Saved!"* : **Z**^{3}eke's **B**^{8}reath *extended*

[39] Hezekiah Shows Off Loot then Judged : *Isaiah: "Decline Coming!"* : **Z**^{3}eke's **g**^{9}old *sent to Babylon*

[40] Comfort My People! (2-3) : *Zi's Warring done* : **W**^{4}ars **O**^{0}ver

<u>OT</u>   Isaiah   <u>NT</u>

[40] Who is like God? (12ff) : *Size Glory?* : M^4e O^0nly!

Big Nations Nothing (15) : *Rise for "0"!* : M^4ights 0^0s!

Mount Eagles' Wings (30-31) : *Flies O'er Roads* : M^4ounted O^0n *eagles' wings*

[41] I Alone Help You, Israel! (8-10) : *I Lord One and Only!* : A^1lone/A^4ids/A^4ssists I^1srael

Idols Futile (23) : *Id[ol]s For None* : M^4eaningless I^1dols

[42] Behold My Servant! (2-4) : *I Lord's Tool* : "M^4y T^2ool!"

I Give My Glory to None! (8) : *My Glory To no one!* : E^4xcellence n^2o-one *else!*

Sing New Song (10) : *My Lord's Tune* : M^4usic n^2ew

Israel Blind/Deaf (18-20) : *Eyes/Aurals Through (Done)* : E^4yes/E^4ars V^2oid

[43] Our Creator/Redeemer : *"I Formed/Stored Thee"* : M^4ade/M^4anumit Y^3ou

Vicarious Atonement (3-4) : *Hires For Thee* : A^4tonement F^3ill-ins (subs)

[44] My Elect (1-5, 21) : *I Form For Myself* : M^4y E^4lect/W^4illed

I Declare Future (7-8) : *I Form Course of events* : M^4y A^4genda

Idols Good for Nothing (9ff) : *Id[ol]s Formed For nothing* : W^4orthless W^4orship

Isaiah

[45] Cyrus My Anointed (1) : *Cy's Formed Messiah* : **A⁴**nointed **S⁵**ervant

I Form Light/Darkness (7) : *I Form Light/Night* : **A⁴**rrange **S⁵**un/**S⁵**hadow

I Make Peace and Create Calamity (7) : *I Form Right/ Smite* : **A⁴**rrange **S⁵**erenity/**S⁵**tress

[46] Babylon's Idols : *Shrines For Smiths* : **W⁴**orship **b⁶**el/ **b⁶**abylonian *gods*

I Declare End/Beginning (10) : *I Form Ticks* of clock : **E⁴**nds/**b⁶**eginnings

[47] Babylonian Empire Destroyed : *Dies For Ever* (5, 9, 11) : **E⁴**mpire **L⁷**eveled

[48] I Declare Events (3-7, 16) : *I Form Date/Place* : **E⁴**vents **d⁶**etermined/**b⁶**roadcast

[49] God Forms Bodies in Womb (1, 5) : *I Form Spines* : **W⁴**omb **g⁹**eneration

Israel Restored : *I Restore Mine* : **M⁴**end/**M⁴**y **g⁹**alilee/ **P⁹**alestine/**P⁹**eople

[50] God Vindicates His Servants : *I Drive Foes* away : **S⁵**ervant **O⁰**pposition

[51] Comforting Zion! : *Zi's Lifting Up* : **S⁵**oothing **I¹**srael

[52] Salvation Coming to Zion! (3, 7-9) : *Zi's Thrive-News* : **S⁵**alvation **n²**ews/**n²**ears

[53] Healed by His Stripes : *My Stripes Heal* : **S⁵**tripes **H³**eal

OT   Isaiah   NT

[54] **Scorned Wife** (6-17) : *My Wife Scorned* : S^5corned W^4ife

   Weapons Against Zion Formed in Vain (17) : *Zi's Life Force/Fort/Lord/Sworn / Tries 5 Swords* : S^5terile W^4eapons

[55] **Come to the Waters** (1) : *Rise Life Tides!* : S^5aving S^5treams

   My Thoughts/Ways High as Heavens (8-9) : *Skies-High Sight* : S^5uperior S^5ight

   Word Returns not Empty (11) : *My/Wise Bytes Strike* : S^5peech S^5trikes

[56] **Foreigners Saved** (6-7) : *My Wife Mixed* (breed) : S^5trangers b^6rought *into Bride of Christ*

[57] **Righteous Die Peacefully** (1-2) : *"Right's" Life Restin/ Heavened* : S^5till L^7ife *(rest)*

   Israel's Idols are Futile : *Zi's Ids Deadened* : S^5terile L^7ords

   I Revive Contrite (15) : *Rise My Servants!* : S^5orrowful L^7ivened

[58] **"Fast" = Share Food** (6-7) : *Rice I Take to others* : S^5hare B^8read/S^5erve B^8eggars

[59] **Sins Hide God's Face** (2) : *Lies Hide Shine* : S^5hroud g^9od/ S^5in g^9losses *God*

   Redeemer Saves Zion (20) : *Zi's Thrive Time / I thrive Zion* : S^5avior g^9od

   My Spirit/Words for Life (21) : *Wise Life-Time* : S^5pirit S^5peech g^9o-on *(won't leave you ever)*

OT   Isaiah   NT

[60] Zion's Enemies Serve Them : *Zi's Whipped/Licked Foes* : b⁶oast O⁰ver *them!*

[61] Captives Liberated : *Rise "Libbed" Ones!* : b⁶ondage-l¹iberated!

[62] Zion's New Name (2, 5) : *I Give New* name : b⁶rand-new n²ame

[63] Vengeance on Edom and Others : *I Kick Edom* : b⁶eats N³ations

Salvation History (7ff) : *Zi's History / I Split Sea* (11) : b⁶ailout H³istory *of Israel*

[64] God Hid Forever? (7) : *I Hid For* ever? : b⁶uried E⁴ternally?

[65] Stubborn People (1) : *Zi's Stiff Lives* : b⁶eings S⁵tubborn

God Creates New heavens/Earth (17) : *I Give Life* : G⁶od S⁵pawns *new world*

People Live Longer : *I Give Life* (20) : b⁶eings S⁶ustained

Wolf and Lamb Graze Together *(25)* : *I Mix Lives* : b⁶easts S⁵hare *space*

[66] Nation Born in One Day (7-8) : *Zi's Crib Kids* : b⁶irthed b⁶abies

Burn Unbelief (16, 24) : *I Lit/Wick/Grill Sticks* : b⁶urn b⁶lasphemers

Gather All Nations (20) : *I Bid Kids* from everywhere : b⁶ring b⁶rothers *to Jerusalem*

Jeremiah
[*er*]

[01] **I Appointed You Prophet in Womb** : *Birthed One* :
I¹nstalled *from womb*

I Made You Iron to Judah (18) : *Ironed One* : I¹ron

[02] **Judah: Idolater From Birth** : *Err Womb* : n²ascent *idolatry*

[03] **God's Call: Return!** (12) : *Turn Ye back!* : "H³omecome!"

[04] **Destruction from North coming** (6): *Bear North / Burn
North* : A⁴nnihilation *coming*

Earth Formless/Void (23) : *Earth's Form* : E⁴arth/
A⁴morphous/E⁴mpty

[05] **Jerusalem Won't Repent** (1-13) : *Jerusalem Strives with
God* : S⁵tubborn *nation*/S⁵trives

Jeremiah: "Judgment Coming!" (14-31) : *Jer Strives with
Jerusalem* : S⁵trives

[06] **Babylon Encircles Zion** (2-3) : *Jerusalem Pitched* :
b⁶abylon *coming*

[07] **"Temple" Lies: Do not Trust** (4) : *Jer[usalem's] Deceptions* :
L⁷ies/T⁷emple

Topheth – Death Valley (31) : *Burn Oven* (30:33) : T⁷opheth

[08] **Refuse to Repent** (4-6) : *Berate Word of God* (8-9) :
B⁸ullheaded/B⁸erated *for stubbornness*

Unjust Gain (10) : *Cursed Gain* : B⁸leed/B⁸urgle/B⁸ooty

Jeremiah Grieves : *Jer Aches/Wails* : B⁸ewails/B⁸emoans

OT   Jeremiah   NT

[09] Jeremiah Laments : *Jer Pines* : g^{9}rieves/g^{9}roans

[10] Jerusalem's Living God (10-13, 16) : *Jerusalem's Friend* : l^{1}iving O^{0}mnipotence

    Dead Idols (8-9, 14-15) : *Jerusalem's End* : l^{1}dols O^{0}verthrown

[11] Covenant Broken by Idolatry (13) : *Turned From Cov* : l^{1}eft l^{1}egal *Agreement* : l^{1}nnumerable l^{1}dols

[12] Wicked Prosper (1-2) : *Worst Well off* : l^{1}oaded/ l^{1}uxuriating ...V^{2}illains

[13] Jer's Loincloth Sign (4-9) : *Jer's Girdling* : l^{1}oincloth F^{3}orecast

    Jer's Wine Jar Sign (12-14) : *Jer's Chablis/Bubbly* : l^{1}iquor F^{3}orecast

    Exile Coming (17-21) : *Jerusalem Serving Babylon* : l^{1}and F^{3}ugitives

    Leopard Change Spots? (23) : *Fur Turning?* (Furturnity?) : l^{1}eopard F^{3}lecks/F^{3}reckles?

[14] Judah: Famine, No Rain (3-6) : *Burn, Soaring temperatures* : l^{1}ocal M^{4}alnutrition

    Lying Prophets (13-18) : *Err Storying* : l^{1}ying A^{4}ugurs

[15] Lord Will Not Turn (1) : *Turn, Shifting none* : l^{1}ord S^{5}et *on judging*

    Lord Stiffens Jeremiah (19-21) : *Jer's Stiffing* (20) : l^{1}ord S^{5}tiffens

[16] Deadly Diseases Coming (4) : *Germ Afflictings* : l[1]ethal b[6]acteria/d[6]iseases

Israel Will Be Restored (14-19) : *Jerusalem Fixings* : l[1]srael b[6]uilt/b[6]ack

[17] Heart is Deceitful (9) : *Coeur (French: heart) Deception* : l[1]nner *L*[7]ies

Honor Sabbath (19-22) : *Work None 7th* : l[1]aborless *7*[7th]

[18] Potter Reshapes Clay : *Turn Some Clay* : l[1]oam B[8]uilding

[19] Potter's Flask Broken (10) : *Burst A Stein* : J[1]ar g[9]round *to pieces*

[20] Pashhur Puts Jeremiah in Stocks (2) : *Jer To Hold / -Shur To Scold* : n[2]o O[0]ut! *Pashhur pillories (ridicules) Jeremiah*

[21] Neb to Take Jerusalem (4-7) : *Jerusalem To Gun* : n[2]eb l[1]evels *Jerusalem*

Message to House of David > Justice or Else! (8-14) : *Turn To Just*ice! : T[2]o J[1]ustice! / V[2]indicate l[1]njured!

[22] Josiah's King-Sons to Die (11-12, 18-23) : *Ne-er To Rule* *again* : n[2]ever T[2]hroned *again*

[23] The Righteous Branch (1-8) : *Virtue Tree* : V[2]irtuous F[3]ork *for birds*

Dreamer Prophets (27, 32) : *Turn To Dreams* : V[2]ision H[3]eralds / T[2]ruthless F[3]akes

[24] Good Figs to Babylon (5-7) : *There To "Score!"* : n[2]ourishing M[4]eals—*will prosper in Babylon*

OT Jeremiah NT

[24] Bad Figs Stay in Land (9-10) **: *There To "Sword!"* : n^{2}oxious M^{4}eals**—*will <u>fail</u> in Babylon*

[25] 70-Year Captivity (1-14) **: *Years To Bide*** *in Babylon* **: n^{2}ebs S^{5}laves**

The Cup of Wrath (15-38) **: *Slurp To Die* : n^{2}ations S^{5}ip** *poison*

[26] Judah Warned to Repent (1-6) **: *Turn To Rid*** *judgment!* **: T^{2}urn b^{6}ack** *to Lord!*

Plan to Murder Jeremiah (7-15) **: *Jer To Rid/"Hit"* : n^{2}o b^{6}ad** *news from him anymore!*

Jeremiah Spared (16-24) **: *Jer To Live* : n^{2}ot b^{6}umped-off** *Micah prophesied the same coming judgments (*18)

[27] Nebuchadnezzar's Yoke : *Jerusalem To Slavin* : n^{2}eb's L^{7}ands**

[28] Hanan[L]iah's 2-Year Forecast (3, 11) **: *"Learn To Wait!"* :** "**T^{2}wo B^{8}irthdays** *or less to the captivity!" The Lord takes him out within the year*

[29] Prosper in Babylon (5-7) **: *Learn To Climb*** *in Babylon* **: T^{2}o g^{9}row / T^{2}o P^{9}ray** *for the city* (7)

I Will "Return You" to the Land (10-11) **:** *[Re]**turn-You Time* **: T^{2}o g^{9}o** *back in 70 years*

Shem[L]iah's Prophecy (24-32) **: *"Miah's To Lyin* : T^{2}ruthless P^{9}rophet** *("I'm priest, not Jehoiada!")*

[30] Return Promised : *Jerusalem's Journey* home **: H^{3}omecoming O^{0}ccasion**

[30] Fortunes Restored : *Jerusalem's "Fertile[y]" again* : F^{3}ortune/F^{3}ertility O^{0}ccasions

[31] Israel Rebuilt for Joy : *Jerusalem Turning Fun again* : F^{3}un O^{0}ccasions

New Covenant with Israel (27-40) : *Her Mercy-Cov* : N^{3}ew l^{1}aw/l^{1}ord/l^{1}ives (33) **//** K^{3}now l^{1}ord/F^{3}orgive l^{1}srael / F^{3}orget l^{1}niquities (34) **//** F^{3}ixed l^{1}aw (35-37)

[32] Zedekiah Imprisons Jeremiah (3) : *Jeremiah Removed from society* : Z^{3}ed T^{2}raps *him*

Jeremiah's Field Deed Sign (9-15) : *Jer's Deed Proof/Field Booked* : F^{3}ields T^{2}itled—*fields and vineyards will exist again!*

Exiled Then Home (16-44) : *Jerusalem Removed then returned* : F^{3}oreign T^{2}rip **//** H^{3}ome T^{2}rip. *Israel will be punished but then restored*

[33] Jerusalem Cleansed/Healed : *Jerusalem Recleaned* (8) : H^{3}er H^{3}ealing *from sin* (8) / F^{3}locks F^{3}lourish (13)

David's Seed/Throne Restored (14-26) : *Jerusalem Re-Seed* : N^{3}umerous K^{3}ids / K^{3}ingdom F^{3}ixed

[34] Babylon Enslaves Judah : *Serfs Deport to Babylon* : F^{3}ree E^{4}nslaved

Zedekiah Extradited : *Serf Deports to Babylon* : Z^{3}edekiah E^{4}xtradited

[35] Rēchabītes Obey their Father from the Beginning:

No houses : *They're Free [of] Hives* (homes) : N^{3}o S^{5}hacks / H^{3}ouseless^5

<u>OT</u>   Jeremiah   <u>NT</u>

[35] Rechabites: No Drinks : *They're free* [of] *"Spiked"* drinks **:** N^3o "S^5pirits"**/** H^3oochless^5

[36] Jeremiah's Scroll Burned then Rewritten : *Burn The Writ!* **:** F^3olio b^6urned **:** *Letter He Writ* **/** *[Let]ter King Lit* **/** *Letter Re-writ* **:** F^3olio b^6ackup

[37] Jeremiah Warns Zed : *Jer-ry Threatens* Zed **:** Z^3ed T^7hreat

Jeremiah Imprisoned (20-21) **:** *Jer-ry Hemmed-in* **:** Z^3edekiah L^7ocks *up*

[38] Jeremiah "Cisterned" (6) **:** *Jer-ry Wades* in mud **:** F^3ilthy B^8ath

Rewarns Zedekiah (17-23) **:** *Jer Berates* Zed **:** Z^3edekiah B^8erated, *not persuaded*

[39] Jerusalem Falls : *Jeru Declines* **:** F^3allen g^9ates

Zedekiah Blinded (7) **:** *Hurt—He's Blind* **:** Z^3ed g^9ouged

Jeremiah Stays with Gedaliah (14) **:** *Jer Reclines* **:** H^3ost g^9edaliah

[40] Jeremiah Helps Poor in Judah (5-7) **:** *Jer's/Serves Poor Souls* **:** A^4ssists O^0utcasts

[41] Officer IshM^4ael^1 Murders Gedaliah (2) **:** *Officer "Murds" One* **:** M^4urders -I^1iah **/** M^4urder < I^1shmael's

[42] "Don't Go to Egypt!" (19) **:** *Jer Warns Jūd* **:** E^4gypt n^2o!**/** V^2etoed

[43] Johanan Forces Jeremiah to Egypt : *Jer Forced > Egypt* **:** E^4gypt-T^2aken

OT　　　　　Jeremiah　　　　　NT

[43] **Nebuchadnezzar to Burn Egypt** (12) : *Z[a]r Torch Egypt* : E^{4}gypt K^{3}indled

[44] **Remnant's "Queen of Heaven" Judged** (17) : *Her For Sword* : E^{4}gyptian W^{4}orship

Egypt will be Conquered by Babylon (30) : *Her For Sword* : E^{4}gypt's E^{4}nemy

[45] **"Baruch: Seek Not Greatness!"** (5) : *Earn/Learn Poor Life* : M^{4}ajesty S^{5}eek *not!*

[46] **Nebuchadnezzar to Exile Egypt** (13) : *Herd Tourists* to *Babylon* : E^{4}gypt b^{6}aggage (19)

[47] **Shore Cities Philistia/Ashkelon Judged** (4-7) : *Burn Shore Settlins* : A^{4}shkelon J^{7}udged

[48] **Moab Broken** (4, 38) : *Burn/Spurn More-āb* : M^{4}oab B^{8}roken/B^{8}urned

Moab Restored (47) : *Turn/Spur More-āb* : M^{4}oab B^{8}uilt

[49] **Nations Judged/Restored** : *Burn for Time* (39) : E^{4}dom/ E^{4}lam P^{9}unished/P^{9}urged—*also: Ammon, Damascus, Hazor, Kedar)*

[50] **Babylon Judged Quickly like Sodom** (31-32) : *Burn Swiftly* : S^{5}odomic O^{0}verthrow (40)

[51] **Babylon's Pride Killed** (1, 12, 53, 58) : *Burn High One* : S^{5}lay l^{1}ofty *one!*

[52] **Jerusalem Falls** : *Jeru Dives To* Babylon : S^{5}alem T^{2}orched

Temple Burned : *Burned My Room/Roof* : S^{5}anctuary T^{2}orched

Lamentations
[Descent, Ascent]

[01] Exiled City Lament : *Lament One* **: I**^{1}ament **/ I**^{1}mmigrants *to Babylon*

[02] City Ruined : *Lament Ruin!* **: T**^{2}rampled

[03] Will be Freed Someday (19-36) **:** *Amended: Free* *some day* **: F**^{3}ree

[04] Ruin To > Restoration 11 **:** *Amended One* **: M**^{4}angled > **M**^{4}ended

[05] Restore us! : *Amend: Thrive* *us!* **: S**^{5}ave *us*

OT   Ezekiel   NT
[*Zeke* *eef* *eek* *eeks* *eace* *eez* *eats*]

[01] Visions: Four Living Creatures and Lord's Glory : *Sees Some creatures* : l¹mages / l¹iving *beings* / *and the* l¹ord

[02] God Calls Ezekiel to Preach : *Zeke To preach* / *"Speak to Israel!"* : V²ocalize!

[03] Scroll Swallow (1-15) **:** *Zeke Eats* : F³olio/F³ood

Watchman to Warn (16-27) **:** *Zeek: "Cease sin!"* : ω³atchman/ω³arn/ω³icked

[04] Siege Wall Symbol (1-3) **:** *Seige-Fort symbol* : W⁴all/A⁴ugur

Ezekiel Bears sin (4-17) **:** *Zeke Bore sin* : A⁴tones *for Israel and Judah*

[05] Jerusalem's 3 Judgments (12) **:** *Sees Three Knives // Fire/ Knife/Dice* : S⁵corch/S⁵tab/S⁵catter-S⁵pread (1/3 each 2-3) : *pestilence/famine + sword + scatter* (12)

[06] Idols judged : *Deities Rid* : b⁶aals/b⁶usted

[07] Prosperity Ending (2, 12) **:** *Ease Endin* : L⁷ooters/T⁷rade *Ends* (11-13)

[08] Temple Abominations : *Tease-Hate (provoke hatred)* : B⁸uilding/B⁸ads/aB⁸ominations/B⁸adgering *God*

[09] Angel Marks Mourners to Protect (1-4) **:** *"Keep" Sign* : g⁹uards *them against death*

Idolaters Killed (5-11) **:** *"Cease" Sign* : g⁹unned *down!*

[10] Glory Leaves Temple (18) **:** *Leaves Temple* : l¹ord O⁰ut!

OT   Ezekiel   NT

[11] God Judges Evil Rulers (1-13) : *Beats malevolent//Chiefs leveled* : I^{1}niquitous I^{1}eaders/J^{1}udges

God Seeks/Gathers His People (14-18) : *Seeks "Left-ins"* *(left in foreign lands)* : I^{1}ocates I^{1}ost—*gathers them to Israel*

New Heart/Spirit (19-21) : *Peace/Meek-Leavened* : I^{1}nner I^{1}ife *renewed*

[12] Baggage Sign of Exile: Packed > : *Valise Tells* : I^{1}uggage T^{2}oken

[13] False Prophet : *Speaks Erring/A Dream* : I^{1}ying H^{3}erald

[14] God Judges Elders' Idolatry (1-11) : *Beats Whoring after other gods* : I^{1}dolatrous E^{4}lders

God Sends Sword Through Jerusalem (12-23) : *Peace Swording (attacks peace)* : I^{1}and M^{4}achete

[15] Burn Useless Vine (7) : *Heats The Ivy* : I^{1}vy S^{5}corched

[16] Faithless Bride (1-43) : *She's Kissing other men/Mixing-it-up with other men/"Tricksing" her husband* : I^{1}oose b^{6}ride

God will Restore Israel's Sisters Samaria/Sodom (44-58) : *Seeks The Sis of Israel* : I^{1}iberates g^{9}als

Everlasting Covenant (59-63) : *Seeks A "Stick!"* : I^{1}asting b^{6}ond/b^{6}lessing *(He will "stick with" His covenant)*

[17] Two Eagles, One Vine : *"Eagles" From Heaven 3 & 7* : I^{1}vy & T^{7}alons

Trees Exalted then Abased (22-24) : *Trees From Heaven* : I^{1}ofty/I^{1}eveled T^{7}rees

OT   Ezekiel   NT

[18] **Father's Eat Sour Grapes > Kids Teeth Crooked :** *Teeths From Grapes* crooked? **:** I^1mputed B^8uck-teeth?

[19] **Lament for the Vine's Princes/Leaders:** *Leads Of Vine / Weeps Timing* **:** I^1ament P^9rinces

[20] **Israel's Long History of Provoking God** (1-32) **:** *Tease Plenty* **:** T^2ease O^0wner *of the nation /* n^2ation's O^0ffenses

    God to Restore Israel > Will Loathe their sins (33-44) **:** *Trees To Loathe* their sins (43)**:** T^2rees O^0dious *in own sight*

    God to Burn Israel (47) **:** *Trees To Roast/Toast* **:** T^2rees O^0vened

[21] **Lord Draws Sword :** *Seized To Run* through **:** T^2akes I^1ance

[22] **Jerusalem Sheds Innocent Blood** (1-17) **:** *Bleeds "True-Blues"* **:** V^2irtuous V^2ictims

    Furnace Purges Dross (18-22) **:** *Treats Fused Fluids* **:** T^2orch T^2rash

[23] **Oholah/Oholibah OHarlots!** (4) **:** *Speaks To Street*walkers **:** $2^2/T^2$wo H^3arlots

[24] **Jerusalem: Nebuchadnezzar's Boiling pot :** *Siege To Scorch* city **:** n^2eb A^4ttack **/** V^2aporous W^4ater

    Don't Mourn for Dead Wife : *Zeke To Mourn? No!* (16) **:** n^2o M^4ourning *[for]* T^2erminated W^4ife

[25] **Five Rebel Nations to be Judged :** *Speaks To Five* **:** n^2ations 5^5

[26] **Judge Tyre's Greed :** *Greed To Pit* (20) **:** T^2yre b^6attered

[27] Tyre's Sea Trade Ruined (34) : *Sea's Routes Severed* :
T^2yre's T^7rade/L^7adings // T^2erminate/V^2oid L^7anes

[28] Tyre's Proud King : *Seeks To Praise* himself : T^2yre's
B^8oaster *prince*

Sidon to be "Pestilenced" (23) : *Disease To Raid* : T^2o
B^8illious *condition* / T^2o B^8edridden

Israel Dwells Safely (25-26) : *Peace To Reign* : n^2o B^8attles

[29] God will Judge Pharaoh's Pride (1-12) : *He's Too "Mine!"*
but *He's to Dine* with beasts (5) : n^2o P^9haraoh *soon!*

Egypt Restored to Less Glory : *Egypt To Shine* less brightly
(13-16) : n^2ot g^9lory *like it did*

[30] Nebuchadnezzar Takes Egypt (13, 16) : *Ēg He Smote* :
N^3eb O^0verran / N^3ile O^0verturned

[31] God "Fells" Proud Cedars (3-14) : *Trees/Cēds He Cut* down :
F^3elled/F^3allen l^1imbs *(Assyria, Egypt, Lebanon)*

[32] Lament Over Pharaoh/Egypt (1-21) : *Ēg King Ruined* :
H^3eartbreak n^2ile

Other Fallen Nations (Trees) (22-32) : *Trees Removed* :
F^3allen n^2ations *to Sheol*

[33] Ezekiel the Watchman (1-9) : *Zeke Sees Grief* coming! :
$ω^3$atchman Z^3ek!

The N^3ight $ω^3$atchman *to* $ω^3$arn $ω^3$icked *of coming judgment*

God Prefers the Wicked to Repent than to Die (10-20) :
Seeks Re-Seeks (repenters) : F^3avors F^3orsakers *of sin*

OT   Ezekiel   NT

[33] God Strikes Jerusalem's Proud Down (21-33) : *Beats The Trees/Peaks down* : F³allen F³orest

[34] Self-feeding Shepherd (2-4) : *Feeds/Eats Before others* : F³eed M⁴e *first!*

Neglect Sheep (5-10) : *Sheep Ignore* : N³eglect E⁴ewes

Lord Seeks His Sheep (11-31) : *Seeks-Sheep Lord* : F³inds/ F³eeds ... E⁴wes

[35] Mount Seir Desolated : *Peak Seir's Dive* : m³ount/H³ill S⁵eir *Barren*

[36] Israel's Mountains to be Blessed (1-21) : *Peaks He Lifts up* : m³ountains/H³ills b⁶lessed/b⁶ranches (10) / H³e b⁶lesses *mountains*

God Puts His Spirit in Us (22-37) : *Leads Th[e] Kids (sheep)* : H³is b⁶reath

[37] Dry Bones Come Together (1-10) : *Cheeks Re-Settin* : H³eals L⁷igaments

My People in My Land (11-23) : *He's Re-Settlin His people* : H³is L⁷and/T⁷eam

[38] Gog Attacks Israel : *Eas-y Prey / Seize Th[e] Prey* (11-12) : F³inal B⁸attle?

[39] God Orders Birds to Eat Gog (1-24) : *He speaks "Dine!" / Eagles" He dines* (17) : F³lesh g⁹og *eaten*/F³alcons g⁹orge *themselves*/F³lesh-g⁹obblers/g⁹rinders/g⁹nashers

God Restores Glory (25-29) : *He Refines/Re-Vines* : H³is g⁹lory *in nations*

[40] Outer Temple : *Sees Court Scope* : W^{4}orship O^{0}uter

[41] Inner Temple : *Sees Court Hub* : W^{4}orship I^{1}nner

[42] My Temple Chambers : *Sees Lord's Rooms* : M^{4}y T^{2}emple

[43] God's Glory Fills Temple : *Sees Glor-y* : M^{4}ajesty F^{3}ills / M^{4}y F^{3}ullness

[44] The Prince Serves God (1-14) : *Eats Toward Lord* (3) : M^{4}inisters A^{4}lmighty

       Levites Serve Men (15-31) : *Lēvs For Lords* : M^{4}inister M^{4}en

[45] Priests' Permanent Districts (1-6) : *Deeds/Priests For Life* : A^{4}reas S^{5}acred

       Prince's Permanent Portions (7-25) : *Deeds For Life* : M^{4}onarch's S^{5}hares

[46] Prince's Feasts (1-18) : *Feasts For Prince* : M^{4}onarch's b^{6}anquets

       Boiling to Fix Sacrifices (19-24) : *Heats For Fix*[ing] *sacrifices* : M^{4}eat b^{6}oilings

[47] Temple's Waters Flow East (1-12) : *East-ward Ebbin* : W^{4}ater FL^{7}ow / E^{4}astern *T*^{7}emple

       Eastern Land Division (13-24) : *East For Severin* (dividing) : A^{4}pportioning *L*^{7}ands

[48] Tribe's Metered Allocations (1-29) : *Metes For States* : E^{4}thnic B^{8}orders

       3 Gates on each of 4 Sides (30-35) : *Three* x *Four Gates* : E^{4}ntry B^{8}arriers

OT   Daniel   NT
[Dan, *am* *an*]

[01] Daniel Fasts in Babylon [8-21] *Dan Shuns* king's food :
l^{1}imits *intake*

[02] Nebuchadnezzar's Dream (1-18) : *Man's View* of future :
n^{2}eb/V^{2}ision/T^{2}rance

Dan Interprets (19-45) : *Dan Knew* : T^{2}ranslates/V^{2}ision

Dan Promoted (46-49) : *Dan Rules* in Babylon : T^{2}hroned/
V^{2}iceregent

[03] "Bow to the Golden Image!" : *Plant Knee!* : ω^{3}orship /
F^{3}igure

Three Cast into Fiery Furnace : *Tan 3!* : F^{3}iery/F^{3}urnace/
H^{3}eated *7x* H^{3}ot!

[04] Nebuchadnezzar's Axed-Tree Dream : *Branch Torn* (14) :
A^{4}xed/M^{4}ind *of beast given to him* (16)

[05] Hand Writes on Wall : *Hand Writes* : S^{5}cript/S^{5}idewall

Dan Interprets : *Dan Cites* meaning : S^{5}ign/S^{5}ignificance

[06] Lion's Den : *Dan Pitched* into > : b^{6}east/b^{6}urrow/d^{6}en

Mede laws are Permanent : *Bans "Stick"!* : b^{6}ans/b^{6}roken
never!

[07] Four Beasts : *Rant Heaven* (25) : L^{7}ion + *3 more*

Son of Man Reigns in Heaven (13-14) : *Man-Heaven* wins :
L^{7}ord *of all*

[08] B[8]elshazzar's Ram/Goat : *Ram Raids/Rage* *(charges)* : **B**[8]illy *goat*/**B**[8]attering ram

[09] Daniel Mourns : *Dan Pines* : **g**[9]rieves

Gabriel Reveals God's 70-week Plan (20-27) : *Planned Times* *(70 weeks)* : **g**[9]abriel/**e**[9]nd *sin* (24) in 49**9**0 *"year"s* (24)

[10] Angels Rule Nations (13, 20-21) : *Transcend* nations : **l**[1]ords **O**[0]ver *nations*

[11] North/South Kings Fight: *Land Leverag*ings : **l**[1]and **l**[1]nvasions

[12] Resurrection/Judgment (1-3, 13) : *Dan's Self* raised : **l**[1]ife **n**[2]ever-ending

OT   Hosea   NT
[*oze* *ose* *ost*]

[01] Hosea's Children of Harlotry (2) : *Hosea's Sons* : I^{1}llegitimate

Infants (6-9) : I^{1}o-Ruhamah *(girl: No Mercy)*/I^{1}o-Ammi *(boy: No People)*

God to Restore Israel (9-11) : *Chosen/Hosed One (cleansed)* : I^{1}nstate/I^{1}srael

[02] Israel Plays Harlot (1-13) : *Chose Lewd* : T^{2}rollop(s)

God to Restore Israel (14-23) : *Chose New* : "n^{2}ewed"/ T^{2}ransformed

[03] Hosea Redeems Wife : *Hosea Frees* adulteress : F^{3}rees *her*

[04] God Accuses Israel of Whoredom : *Chose Whore*dom : W^{4}hore[dom]

[05] Spirit of Whoredom (4) : *Chose Life* of a whore : S^{5}pirit [of] S^{5}trumpetry

[06] God Tears then Heals (1, 11) : *Mows It/Grows It* : b^{6}reaks/ b^{6}uilds

[07] Ephraim Lies to God : *"Woe!"s Ephraim!* (7, 11, 13, 16) : L^{7}iars

[08] Whirlwind Coming on Israel (7) : *"Blow!" Fate* : B^{8}last/ B^{8}lowings

[09] Ephraim will Go to Egypt (3) : *Goes Time* : g^{9}oes/Eg^{9}ypt-bound

Detestable Grapes (10) : *Gross Vine/Wine* : g^{9}rapes *go bad*

[10] **Israel's Idols (1-3:** *Chose Men gods***/***Chose Dumb Molds* : I^{1}dol O^{0}fferings

[11] **God's "Son" Since Egypt** (1) **:** *Chose A Son* out of Egypt **:** I^{1}ord's I^{1}ad

[12] **Jacob Takes Hold of Brother's Heel** (3) **:** *Toes/Sole Held?* **:** J^{1}acob T^{2}akes *heel*

    Jacob Tackles Angel (4) : *Toes/Sole Held?* (4) **:** J^{1}acob T^{2}ackles *angel*

[13] **Your God Since Egypt** (4) **:** *Knows From Eg*ypt **:** I^{1}ord F^{3}rom *Egypt*

    But Jacob Forgot Me (6) **:** *Chose "None Me!"* **:** I^{1}ord F^{3}orgotten **// Jacob** *Knows Of Me* but opts for I^{1}dol(s) m^{3}ultiplied**/N^3**umerous (2)

[14] **I Will Heal their Apostasy** (4) **:** *Chose Curing* **:** I^{1}ord M^{4}ends *His People*

OT   Joel   NT
[*ol* *all* *ell*]

[01] Locusts Invade (4) : *Locals/Stole Lunch* : l^{1}ocusts/ l^{1}nvasion/l^{1}nfestation

Drought/Famine (17-20) : *Sole Sun—no rain* : l^{1}ifeless

[02] Day of the Lord: Invasion (1-11) : *Bold Troops* : n^{2}ation/ T^{2}roops *invading*

Repent! (12-17) : *Stroll (back) To God!* : T^{2}urn *back!*

Lord will Restore Us (18-27) : *Soul New* : T^{2}ransformed n^{2}ew

Will Pour Out Spirit (28-29) : *Soul New* : T^{2}ransformed /"n^{2}ewed"

Sun Dark, Moon Blood (30-32) : *Sheol (Death) Cues/Hues* : n^{2}otations *(signs) of death coming*

Whoever Calls on the Lord will be Saved (32) : *C[a]ll New, Soul New* : V^{2}ocalize > n^{2}ew

[03] Multitudes Judged (14) : *Souls Deemed good or bad* : m^{3}ultitudes/H^{3}ordes *in the Valley of Decision* = Decision Valley = F^{3}indings/H^{3}ollow

OT   Amos   NT
[*aim * *ane* *famous*]

[01] God Faults Surrounding Nations : *Blames/Shames Ones* : **I**[1]ndicted **D**amascus, **G**aza, **T**yre, **E**dom, **A**mmon, **M**oab [**D**o**GTEAM**)

[02] God Faults Judah and Israel : *Blames/Shames Jews* : **V**[2]ituperated

[03] You Only I Knew So I will Punish You : *Named Thee/ Shamed Thee* : **K**[3]new *you* / **H**[3]umiliated you

[04] Israel Judged for Idolatry but Didn't Return : *Blames For idolatry* : **A**[4]postasied

[05] Seek Me and Live : *Aim High/Gain Life!* : **S**[5]eek & **S**[5]urvive!

[06] Judging Those at Ease : *Blames Bliss* : **b**[6]lames/**b**[6]liss

[07] Plumbline Vision (8-9) : *Blame Severance* : **L**[7]ine *divides /severs* **L**[7]ord *from the* **L**[7]and (8, 17)

    Amos Falsely Accused (10) : *Amos Censured* : **L**[7]ies/**L**[7]ibel/ **T**[7]reachery

[08] Famine/Thirst for Word (11-12) : *Phrase Slake (Thirst for Biblical Phrases)* : **B**[8]ible *Thirst*

[09] Israel Destroyed : *Flame Time* (1-10 esp. 5 and 7:4) : "**g**[9]rilled"/"**g**[9]utted"

    Israel Restored (11-15) : *Fame Time* : **g**[9]lory/**g**[9]rowth/ **g**[9]rapes/**g**[9]ardens (13-15)

OT   **Obadiah**   NT

[01] **Ed[o]m to be Humiliated** (1-9) : *O Bad D[o]m [Dumb]*

  Ed[o]m's Violence Toward Jacob : *O Bad D[o]m*

  Day of the Lord Approaching : *O Bad One*

  Lord's KingDom : *O Glad-D[o]m*

Jonah

[01] **Jonah Flees to Tarshish** (3) : *Jonah Runs* : **J^1**onah/**l^1**opes/ **l^1**eaves

  Swallowed by Fish : *Jonah Gummed/Gulped* : **l^1**ngested/ **l^1**arge *fish*

[02] **Prays from Belly of Fish** : *Jonah's/Alone-a's Gloom/Room* : **T^2**ummy / **T^2**urns *to God*

  Fish Vomits Him : *Jonah Spewed* : **V^2**omited *(the good kind!)*

[03] **Nineveh Warned** : *Jonah Preached/Speaks* : **N^3**ineveh / **W^3**arned

  Nineveh Repents : *Groans, Weeps* : **N^3**ineveh / **ω^3**eeps

[04] **Jonah Angry** : *Jonah Sore* : **M^4**an *of God* / **A^4**ngry

OT   Micah   NT
[*ike*]

[01] Judgment Coming on Israel (15) : *Strike One* on Israel :
I¹srael I¹nvasion

[02] God Will Judge Israel's Oppressors (1-11) : *Strike Two* :
V²engeance

God Will Gather the Sheep Back (12-13) : *Tykes/Hike To*
Israel : T²end *sheep*

[03] God Will Judge Israel's Leaders : *Strike Chiefs/"Leads"* :
H³eads *of Israel*

God Will Judge Israel's Seers (Mediums: 7) : *Strike Seers* :
F³ortune-tellers

[04] "Go to the Lord's Mountain!" (1-2) : *Hike Horeb!* :
M⁴ountain *climb!*

SW⁴ords to ploW⁴shares (3) : *Strike Swords! / Hike Forks!*
(pitchforks; as in "hike the number of") : W⁴ar > A⁴griculture

Spears to Pruning Hooks (3) : *Strike "Forks"! / Hike*
"Shorns"/"Shorts" : W⁴ar > A⁴griculture *(pruning hooks for*
trimming)

The Lord Beats Zion's Enemies (13) : *Strike Force(s)* :
E⁴nemies/E⁴liminated

[05] Bethlehem's Shepherd will Shepherd His Flock: *Tykes*
Lives protected : S⁵hepherds *flock* (4)

Lord will Strike Atheists (10-15) : *Strike Life* from them :
S⁵trike at S⁵keptics and S⁵coffers

[06] The Lord Likes Justice, Kindness, Humility (6-8) : *Likes Kids* (sheep) that are *Like Him/Likeness* : b[6]eauty *inner*

The Lord Strikes Injustice (11) : *Strikes Sins* : b[6]ad/ b[6]alances *(scales)*, d[6]eceit

[07] Wait For the Lord (7-9) : *Like Heaven's times* : L[7]ord's/ T[7]iming

OT Nahum NT
[Nineveh "Named" for "Blame"]

[01] God's Wrath on Nineveh (1-3, 6) : *Blamed One* : I^{1}ashes

[02] Nineveh Destroyed : *Name Ruined* : T^{2}rashed *(by Babylon)*

[03] Nineveh's Woe/Grief : *Blamed > Grieves* : F^{3}aulted >
H^{3}eartbroken

Habakkuk
["ack*]

[01] God Raising up Babylon to Punish Judah's Injustice :
Whack/Smack One coming : I^{1}nvaders *(Chaldeans)*

[02] Righteous Live by Faith : *Facts Rule* the righteous : T^{2}ruth/
T^{2}rust/V^{2}itality

Greed : *Black Boon/Loot/Boot*y (8-9) : V^{2}oracity/T^{2}heft

[03] Habakkuk Prays : *Habakkuk Pleads/Pleas* : H^{3}abakkuk/
K^{3}neels

Rejoices: *Habakkuk Glees* : E^{4}xults *(The Lord will save!)*

Zephaniah
[*ef* *eth* "Left"s = remnants; death]

[01] Judah's Idolaters will be Cut Off (1-6) : *Left None* (2-3) :
J^{1}udah/I^{1}eft *none*

[02] Judah's Enemies will be Destroyed : *Left Ruined* :
n^{2}ations / T^{2}rashed

[03] Judah's Princes/Prophets/Priests Judged (3-4) : *Deaf
Lead*er*s* : H^{3}aughty/H^{3}ypocritical/H^{3}eartless/K^{3}leptocracy

OT   Zephaniah   NT

[03] **Nations Desolated** (6) : *Left Bleak* : **N³**ations/**F³**orsaken

Nations Restored (9-11) : *Left Healed* : **N³**ations/**F³**orgiven /**F³**ixed /**H³**ealed/**F³**iltered, **F³**iltrated *(purified 9)*

Haggai
[*ag*]

[01] **Trees to Rebuild Temple** (8) : *Drag Trunks to Israel* : **l¹**umber *needed*

Zerubbabel/Joshua (14) : *Flag Jews to come and build Temple* : **l¹**eaders

[02] **Nations will Bring Wealth into the Temple** (7) : *Drag Loot to it* : **n²**ations'/**T²**reasures/**V²**aluables

Temple's Latter Glory (9) : *Brag/Flag New coming!* : **n²**ew/ **T²**emple *greater*

Zerubbabel (Judah's governor) : *Drags Jews to Judah* : **T²**akes *them back*

OT   Zechariah   NT
[*eck* *es* *etch*]

[01] Return to the Lord! : *Beckon Him* **: l¹**ook *to* **l¹**ord

    4 Horsemen Inspect Earth (10-11) **:** *Trek/Check/Spec Ones* **: l¹**nspect *earth*

    4 Horns Scatter Judah's Proud (21) **:** *Wreck Ones* **: l¹**ntersperse *the* **l¹**ifted-up *heads*

[02] Measure Jerusalem : *Check/Spec Jeru/Stretch Tool* > **: T²**ape-measure?

    Nations will Become My People (11) **:** *Elect Too!* **: n²**ations**/V²**oted *(elected)*

[03] Satan Accuses Joshua : *Heckles Priest* **: F³**aults**/H³**igh *priest*

[04] Golden Lampstand : *Deck Ore/Aur* > **: A⁴**uriferous *(golden)* **/ M⁴**enorah

    7 Lamps on Lampstand See All : *Spec-Lord* **: E⁴**yes *of Lord*

    2 Anointed Olive Trees (3, 12, 14) **:** *C[a]tch For oil* **: A⁴**nointed**/A⁴**ngels?

[05] Flying Scroll of Curses (1-4) **:** *Wreck Fly* **: S⁵**croll**/S⁵**wears

    Woman: "Wickedness" (5-11) **:** *Wretch/Wreck Flies* to *Shinar* **: "S⁵**in" *itself*

[06] Four Chariots/Horses Patrol : *Trek Width of the earth* **: b⁶**uggies**/b⁶**roncos

    "The Branch" who Branches and Sits on Throne (11-15) **:** *Stretch, Sit* **: b⁶**ranches *out and sits*

OT   Zechariah   NT

[07] Hearts Like Flint Against God (12) : *Peck Heaven* : *L⁷ithic hearts* / F**L**⁷int // **L**⁷ed *away Into the nations* (14)

[08] God Takes Remnant Back to Zion (7-8) : *Elect Takes to Zion* : **B**⁸ack *Home!*

[09] Nations Judged (1-8) : *Decline of nations* : g⁹odless/g⁹ored

King Coming On a Colt (9) : *Equine appearance* : g⁹allop?

King Rules From Sea To Sea (17) : *Spec Line* : g⁹overns

[10] Judah/Ephraim Gathered/blessed : *Fetch Men from nations* : l¹and O⁰ccupied

[11] Slaughter Sheep (4) : *Wreck Dumb Ones* : l¹ynch l¹ambs!

[12] Lord Defends Jerusalem (1-9) : *Wrecks Troops/Expels enemies* : l¹evels T²roops

Israel Mourns the Pierced One (10-14) : *Staked One Rued* : l¹ament V²ictim/n²azarene

[13] Fountain to Cleanse Sin (1-6) : *Etch Unclean/"Dirteen"* : l¹aunder F³ountain/F³ilthy

Smite Shepherd, Scatter Sheep (7-9) : *Wreck Herding/ Trek The Sheep* : l¹ambs F³lung/F³ar

[14] Day of the Lord 1-7) : *Wreck of Lord* : l¹ord W⁴recks *nations*

Zion's Living Waters Flow to Nations (8) : *Stretch Watering* : l¹iving W⁴aters

Lord is King Over All (9-21) : *Stretch Lording* : l¹ord W⁴orshipped *or He* **Wrecks Pouring** (rain)

Malachi
[*al* *mal* = "bad"]

[01] Priests Bad offerings (8) **: *Mal Ones* :** l^{1}ame *offerings*

[02] Corrupt Priests (1-9) **: *Mal Jews* :** n^{2}egate *the Law* (8)

Judah Profanes Sanctuary (11) : *Mal Judah* **:** T^{2}arnish/ T^{2}emple

Bad Husbands: Treacherous (14-16) **: *Mal Dudes* :** T^{2}reachery

[03] Messenger of the Lord Coming (1-7) **: *Shall Preach* :** H^{3}erald

Refiner's Fire will Purify (2-7) **: *Shall Clean/Free* metals *from impurities* :** m^{3}etals/F^{3}reed *from contaminants*

Shall Rob God's Tithes (8-15) **: *Shall Steal* :** H^{3}eist/F^{3}unds

[04] Day of Lord will Melt Evil : *Shall Scorch* : M^{4}elts/E^{4}vil

<u>OT</u>   **Matthew**   <u>NT</u>
                       [*ath* *av*]

[01] Jesus' Genealogy : *Path Son* : l^{1}ineage

[02] Wise Men Search (1-12) **: *Magi Look*** *for Son of God* **: T^{2}our**

   To Egypt (13-15, 19-23) **: *Path To*** *Egypt* **: n^{2}ile/T^{2}rip**

   Herold Kills Children (16-18) **: *Shaft Youth* : T^{2}ots/V^{2}ictims**

[03] John: Ax Laid at Root (10) **: *Shaft Trees* : H^{3}ack** *bad trees*

   Wheat to Barn; Burn up Chaff (12) **: *Chaff Heat* : K^{3}indle
   F^{3}ire/H^{3}eat / H^{3}usks/K^{3}ernels/K^{3}nubs**

   John Baptizes Jesus (13-17) **: *Bath/"Bap" Jes*us : ω^{3}aters**
   *Him/***H^3**oly *Spirit descends*

[04] Jesus Tempted by Devil (1-11) **: *Have Force*** *to eat, fly, rule?*
   : A^{4}llured/E^{4}nticed/W^{4}ooed/W^{4}iley

   First Disciples (18-22) **: *Path Toward*** *Jesus* **: A^{4}ccompany/
   W^{4}alk** *after (toward) and with Him*

**[05] Sermon on the Mount : *Path Life* : S^{5}ermon/S^{5}ervice/
   S^{5}ervant/S^{5}lope** *(mount)***/S^{5}ummit**

   Salt & Light (13-16) **: *Path Light* : S^{5}alt & S^{5}un**

   Christ Fulfills Law (17-20) **: *Satisfies* : S^{5}atisfies/S^{5}tatutes**

   Anger (22-26) **: *Wrath Strife* : S^{5}eethe/S^{5}tew/S^{5}molder/
   S^{5}hort-tempered**

   Lust/Adultery/Divorce (27-32) **: *Have Wife!* : S^{5}ensual/S^{5}ex
   /S^{5}eparate**

<u>OT</u>   Matthew   <u>NT</u>

[05] Oaths Not Kept (33-37) *Have Lied* : S^5wore

Retaliation (38-42) : *Wrath-Life* : S^5atisfaction *(bad)*

Love Enemies (43-48) : *Path Life* : S^5elflessly

[06] Hypocrisy—External Righteousness : *Have/Stash Sin* inside : b^6ury *sin*/b^6eneath/b^6oastful/d^6uplicitous

Alms (2-4) : *Have Gifts!* : b^6enefit *others!*

Closet Prayers (5-7) : *Have Bids* to God : b^6ackroom/b^6ids

Earthly Treasure: Moth, Rust, Stolen (19) : *Have Riches* earthly : b^6rief/b^6reak-ins/b^6ooty

Heavenly Treasure Lasts (20-21) : *Have Riches* heavenly : "b^6anked" *(vaulted)*/b^6reak-in-proof/b^6ulletproof/d^6urable

Two Masters (24) : *Half-Split?* : b^6ifurcated *commitments*

[07] Judgment Metri<u>c</u>s (1-12) : *Maths Several? / Math Metrics?* : L^7engths? / L^7ogs *in your own eye*

Narrow Path to Life (13-14) : *Path Heaven* narrow : L^7ife /L^7ane

Burn Bad Trees (15-20) : *Wrath Heaven* : L^7ight *bad* L^7ogs

"I Never Knew You!" (21-23) : *Wrath Ever/Heaven* : L^7ong unknown/L^7ost

House Built on Rock (24-27) : *Bath/Wrath Haven* : L^7asting /L^7odge *in rainstorm (bath)*

[08] Centurion's Faith (5-13) : *Have Faith* : B^8rigadier's/B^8elief

OT   Matthew   NT

[08] Jesus Calms Storm (23-27) : *Wrath Waves* : B^{8}illows/ B^{8}luster

Demonized Pigs Drown (28-34) : *Have Rage* : B^{8}oars/ B^{8}reathless

[09] Paralytic: Go Home! (1-8) : *Path [Walk] Time!* : P^{9}aralytic/ g^{9}o *home!*

Jesus Calls Matthew (9) : *Matthew's Time* : g^{9}athers *taxes*

Sick Need Doctors (11-13) : *Have Spine issues?* : P^{9}atients / P^{9}hysicians/g^{9}ynecologists/g^{9}eriatricians

Fasting (14-15) : *Fast Time* : g^{9}rowling *stomachs*

Wineskins (16-17) : *Draft Wine from new skins* : g^{9}amay / g^{9}oatskins

12-year Hemorrhage (18-22) : *Path (Flow) Time* : g^{9}ory / g^{9}lanulocytopenia/g^{9}amma g^{9}lobulin

Dead Girl Raised (23-26) : *Nap Time ("asleep": 24)* : g^{9}irl *raised up!*

Two Blind Men Healed (27-31) : *Have Blind eyes no more* : g^{9}aze/e^{9}yes *restored*

Mute Man Healed (32-34) : *Have Mime condition no more* : g^{9}estures > g^{9}abs

Harvest is Plentiful (36-38) : *Chaff Time* : g^{9}athering g^{9}reat

[10] Sends 12 to Lost Tribes (7-8) : *Tasks Men >* : I^{1}srael O^{0}nly

Cast out Demons! (8) : *Cast Them out!* : I^{1}eave O^{0}ppressed!

OT Matthew NT

[10] Shake Dust Off Feet/Shoes as A Sign (13-15) *Cast Them* (dusts?) off : l^{1}eave O^{0}men

Wise as Serpents (16) : *Asp Men* : l^{1}ntelligent O^{0}phidians

All Concealed will be Revealed (26) : *Stash Them* (secrets) to no avail : l^{1}ies O^{0}pen to God

Men Kill Body Not Soul (28) : *Half Men* killed : l^{1}imbs O^{0}nly

I Bring Division, Not Peace (34-39) : *Halves Men* : l^{1}solates O^{0}ne from another

[11] John Prepares Path for Christ (10) : *Path Leveled* for Christ : l^{1}eveled l^{1}ane

The Violent Seize Kingdom (12) : *Wrath Levers* kingdom : l^{1}awless l^{1}ever kingdom for themselves

More Tolerable for Sodom (20-24) : *Wrath Elevates* judgment : l^{1}ighter l^{1}ndictment for less sin

Yoke Easy, Learn Me/Humility (29) : *Path: Lessen* self : l^{1}earn l^{1}owliness / All^{11} you who are heavy laden!

[12] Lord of the Sabbath (8) : *Sabbath Held* by Lord : l^{1}ord's n^{2}ap (rest) day

Heals Withered Hand (10) : *Half Held* things : l^{1}ean/l^{1}imp T^{2}humb

Lamb-like Messiah until Victory (19-20) : *Wrath held* : l^{1}amb's n^{2}ature

Blind-Mute Healed (22) : *Lacked "Tell"* ability : l^{1}acked V^{2}ision/T^{2}ongue

[12] Satan Against Satan (25-28) : *Casts Self out? If so > :* Kin^{12}gdom IT^{12}self *divided?* **1^1** becomes **2^2?**

Blaspheme Spirit (30-32) : *Have Hell for this!* : **F^3**orgive n^{2}ot

Bad Tree, Bad Fruit (33-37) : *Bad Self, bad deeds* : l^{1}ike T^{2}ree > *like fruit*

Sign of Jonah (38-40) : *Bath belly* : l^{1}n T^{2}ummy

Last State of 8 Demons (45) : *Have Hell[ier] condition* : l^{1}ast/l^{1}ot n^{2}astier

Jesus' True RELatives (46-50) : *Have "REL"s?* : l^{1}ord's n^{2}ext-of-kin

[13] Kingdom Seeds (3-23) : *Cast Some Seed / Flaxseed Hurling* **4 Soils** = *Paths Dirting/Dirteen* : l^{1}aunch K^{3}ernels

Kingdom Weeds (24-30; 36-43) : *Gather The Weeds* : l^{1}ift ω^{3}eeds/N^{3}ettles

Mustard Seed (31-32) : *Cast Some Seed* : l^{1}ittlest K^{3}ernel

Large Tree for Birds (32) : *Have The Tree for a roost* : l^{1}arge N^{3}est

Kingdom: 3 Measures of Leaven Hidden (33) : *Stash The Three measures in the dough* : l^{1}eaven H^{3}idden

Kingdom: Bury Treasure! (44) : *Stash The "Green"* : l^{1}oot H^{3}idden

Kingdom: Pearl (45-46) : *Stash The Bead!* : l^{1}agoon N^{3}acre

Kingdom: Net (47-50) : *Cast A Screen* : l^{1}aunch N^{3}et!

Matthew

[13] Old/New Treasures > (2) : *Have The Green* : I¹oot F³ormer/ N³ew

Nazareth Rejects Jesus (53-58) : *Naz Skirting Jesus/Naz Turning Jesus away* : I¹eery N³azareth

[14] John Beheaded (1-12) : *Halved From Sword* : A⁴xed

5000 Fed Fish (13-21) : *Have Some Sword(fish) / "Math" Some Sword(fish)* > *fish multiplied* : I¹chthus M⁴ultiplied

Craft From Shore (24) : I¹ake M⁴iddle // *Draft From Storm* : I¹ake W⁴inds // *Av[id] "Oaring"*

Jesus Walks on Water (22-36) : *Path "Un"/None-Water"* : I¹ake W⁴alk *dry ("unwater"/"none-water")*

[15] Tradition: Wash Before Eating (1-9) : *Bath Life?* : I¹aver S⁵oap

The Inside Defiles Us! (11-20) : *Graft D[e]files* : I¹nside S⁵ullies

Lost Sheep of Israel Ministry (24) : *Have Driftings* : I¹srael's/I¹ost S⁵heep

4000 Fed Bread (32-39) : *Have A Slice!* : I¹oaves S⁵erved

[16] Can You Discern the Signs of the Times? (1-4) : *Have Wittings/"Signalings"?* : I¹nterpret b⁶ible: *prophetic times*

Sadducee Leaven (6) : *Have Mixings (truth and lie)* : I¹eaven b⁶lends/b⁶ad

Peter Confesses Christ (13-20) : *Have Admittings* : I¹ord b⁶orn *of the Father*

[16] Whatever You Bind on Earth (19) *Have Fixings to do* : l^{1}ord b^{6}inds *in heaven what we bind on earth*

Get behind Me Satan! (23) : *Aft "Gitting!"* : l^{1}apse b^{6}ehind!

Take Up Your Cross (24) : *Grab The Sticks* : l^{1}ay b^{6}urden *on back*

[17] Transfiguration (1-8) : *Have View Of Heaven!* : l^{1}it-up L^{7}ord / l^{1}ord T^{7}ransfigured

Casts out Boy's Demon (14-18) : *Casts A Devil out* : l^{1}eave L^{7}ucifer!

Mustard Seed of Faith Moves Mountains (20-21) : *Fa[i]th From Heaven* : l^{1}ittle L^{7}ifts *much (even mountains)*

Temple Tax (24-27) : *Half A Shekel!* : l^{1}evy T^{7}emple

[18] Who Is Greatest in Kingdom? (16) : *Who Grabs/Hath/Has The Great?* : l^{1}ittle B^{8}oy!

Better to Enter Life Crippled (7-11) : *Have One Leg* (9) : l^{1}imbless B^{8}ody *better than whole body into hell*

1 of 100 Sheep Goes Astray (12-14) : *Path Straying* : l^{1}ost B^{8}aaah! / l^{1}eaves B^{8}unch

Forgive Brother 70 x 7 (23-35) : *Wrath Abating!* : l^{1}apsed B^{8}rother/l^{1}oan B^{8}reak (*10,000 talents owed* = l^{1}arge B^{8}ond)

[19] Divorce (1-9) : *Path Untwine >* : l^{1}oose g^{9}al *only case (adultery)*

Eunuchs/Celibates : 3 kinds (10-12) : *Castrated: One Kind* : l^{1}ose g^{9}enitals/g^{9}onads *for kingdom*

[19] Let Kids Come to Me! (13-15) : *Gather-Sons Time* : l**¹**et g**⁹**randkids *come!*

Rich Ruler: Sell All You Have! (21) : *Cash What's Mine!* : l**¹**iquidate g**⁹**oods *I own*

[20] Vineyard Workers: Last First (1-16) : *Last Plenty/Many more per hour* : V**²**ineyard O**⁰**peratives

Grant My Two Sons Thrones (20-28) : *Have Two Thrones? We'll take them!* : T**²**wo/T**²**hrones O**⁰**kay?

Two Blind Men Healed (29-34) : *Path Two Stroll!* : T**²**wo O**⁰**bserve *again (can walk a path)*

[21] Triumphal Entry! (1-11) : *Path Entry Son/Path to Son* : T**²**riumphal l**¹**ngress

Cleanses Temple (12-17) : *Graft To Run out!* : T**²**emple l**¹**aundered

Curses Fig Tree (18-22) : *Have Fruit None?* : T**²**ree l**¹**anguishes

Who Gave You this Authority? (23-27) : *Have Rule, Who From?* : V**²**alidate l**¹**ordship!

Parable: Two Sons (28-32) : *Man's Two Sons* : T**²**wo l**¹**ads

Parable: Landowner/Tenants/Son (33-46) : *Wrath—Slew Son* : T**²**enants l**¹**iquidated Him to / T**²**ake l**¹**and / V**²**indictive l**¹**and-owner / V**²**ineyard l**¹**eased *to new* Vl**²¹**ne-*growers*

[22] Parable: Wedding Feast invitation (1-14) : *"Have To Do other things!"* : *"*n**²**o-T**²**hanks!" // *Have To Woo others* : T**²**ake T**²**hem *in!* *Have To Boot some out* : T**²**ake T**²**hem *out!*

[22] Pay Caesar Taxes? (15-22) : *Have/Half To "Boon" Caesar?* :
T^2ax V^2oid/n^2ecessary?

Resurrection Marriage (23-33) : *Have Two+ Grooms?* : n^2o
n^2uptials—*all gone after the resurrection*

Two Greatest "Do!"s (34-40) : *Have Two "Do!"s/To Do* : 2^2
T^2o *obey*/T^2opT^2wo *on which the whole Law hangs*

Whose Son is Christ? (41)-46): *Lad To Whom?* : T^2o n^2one
on earth!

[23] 8 Woes on Pharisees! (13-36) : *Wraths To "-Sees"/to see* :
V^2iperous/V^2ituperous ... H^3ypocrites (13, 14, 15, 25, 27,
33) / V^2ision-less N^3avigators (blind guides: 17, 19, 24)

Jerusalem Kills Prophets (37-39) : *Wrath to Seers* :
T^2erminates H^3eralds

[24] Tribulation in the World (1-24) : *Wrath To War on saints* :
T^2ribulation W^4orld

Idol Abomination in Temple (15) : *Wrath To Form in
temple* : T^2emple A^4bomination

Son of Man Returns to Judge (29-31) : *Have To "Court"* :
T^2o W^4orld / T^2o A^4djudicate/W^4eigh/E^4valuate

Fig Tree Sign (32-41) : *Flag To Lord's return* : T^2ree W^4ild-
fig/M^4ark

[25] No One Knows Hour (42-51) : *Math To Hour incalculable* :
T^2ime M^4ystery

Foolish Virgins (1-13) : *Have You Fueled Lights?* : V^2irgins
S^5enseless

[25] Talents Multiplied? (14-30) : *Have You "Two To Five"ed?* :
"2² to **5⁵**ed *your talents (multiplied them)?"*

Hungry/Thirsty/Stranger, You Fed/Hydrated/Invited Me
: *Had Food/Fluid/Roof Life* : **n²**o **S⁵**tarving/**S⁵**helterless
/**S⁵**trangers

Naked You Clothed Me (36) : *Had Nude Life . . . Had "Suit"
Life* : *When I was* **n²**aked/**n²**ude . . . *you* **S⁵**uited *Me!*

[26] Plan To Kill Jesus (1-5) : *Trap To Rid* Jesus : **T⁶**ermination
b⁶lueprint

Anointed For Burial (6-13) : *Have To Fix body for burial* :
T²allow **b⁶**ody

Last Supper (26-29) : *Have To Fix meal* : **T²**erminal
b⁶anquet

Peter and Others: "Never Deny You!" (31-35) : *Have To
Stick it out!* : **n²**o **b⁶**etrayal *from me!*

If You will, Let this Cup Pass (39) : *Path To Bliss?* : **T²**his
b⁶itter *cup*

Swords and Clubs to Take Me? (47) : *Have You Sticks?* :
T²o **b⁶**eat Me? / *I'm* **n²**o **b⁶**ankrobber! (55)

Caiaphas's Trial (57-68) : *Accused To Spit on* : **T²**rials **b⁶**egin
(first one)

[27] Judas "Fesses" up (1-10) : *Have You "Fessins"?* : **n²**ot-
L⁷awful *money made!*

Barabbas, Not Jesus! (19-26) : *Have Two To Settin free!* :
"**n²**ot *J⁷*esus!"

[27] Jesus Nailed to Cross (33-56) **:** *Accused To Peggin* to cross **:** n^{2}ailed *J^{7}esus/L^{7}ord* to cross

Joseph Offers his Tomb (57-60) **:** *Have Tomb To Settin* body in? **:** V^{2}acant *T^{7}omb/T^{2}omb J^{7}os*eph

[28] Angel Shakes Tomb (1-7) **:** *Have Tomb To Shake* (2) **:** T^{2}omb B^{8}uckles

"Stolen Body" Story (11-15) **:** *Myth: Jews To Prate* **:** "T^{2}ook B^{8}ody!" (the disciples)

Teach & Baptize All (18-20) **:** *Craft You To Make* disciples! **:** T^{2}each B^{8}aptize (I gifted you to do this)

OT   Mark   NT
[*ar*]

[01] **John Announces Jesus** (2) : *Hark, One coming !* : l**¹**nformer

Make His Paths Straight (3) : *Mark One path for Him* : l**¹**ineal *paths (no curves!)*

Voice at Jesus' Baptism (9-11) : *Hark Son! Well pleased!* : l**¹**isten *to Him!*

Satan Tempts Jesus (12-13) : *Dark One tempts* : l**¹**ures

Fishers of Men (17) : *Barb One (Hook them, ouch!)* : l**¹**urers

Cast Out Evil Spirits (32-34, 39) : *Dark Ones (evil spirits) run!* : l**¹**ucifer *et.al.*

Lepers Healed (40-45) : *Scarred/Marked Ones healed* : l**¹**epers / l**¹**eap!

[02] **Paralytic Takes up Bed** (1-13) : *Arms Move!* : T**²**ake up bed!**/n²**euromuscular *healing*

Levi, Tax-Booth-Man, Follow Me! (14) : *Park Booth and come!* : T**²**ax-Man / T**²**rail *Me!*

Fast When Groom Leaves (19-20) : *Starve Soon* : n**²**ourish/ n**²**one

New Wineskins (21-22) : *Sarx* [Greek: *flesh*] *New* : n**²**ew *wineskins*/T**²**hermos?

David Ate Forbidden Showbread (25-27) : *Barred Food* : n**²**ot-lawful

Lord of the Sabbath (28) : *L[o]rd Rules it* : T**²**ranscends *Sabbath*

OT   Mark   NT

[03] Harm or Heal on Sabbath? (1-6) : *Harm, Heal?* (4) : H³arm/
H³eal? *Lord?/*H³*eals/*H³*and/*F³*ingers (withered)*

Twelve Apostles Chosen to Preach (13-19) : *Hark Team* :
H³eralds *of Gospel* Marked *[to]* Preach/Teach

Casts out Demons by Prince (22) : *Arch Dem*on *needed* :
H³ighest *demon*

[04] Parable: Sower (1-12) : *Farm Spores/Sower* : E⁴xpel *seed*

Purpose of Parables (10-12) : *Dark Forms* : M⁴ask *truth*

Parable: Lamp Under Basket (21-22) : *Dark Torch* : M⁴asks
light

Parable: Seed Growth (26-29) : *Farm Spores* : M⁴ature

Parable: Mustard Seed (30-34) : *Must[ar]d Soars* :
M⁴ustard *seed grows into tall plant*

Jesus Calms Storm (35-41) : *Dark Storm* : W⁴ind/A⁴bates

[05] Demons into Pigs (1-20) : *March-Dive* over cliff : S⁵wine /
S⁵pirits

Blood-Discharging Woman (25-34) : *Discharge Life* :
S⁵ecrete *life*

Jairus' Daughter Dead (35-43) : *Discharged Life* :
S⁵leeping, *not dead!"*

[06] Nazareth Rejects Jesus (1-16) : *"Bar/Mark Him!"* : b⁶ar/
b⁶erate *Him*

Twelve Sent Out 2 x 2 (7-13) : *March Six sets of 2* : 6⁶ x 2

[06] John Beheaded (14-32) : *Martyr Fixed on platter* : **b⁶**ehead

Jesus Feeds Fish to 5,000 (33-44) : *Shark Dish/Fixed* : **b⁶**ullshark *or* **b⁶**lue-shark?

Jesus Walks on Water (45-52) : *Jars Fish!* : **b⁶**reakers *(waves)* **/ b⁶**elow

Bedridden People Healed (53-56) : *P[a]ralytics* : **b⁶**edridden/**b⁶**etter

[07] Defy Law For Tradition (1-8) : *Bar Heaven for tradition* : *T⁷*radition *for L⁷*aw

"Corban" ("for God") (9-13) : *Marked "Heaven" on it!* : "*L⁷*ord-allocated"

Heart Defiles Man (14-23) : *Heart Devil* : *T⁷*aints *the man*

Unclean Spirit Torments (24-30) : *Dark Devil* : *T⁷*ormentor

Deaf Healed (31-37) : *"Hark Deafened one!"* : *L⁷*isten!

[08] Jesus Feeds Fish to 4,000 (1-10) : *Shark Ate/Plate // Starved Ate* : **B⁸**ullshark or **B⁸**lue-shark *(again)?*

"Show Us a Sign (mark)!" (11-12) : *Mark Make us!* : **B⁸**ewilder us!

Pharisee's Words = Leaven (16-21) : *Pharisee Cakes* : **B⁸**aker's *yeast*

Healed a Blind Man (22-26) : *Dark Gaze* : **B⁸**lind *healed*

Who Do You say I "Art"? (27-30) : *Art Babe/Mate of God* : **B⁸**oy *(Son) of God (cf. Matthew 16:16; John 11:27, 20:31)*

OT   Mark   NT

[08] **Get Behind Me Satan!** (33) : *March Sāt / Dark Wake* :
B^8ehind!

Gain World > Lose Soul (34-38) : *Dark Gain > Dark Pain* :
B^8illionaire > B^8usted/B^8roken/B^8ereft

[09] **Transfiguration** (1-13) : *"Garb" Shine (Gar*ment*)* : g^9lory
event; Luke **9^9** *too*

Demon of Convulsion Hard to Cast out! (14-29) : *Hard
Kind to cast out* (28-29) **/ *Hard Grinds*** (teeth) **/** g^9host/
g^9houl/g^9rinds *teeth* (18)

"Help My Unbelief!" (24) *Dark Mind* ; q^9uestionings
(doubts)

Who's Greatest? Child! (33-37) : *Heart 9 year-old?* :
g^9reatest

Offend Little One > Hell! (38-50) : *Mar/Harm Crime* :
P^9rofane/P^9ollute > q^9uenchless *fire*

[10] **Divorce** (1-12) : *Part? Mend?* : l^1oose O^0nly *for
fornication*

Kingdom Belongs to Children (13-16) : *Hearts Ten*der :
l^1ads O^0nly **/** l^1ord's O^0wn!

Hard for Rich to Enter Kingdom (17-31) : *Hard Ent*ry (23)
: l^1ean O^0pening *(eye of a needle: 25)*

Zebedee's Sons Ask for Thrones (35-40) : *Mark Sons'
Thrones!* : "l^1ordships O^0rder!" *Not Mine to Give!*

Blind Bartimaeus (46-52) : *Bart's Lens was bad* : l^1ens
O^0pened *by Jesus*

OT   Mark   NT

[11] **Triumphal Entry** (1-10) : *Hark, The Son comes!* : l¹aud l¹ord *(Hosanna!)*

Curse Figless Tree (12-14) : *Bars Livin* : l¹et l¹eaves *die!*

Lenders in Temple (15-18) : *Bars Lendin* : l¹enders l¹eave!

Jesus' Authority Questioned (27-33) : *Are Levered by Whom?* : l¹ord's l¹ord?

[12] **Parable: Tenants/Vineyard** (1-11) : *Yard Held by tenants / Farm's Son Slew* (8) : l¹eased T²enants / l¹iquidate l¹nheritor

Taxes to Caesar? Whose Inscription and Likeness is this? (13-17) : *Marks Self on coins (Caesar)* : l¹ikeness T²o *Whom?*

Whose Wife Next Life? (18-27) : *Mar[ried] selves no longer*: l¹inks/l¹overs n²one = *no marriages, no pairings*

Two Greatest Love Commands (28-34) : *Heart Selves / Hark/Mark the Two* : l¹ove T²rinity/n²eighbor *as self* / l¹ove T²wo *selves (God and neighbor)*

Whose Son Christ? (35-37) *Are/Art Son To Whom? / Are/Art El*ohim's *Son?* : l¹ad T²o *Whom?*

David Calls Him Lord (37) : *Are/Art El*ohim? : l¹ord T²o *me!*

Widow Offers her Life (41-44) : *Parts Self/From Food* : l¹ife V²itals

[13] **End-Time Deceivers** (5-6) : *Dark Erring/Deceit* : "l¹ H³e!" (6) / l¹ords F³alse/F³rauds / l¹ying m³essiahs (cf. 21-22)

OT   Mark   NT

[13] Abomination of Desolation (14) : *Dark One's Feet* in *temple* : I¹nfiltrates H³oly *place*

Stars Fall from Heavens (25) : *Stars Careen/Erring* from *course* : I¹ights F³all

Watch Fig-tree Leaves (28-29) : *Mark The Leaves!* : I¹ook-at F³ig-tree / I¹eaves F³ig-tree

Stay Awake (Alert)! (33-37) : *Guard From Sleep! / Guard Alerting* (36) : I¹ess Z³s! / I¹ess H³ibernating

[14] Judas: Sell Perfume for Poor? (3-21) : *Nard Pouring / Guard The Poor?* : I¹iberate M⁴isfortunate?

Last Supper (12-31) : *Parts Of Lord (body)* : I¹ast M⁴eal

Judas's Signal Kiss (44) : *Mark The Lord* with a kiss : I¹dentification M⁴ark

Remove This Cup? (36) : *Hard/Dark Warring* of wills inside *Me* : I¹ift M⁴ug from Me?

Gethsemane Sleeping (37-42) : *Hark, Snoring I hear? Hark, One More* hour you couldn't stay awake? : **1¹ M⁴ore** hour?

Jesus' Arrest (43-52) : *Cart The Lord* away! : I¹ord's A⁴rrest/ M⁴anhandling

Jesus: Accused and Silent (60-61) : *Charge Of Lord (charges against)* : I¹ord's M⁴ute before I¹ord's A⁴ccusers

You'll Deny Me 3 Times! (66-72) : *Dark/Part Foreseen* ("I *don't know the man!*" I¹ord A⁴bnegated/A⁴bandoned/ E⁴schewed

[15] Barabbas Released (6-15) **:** *Bar**abbas** **Living** free again* **:** "l**¹**et S**⁵**layer go!"

Burial Garb (46) **:** *Garb Of White / Garb Fitting* Jesus **:** l**¹**inen S**⁵**hroud

Joseph of Arimathea's tomb (42-47) **:** *Ar**imathea's** "Crypting"/Gifting / Park Stiffening* body there! **:** l**¹**oans S**⁵**epulcher

[16] Jesus Raised (1-13) **:** *Sarx Fixing* (Sarx: Greek "body") **:** l**¹**ord's b**⁶**ody *raised*

Great Commission (14-20) **:** *Far Fixing / "[Co]mmishing"/ Visioning* **:** l**¹**ord's b**⁶**ehest

Luke
[*oo* *ou* *uke*]

[01] Mary & Elizabeth Pregnant (1-45) : *Two Sons* : I¹nfants

Mary's Magnificat (46-55) : *Tune Sung* : I¹yrics/I¹iturgy

Zacharias Prophesies (57-79) : *Loosed Tongue* of Zacharias : I¹oosed *from mute*

[02] Angel "Gospels" the Shepherds (8-14) : *Good News—Savior* (10) : n²ews

Jesus Presented at Temple (21-33) : *Took To* temple : T²emple/T²aken

Jesus Appoints Rise and Fall of Many (34-35) : *To Move* many : T²urn *many to rising and falling*

Anna Worships (34-38) : *To Pews* daily : T²emple *night and day*

Didn't you know—I Should Be in My Father's house? (49) : *You Knew* not? : V²ocation

Jesus Grows in Wisdom and Stature (52) : *Truth Grew* : T²ruth / T²all?

[03] John: Ax at Root of Tree (1-9) : *Fruit Tree* axed if no fruit / *Took Tree* down : H³atcheted/H³acked/F³ruit tree F³ruitless

Jesus Gathers Wheat into Barn (16-17) : *Took Wheat* into barn : H³arvest / F³lour ingredient

Jesus' Ancestry (23-38) : *Jewish Genes* : F³orefathers

[04] Devil Tempts Jesus (1-11) : *Wooed Lord* : W⁴ooed/E⁴nticed/A⁴llured

<u>OT</u>   Luke   <u>NT</u>

[04] Isaiah's Prophecy: God Appointed Me (14-21) : *To Poor* to *give Gospel* > (18) : **M⁴**inister**/A⁴**nnounce *Gospel*

Nazarites Try to Cast Him Over Cliff (23-29 : *Took Lord* to *cliff* : **M⁴**ountain**/M⁴**urder

Commands Demons (31-37) : *Spooks Forced* : **M⁴**asters**/W⁴**icked**/M⁴**alevolent**/E⁴**vil

[05] "Fluke Simon! Drop Your Net!" (4) : *Fluke Hive* (6-11) : **S⁵**imon **/ S⁵**everal *others called to Jesus*

Leper's Skin Healed (12-16) : *Took Hives* away : **S⁵**kin *heal*

Paralytic: Rise Up! (17-26) : *You, Rise!* (24) : **S⁵**tiff **/ S⁵**tand!

Matthew the Tax Collector Called (27-29) : *Took Tithes* for *Caesar* : **S⁵**urtaxes?

Only Sick Need Doctors (31) : *Wounds Drives* out! : **S⁵**ick**/S⁵**urgeons**/S⁵**ave**/S⁵**oothe

Fast When Bridegroom Taken Away (33-35) : *Took Bride's* groom : **S⁵**tarve **/ S⁵**lim *down when bridegroom gone*

New Wine > New Skins (36-39) : *New White* wine? : **S⁵**auterne**/S⁵**kins

[06] Forbidden Showbread Eaten (1-6) : *Took It* (David: 4) : **b⁶**read *of Presence*

Heals Withered Hand on Sabbath (6-11) : *Wound Fixed* on *Sabbath* : **b⁶**arren *hand* **/ b⁶**roke *Sabbath?*

Jesus Chooses the Twelve (12-19) : *Took Six* x 2 : **d⁶**isciples **/b⁶**elievers

OT   Luke   NT

[06] Beatitudes (20-45) : ***Do This!*** : **b⁶**eatitudes/**b⁶**lessings

Woe To/Due Rich (24) : ***Rue/Due Rich*** : **b⁶**anes *on* **b⁶**arons

Do to Others What You Wish for Yourself (31-36) : ***Do/Due Wish/Gifts*** : **b⁶**less *others*

Judge Equally (37-42) : ***Use Sticks*** *equal* : **b⁶**aselines

Blind Lead Blind to Ditch (39) : ***Look, Ditch!*** : **b⁶**lind-guides **/ d⁶**itch

Good Trees Produce Good Fruit (43-45) : ***Good Figs*** : **b⁶**enevolent *tree*, **b⁶**enevolent *fruit*

Wise Man's House on Rock (46-49) : ***Rooting Fixed*** : **b⁶**oulder/**b⁶**ase

[07] Jesus Heals Centurion's Servant (1-10) : ***Soothes Slave/Servant*** : **J⁷**esus *heals* **L⁷**ieutenant's *servant*

Raises Widow's Son (11-17) : ***Took Dead Son*** *back* : **L⁷**one *woman/***L⁷***eft son/***L⁷***ifted up!*

John in Fancy Dress? (25) : ***Look/View Dressin!*** : **L⁷**uxury?

John/Jesus: Heavy Drinkers? (31-35) : ***Took 7 & 7s?*** : **L⁷**ushes? *No!*

Forgiven More > Loves More (36-50) : ***Who's Debtin*** *more?* (47) : **L⁷**oves *more*

[08] Parable Sower (4-15) : ***Took/Threw Grain*** : **B⁸**reeder

Lamp Under Bed? (16-18) : ***Put Blaze*** *under bed?* : **B⁸**ed *hidden?*

Luke

[08] Jesus Calms Storm (22-25) : *ReB⁸ukes Waves/Gales* :
B⁸ecalmed**/B⁸illows/B⁸reezes**

Casts Out Legion (26-39) : *Spook Raid* : **B⁸**anishes *him*
"He casts out demons by **B⁸**eelzebub!" *No way!*

Heals Bloody Discharge (40-48) : *Ooze Brakes* : **B⁸**leeding**/
B⁸**locked

Raises Jairus's Daughter (49-56) : *Youth Waked* : **B⁸**ody-lift

[09] Twelve Sent to Preach and Heal (1-6) : *Truth/Soothe Time*
: **g⁹**o *preach and heal!*

5,000 Fed Fish (10-17) : *Fluke Dine* : **g⁹**efiltefish?

Who do They Say I am? (18-20) : *Who I'm?* : "**P⁹**rophet *say
some!"* (19)

Takes Cross, Finds Life (23-27) : *Took/Finds* : **g⁹**utted *self,*
g⁹ains *life*

Transfiguration: Jesus/Moses/Elijah (28-36) : *Group Shine*
: *appear in* **g⁹**lory (Mark **9⁹** too)

Demon Torments Kid (37-43) : *Spook Time* : **g⁹**rand *mal
convulsions*

Who's Greatest? (46-48) : *Who Shines?/Who's Fine?* :
g⁹reatest?

Not Against us = For us (49-50) : *Truth Sign (identity)* :
P⁹roof

Send Fire from Heaven on Rejecters? (54) : *Cook Sign?/
Time?/Nein!* says *Jesus* : **g⁹**od-fire (54)

[10] Jesus Sends 72 Two by Two (1-12) : *Twos Sent* : **I**[1]aunches **O**[0]bedient

More Tolerable for Sodom (13-16) : *Doomed Men* : **I**[1]ess **O**[0]nerous *for Sodom*

"Demons Subject to Us!" (17-20) : *Spooks Bend knee* : **I**[1]ucifer **O**[0]beys us!

Son Alone Knows the Father (21-24) : *True Son Knows the true Father* : **I**[1] **O**[0]nly *knows the Father*

Good Samaritan (25-37) : *Wound Mends* : **1**[1] **O**[0]nly *helps*

Mary Attends Jesus (38-42) : *Who Tends Jesus?* **1**[1] **O**[0]nly *(Mary, not Martha)*

[11] Lord's Prayer (1-4) : *You are in Heaven* (Matt. 6:9) : **I**[1]ord's **I**[1]itany

Parable: Kept Asking! (5-13) : *Shook Heaven!* (8) : **I**[1] **I**[1]nsist

Jesus "Fingers" Demons (14-23) : *Spooks Run From Him* : **I**[1]ord **I**[1]evers *them*

Demons in Deserts (24-26) : *Spooks Come From deserts* : **I**[1]ifeless **I**[1]ocations (24)

Demons Go but Come Back : *Spooks Run > Come back* : **I**[1]eave > **I**[1]odge

Sign of Jonah/Whale (29-32) : *Look, Leviathan* : **I**[1]nside **I**[1]eviathan

Eye = Lamp of the body (32-36) : *Look Levers body* : **I**[1]amp **I**[1]evers *body*

[11] Jesus "Woe!"s the Pharisees (37-54) : *Dooms Leaven* of *Pharisees!* (cf. 12:1) : l[1]ord l[1]ambasts *Pharisees*

[12] Bad Leaven Exposed! (1-3) : *Crooks "Tell"* all on Judgment : l[1]eaven n[2]aked/"T[2]old" on that day

Fear Him Who Casts into Hell (4-7) : *Rules Hell* (5) : l[1]ords n[2]etherworld/T[2]orture/T[2]artarus

Confess Christ Before Men (8-12) : *Truth Tell!* : l[1]ecture T[2]ruth!

Parable: Rich Fool (13-21) : *Food Held* (stored for future) : "Goods laid up for many years" / "l[1]arger V[2]ats needed!"

Don't Be Anxious! (22-34) : *Too "Whelmed"* : l[1]eery T[2]otally/V[2]ery

Thief in the Night (35-48) : *Crook Stealth* : l[1]ord T[2]hief in the night

I Divide Families/Groups (49-53) : *Groups/Broods Felled* dis**pelled** : l[1]ord T[2]ears apart

Discern Weather/Time (54-56) : *Cool Spell* coming! : l[1]nterpret T[2]imes like the weather

[13] Repenting or Likewise Perishing (1-5) : *Crook-Turning* (repenting from evil) : l[1]ikewise K[3]illed!

Parable: Barren Fig Tree (6-9) : *Fruit "Dearthing"* : l[1]acks F[3]igs

Lady's "Bent-over" Demon (10-17) : *Spook Curving* lady : l[1]ady F[3]olded/F[3]lexed. **Jesus Heals Her** : *Spook Hurting* > l[1]ady H[3]ealed

[13] **Small Mustard Seed Grows** (18-19) : *Took Runt Seeds* >
Food Nurturing : l¹ittlest H³usk > l¹arge m³ustard *tree*

Good Leaven Spreads (20) : *Took Some Yeast* : l¹eaven
F³lows/F³ans *out*

Few Saved/Narrow Gate? (23) : *Few Turning toward*
heaven? : l¹ane N³arrow!

Jesus Laments Jerusalem (31-35) : *Mood Stirrings* :
l¹aments K³illing *Prophets*

[14] **Heal on the Sabbath?** (1-6) : *Crooked Curing? / Took*
Horsey out of ditch on wrong day? : l¹llegal M⁴edical!

Take Lowest Seat at Feasts (10) : *Took Fourteenth row* :
l¹owest M⁴ember

Invite Poor to your Feasts! (12-14) : *Book The Poor!* :
l¹nvite M⁴isfortunate

Compel the Poor (15-24) : *Hook the Poor!* : l¹ure
M⁴isfortunate *to my feast*

Hate Family Persecution! (26) : *Book Warring with those*
who war against Christ : l¹oathe M⁴embers *who oppose Him*

Plan Like a Warring King (28-33) : *Rule/Route Warring!* :
l¹ayout W⁴ar

[15] **Parable: Lost Sheep** (1-7) : *Ewe Lifting on shoulders* : l¹ost/
l¹ocated/l¹ifted S⁵heep

Parable: Lost Coin (8-10) : *Sou Drifting* : l¹ost S⁵ilver/S⁵ou

Parable: Prodigal Son (11-31) : *Youth Drifting* : l¹ost S⁵on

Luke

[16] Parable: Shrewd Manager (1-13) : *Shrewd Fixing* bill :
l^{1}owered b^{6}ill

Law Until John, Now Gospel (14-16) : *Rule/Truth Mixing*
(rule and truth) : l^{1}aw > G^{6}ospel/G^{6}ood news *of kingdom* :
Rule Skipping but Law fulfilled not voided (17 cf. John 1:17)

Some Remarriage = Adultery (18) *Two Mixings* :
l^{1}llegitimate b^{6}reakups/d^{6}ivorces

Lazarus and Rich Man Destinies (19-31) : *Two Fixings*
(26) : l^{1}oaded-one b^{6}urning *but* l^{1}azarus b^{6}osom *of Abraham*

[17] Tempt a Little One (1-2) : *Dupe A 7-year-old* : l^{1}ure 7^7-
year old, plan on hell

Forgive 7x? (3-4) : *Loose One 7* times? : l^{1}oose 7^7 times?

Increase Our Faith! (5-6) : *Boost up 7x* : l^{1}ncrease
L^{7}oyalty

Say "Unworthy Servants!" (7-10) : *Due One Heaven? No!* :
Say "l^1'm L^{7}ow/L^{7}oser!"

10 Lepers Cleansed; 1 Thanks! (11-19) : *"Newed"/Spruced
From Heaven / Due From Cleansin* = at least "Thanks!" :
l^{1}aundered L^{7}epers

Kingdom and Kingdom Come Unexpectedly (20-37) :
Boo!/New/Coup From Heaven : l^{1}ightning L^{7}ord

[18] Parable: Persistent Asking (Widow) (1-8) : *Do Praying/
Begging* : l^{1}asting B^{8}eg

Parable: Two Pray (9-14) : *Two Praying* : 1^1 B^{8}rags/1^1 B^{8}egs

OT   Luke   NT

[18] Let Infants Come to Me (15-17) : *Took A Babe* : l^{1}et B^{8}abes

Parable: Sell All You Have and Give to the Poor (18-30) : *Lose Estate* > : l^{1}eave B^{8}illions *to poor!*

Blind Beggar Healed (35-43) : *New Gazing* : "l^{1}enses" B^{8}eggar

[19] Zaccheus's Half Goods to Poor (1-10) : *Goods Consigned/ Consigning* : l^{1}eaves g^{9}oods *to poor*

Parable: 10 Minas Time-Invested (11) : *Loot Timing* : l^{1}oot g^{9}rowth *over time*

Triumphal Entry (28-40) : *Looks Shining!* : l^{1}ord g^{9}lorified

Jerusalem Loses Time Of Visitation (41-44) : *Lose Timing / Jeru's Unwind* : l^{1}ose g^{9}uest *who arrived*

Temple Cleansed (45-48) : *Grooms/Prunes the Shrine* : l^{1}ashes P^{9}eddlars/g^{9}raft *out of Temple*

[20] Who Gave You Authority? (1-8) : *Who's Sending you?* : n^{2}o O^{0}ne *on earth; that's for sure!*

Parable: Wicked Tenants (9-18) : *Crooks To Own vineyard* : T^{2}o O^{0}wn *vineyard* > T^{2}erminate O^{0}wner's *son*

Give to Caesar/God (19-26) : *Loot To Owe Caesar and God* : *Lose Pennies to Caesar/Plenty to God* : T^{2}hings O^{0}wed *each*

Resurrected Spouse Marries Whom? (27-40) : *Who To Own woman?* : n^{2}o O^{0}ne!

Make Enemies Footstool (41-44) : *Stool Enemy /* T^{2}opple O^{0}pponents

OT   Luke   NT

[20] **Devour Widows' Houses** (45-47) : *Loot Plenty* : V[2]ictimize O[0]wners

[21] **Widow Offers 2 Lepta** (1-4) : *Two To Fund* temple : 2[2] l[1]epta

Temple—Not 1 Stone on Another (5-9) : *2 To 1 stones* : 2 > 1/n[2]ot O[0]ne *on the other* / T[2]emple l[1]eveled

Nation Vs. Nation (10-19) : *Nukes To Come?* : n[2]ations l[1]ncited

Jerusalem Destroyed/Scattered (20-24) : *Jeru To Run* : n[2]ations l[1]evel *it*

Sun Signals Jesus Near (25-27) : *Look To Sun/Son* (25) : "n[2]earing" l[1]ight

Fig Tree Sign (29-33) : *Look New/Plenty Buds!* : n[2]ew l[1]eaves

Guard Against Dissipation (34-37) : *"Boozed" Too Drunk to see the signs* : V[2]oid l[1]avishness/l[1]icentiousness/l[1]uxuriance

[22] **Judas Betrays Jesus for $** (3-6) : *Judas To Cue priests with kiss*: T[2]reachery T[2]oken/n[2]otation

Lord's Supper (11-12) : *Booked Group-Room* : T[2]eam T[2]able

New Covenant (15-20) : *Booked New Truce between God and man* : n[2]ew T[2]estament/T[2]reaty

Who is the Greatest? Servant! (24-27) : *Who Rules Whom?* : V[2]assal V[2]alue

Satan to Sift Peter (31-34) : *Spook To Prove Peter* : T[2]o T[2]empt/T[2]est *Peter*

Luke

[22] Cock Crows (34) : *Rooster Doodle Doos* : n^2o n^2oise *until*

Not My Will but Yours (39-46) : *You To Do* Your will : n^2ot V^2olitional

Judas Betrays with Kiss (48) : *Judas To Smooch Jesus* : T^2reachery T^2oken

Jesus Answers Council (66-71) : *You To View* Son at right hand of God : T^2o V^2iew *Him there*

[23] Pilate: Are you King of Jews? (3) : *You Jew King?* : T^2orah K^3ing?/T^2hrone Z^3ion?

Jesus Crucified (18-42) : *Took To Tree* (cross) : T^2ree K^3illing

"Today Paradise for You!" (43) : *Took To Peace/Good To Thief* : T^2oday H^3eaven!

Joseph's Tomb Sealed (53) : *Tomb To Seal* : T^2omb F^3astened

[24] Jesus' Body Gone (3) : *Who Moved Corpse?* : V^2ictim M^4issing/*Tomb To Force* open (angels) : T^2omb W^4ide-open

Jesus' Appears in New Form (4-49) : *Took New Form* (16, 31, 37, cf. Mark 16:12) : n^2ew "M^4orph"

Jesus Ascends to Heaven (50-52) : *You To Soar!* : T^2o M^4ount *of God*

OT   John   NT
[*ah* *aw*]

[01] Word Takes on Flesh (1-18) : *God Comes* to earth : l^{1}ogos = l^{1}ight = 1^1ife (1:4) **/** l^{1}ncarnation (1:14)

John Testifies (19-28) : *John "Spun" Jesus* : l^{1}amb *of God!*

Jesus Calls Disciples (35-51) : *Drawn Ones* : l^{1}earners

[02] Cana: "We're out of Wine!" (3) : *Gone Booze* : n^{2}one *left!*

Jesus Drives Sellers out of Temple (13-22) *"Cons" Threw out!* ("robbers": Matt 21:13) **/ Consumed** by zeal (17) : n^{2}o trade *in here!*

Jesus Knows What's in Man (23-25) : *M[a]n Knew* : T^{2}otal *knowledge*

[03] Rebirth or No See kingdom Nicothreemus! (1-15) : *Non-See* > : K^{3}ingdom

God Gives Son to World (16-21) : *God Treats* world to Son : K^{3}id *given*

John Testifies of Jesus (22-34) : *John Speaks* of Him : K^{3}id/ K^{3}ing of K^{3}ings

Fr[o]m Peak (above) : H^{3}eaven **// God Seals** Him : H^{3}allmark

[04] Jesus Speaks to Samaritan Woman (4-42) : *"Consort with Gentiles?"* : M^{4}utts *(Hybrids)*

She Draws Water for Jesus (7-15) : *Drawn Water* : W^{4}ater *for Jesus*

God is Spirit, not Local (20-26) : *God Free* of location : E^{4}verywhere!

OT John NT

[04] **Fields Ripe for Harvest** (31-38) : ***God's Corn*** *ready* : **M⁴**ature *(ripe) corn*

Heals Dying Son (46-54) : ***Gone Mort****al illness* : **M⁴**ended

[05] **Sabbath Healing at Roofed Pool** (1-17) : *Roof **On Five** (5⁵⁾ colonnades* (2) : **S⁵**abbath **/** *"****None I've*** *got to put me in the pool!"* : **S⁵**tranded!

Jesus has Life in Himself (26) : *[**I]'m Life** itself* : **S⁵**elf-Life

Equal to God (18) : ***God's Iso*** [Greek: "equal] : **S⁵**ame

I Do What the Father Does (19-24) : ***God Drives,*** *I drive* **//** ***God "Life"s, I*** *"Life"!* : **S⁵**ame **/** **S⁵**ource *of eternal life*

[06] **Jesus' Witnesses: John, Father, Moses** (30-47: ***Non-I*** *alone* (30, 37) : **S⁵**ubstantiators/**S⁵**upporters

5,000 Fed Fish (1-15) : ***Codfish? / M[o]nkfish?*** : **b⁶**ullshark/**b⁶**ass/**b⁶**luefin *tuna?*

Jesus Walks on Water (16-21) : ***On Lid/Brim*** *of water* : **b⁶**uoyant/**d⁶**efies *gravity*

Jesus the Bread of life (25-59) : ***God Gives*** *bread of life* : **b⁶**read

My Words Are Eternal Life (60-71) : ***Long Live*** : **b⁶**io-logoi ("life- words") **/** ***Psalms live*** : **d⁶**avid's *God-inspired words*

Judas A Devil (70-71) : *De**monic** / Jesus **"On Him"** already* : **b⁶**etrayer/**d⁶**evil

[07] **Jesus Sneaks into Feast of Booths** (1-24) : *"[**I]'m Gettin** in!"* : ***L⁷***urks *in* (10)

John

[07] **"Christ"—From Where?"** (25-31) : *Fr[o]m Heaven? : L^{7}ocal guy?/L^{7}ocale?*

Spirit: Living Water (37-39) : *Fr[o]m Heaven : L^{7}iving water*

People Divided on Christ's Origin (40-52) : *Bonds Severed : T^{7}ensions/L^{7}oggerheaded over L^{7}ineage*

[08] **Adulteress Caught** (1-10) :*"John" Raid : B^{8}agged in the act!*

No Sin, Cast First Stone! (7) *Non-Blamed bash first! :* B^{8}lameless *can* b^{6}ash

Jesus: Light of the World (12) : *[I]'m Ray/Blaze of light to world :* B^{6}eacon

Truth Sets Free Slaves to Sin (31-37) : *[I]'m Slaved until freed :* B^{8}ondage/B^{8}roken *by* B^{8}ible

Keep My Word, Never Die (51) : *Non-Grave :* B^{8}elieve/ B^{8}eyond *death*

Before Abraham, I Am (48-59) : *Non-Abe/God's State :* "B^{8}efore AB^{8}e I B^{8}e!"

[09] **Jesus Heals Man Born Blind** (1-41) : *Spawned/Long Blind :* g^{9}azeless

[10] **Sheep Never Perish** (11-19) : *God Tends His sheep/Bonds Them to Himself :* l^{1}oses 0^0

I and the Father One (22-39) : *[I]'m One hand with Father* (29, 30) : 1^1 O^{0}peration/*God Them (Father, Son, and Spirit)*

[11] **Lazarus ill^{11} Dies** (1-16) : *God's Lov-ed :* l^{1}azarus / l^{1}oved / l^{1}anguishes

        # John

[11] I am Resurrection/Life (17-37) : *[I]'m Levitator* : I^1'm I^1ifter/I^1ifer

Jesus Raises Lazarus (38-44) : *God Levitates Lazarus* : I^1evitates/I^1ifts I^1azarus

Leaders Draw Plans to Kill Jesus (45-57) : *Drawn malevolent plans* : I^1eaders *plan* / I^1ay *plans*

One Dies for Whole Nation (50-53) : *God's One Son for all* : 1^1 I^1ife *for whole nation*

[12] Mary Anoints Jesus with Costly Ointment (1-8) : *"Balm Sell!" (Judas)/M[a]n Held moneybag* : J^1udas/I^1scariot T^2hief

Leaders: "Kill Lazarus Too!" (9-11) : *"M[a]n 'Fell' too!"* : "I^1azarus T^2erminate!/T^2oo!"

Triumphal Entry (12-19) : *Palm Held (palm branches)* : J^1esus' T^2riumphal *entry* : I^1auded n^2ame *of the Lord*

Grain of Wheat Dies, Bears Fruit (24-26) > *Spawns Some Fruit/Melon* > : I^1aunches n^2ectarines

Satan Cast Out Now (31) : *Join Hell!* : I^1eave n^2ow!

Son Lifted up, Draws All (32-33) : *Drawn Selves* : I^1 I^1ifted *Up* > I^1ure T^2otal

God Reveals/Blinds Some Eyes (37-43) : *God Tells some* (38) */ God Held some from seeing* (40) : I^1mparts V^2iewing/ I^1mpedes V^2iewing

Came To Save, Not Condemn (47) : *Non-Accuse / Non-Hell* (47) : I^1itigate n^2ot

[13] Peter: "Wash My Feet? Never!" (1-19) ***Balm The Feet?*** *No!* (8) **: I**[1]aunder **F**[3]eet?**/N**[3]o!**/N**[3]ever!***/I'm Dirtying*** *feet* **:** **I**[1]nfected **F**[3]eet **/** Jesus**: "I**[1] **H**[3]andwash *feet!"*

Judas to Betray Jesus (21-30) **: *Con The Priests* :** **J**[1]udas **F**[3]orsakes *Jesus***/J**[1]udas's **K**[3]iss

New Command: Love One Another (31-35) **: *Concurring/ Conferring*** *love* **:** **I**[1]ove **F**[3]ellows!

[14] I'm the Way, the Truth, the Life (1-7) **: *[I]'m The Norms* : 1**[1] **W**[4]ay**/1**[1] **W**[4]ord**/1**[1] **W**[4]ell-*being*

Seen Me, Seen the Father (8-14) **: *[I]'m The Form*** *of God* **/ *Conforming*** *to the Father* **: I**[1] **M**[4]odels *the Father*

I'll Send the Helper (15-31) **: *[I]'m Pouring*** *out Spirit* **:** **I**[1]aunch **A**[4]ssistant

[15] I Am The True Vine (1-17) **: *[I]'m The Iv*y : I**[1]vy **S**[5]incere

World Hates You (18-27) **: *Throng Deprives*** *you* **:** **I**[1]oathes **S**[5]aints **/ I**[1]oves **S**[5]elf *only* (19)

[16] Spirit Convicts of Truth (4-15) **: *Convicting*** (8) **:** **I**[1]mpress**/ I**[1]nduce **b**[6]eliefs

Sorrow [Sunk] to Joy [Bliss] (16-24) **: *[I]'m "Blissing"*** *you* **:** **I**[1]ament **> b**[6]liss

I Overcame World/Tribulation (25-33) **: *Conflictings* : "I**[1] **b**[6]eat *the world!"* (33)

[17] Intercessory Prayer (1-26) **: *God's Son's Session* :** **I**[1]nterceding **L**[7]ord *(prayer session)*

OT   John   NT

[18] **Lord Betrayed** (1-3) : *God "Traitoring"* : l[1]ord B[8]etrayed

Lord Arrested (4-11) : *God's Son Raid/God-Raiding* : l[1]ord B[8]ound

Peter Denies Jesus (15-18) : *God's Son? Nay! / God "Naying"/Negating* : l[1]ord B[8]elied

Caiaphas/Pilate Trials (19-32) : *God's Son Blamed / God Blaming* : l[1]ord B[8]lamed

My Kingdom Not of this World (36) : *God's Son's Reign* in world to come : l[1]ord B[8]eyond *this world*

[19] **Lord Crucified** (1-16) : *Consigning* to cross : l[1]ord g[9]ored

"It is finished!" (30) : *God's Timing* : l[1]ord's g[9]oal *achieved*

[20] **Resurrection—Tomb >** (1-10) : *"[I]'m empty!"* : T[2]omb O[0]pened / T[2]omb O[0] *occupants*

Thomas Demands Proof (25) : *Tom: "Plenty* of evidence please!" since he's been *Conned Plenty* : T[2]om O[0]verwary/ O[0]bserver *// wants* n[2]ailprint O[0]bservation

[21] **Many Signs Written for Faith** (21) : *Jots Plenty* : n[2]oted O[0]bservations

Love Me? Feed My Lambs! (17) : *[I]'m To Love* them! : n[2]ourish l[1]ambs

Jesus Comes Before John Dies? (23) : *[I]'m to come* before *John dies?* : n[2]ot l[1]nterred *or* n[2]ot l[1]ive?

OT   Acts   NT
[*a* as in at, act, back, ad, ap(ostles)]

[01] Stay in Jerusalem! (4) : ***Act None!*** *(Wait!)* : l^{1}inger *there*

    Jesus Ascends (10) : ***Tracks/Back Up*** *to heaven* : l^{1}ifted *up*

    Matthias Chosen by Lot (12-26) : ***Matt's Up*** *next* : l^{1}ots

[02] Pentecost's Tongues (1-13) : ***Yak Truths*** (11) : T^{2}ongues/ n^{2}ative *languages*

    Peter: "Jesus of Nazareth" (14-40) : ***Yaks/Naz Truths*** : T^{2}ruths/n^{2}azarite

    Last-Day Signs (17-21) : ***Last Cues*** : T^{2}okens

    Sharing with Poor (42-56) : ***Pass Food*** *out* : n^{2}etworking/ n^{2}eedy

[03] Lame Healed (1-8) : ***Back healed / Back Leap*** (8) : H^{3}ealed/H^{3}andicapped

    Peter: You Rejected Holy One (11-26) : ***[A]greed*** *to reject Him* : H^{3}oly *One denied* (14)

[04] Apostles Peter/John Warned (1-18) : ***Aps Warned*** : W^{4}arned: "No more Jesus!" (18)

    Prayer for Bold Preaching (23-31) : ***Yak Force*** : E^{4}mbolding

    Sharing with Poor (32-37) : "***Back*** *Poor* / ***[A]ccord*** : M^{4}erge *your goods* / A^{4}pportion/A^{4}llocate

[05] Ananias/Sapphira Lie to Spirit (1-11) : ***Saph-Five****ra* : S^{5}apphira / S^{5}pirit / S^{5}cam/S^{5}windle *attempt*

    [Ap]ostolic Signs (12-16) : ***Ap Sights*** : S^{5}ights/S^{5}igns

OT   Acts   NT

[05] [Ap]ostles Arrested/Freed (17-42) **:** *Aps Tied/"Ride"* **:**
S⁵eized**/S⁵**et *free*

[06] [Ap]ostles Pick Deacons (1-7) **:** *Aps Pick* > **:** **d⁶**eacons**/**
b⁶usboys**/b⁶**ellboys *(servants)*

[07] Stephen Speaks/Stoned (8-15) **:** *Yaks//Whack/Smack*
Stephen **:** *L⁷*ob *stones*

[08] Saul Ravages Church (1-3) **:** *Whacks Saints* **:** **B⁸**rutalizes

Phillip to Samaria's Half-Jews : *"Halves" Saved* : B⁸lended
Jews **/ B⁸**reeds

Simon the [Mag]ician (9-25) **:** *Mag's Faith* **:** **B⁸**lack *magic*

Baptize Ethiopian Eunuch (26-40) **:** *Castrated one* **:**
B⁸aptize *me!* (36)

[09] Jesus Appears to and Blinds Saul (1-9) **:** *Flash Shine/Blind*
: **g⁹**lory > **g⁹**azeless

Ananias: "Find Paul!" (10-19) **:** *"Ananias, Find Paul!"* **:** **g⁹**et
Paul!

Paralyzed Aeneas Healed (32-35) **:** *Bad Spine / Aligned* **:**
g⁹et *up!*

Dorcas Raised from Dead (36-43) **:** *"Back" from dead Time*
/ Dorcas Time **:** **g⁹**et *up!*

[10] Cornelius Sends for Peter (1-8) **:** *Lads Sent* to pick up **:**
1¹ads **O⁰**ut

Peter's Reptile Vision (9-33) **:** *Asps Sent* down from heaven
: **l¹**owered **O⁰**phidians (12)

<u>OT</u>   **Acts**   <u>NT</u>

[10] Baptize Cornelius (34-43) : *Bapts "Gent"* : I^{1}aves C^{0}ornelius

Spirit Falls on Gentiles (44-48) : *Bapts Gent[ile]s* : I^{1}aves O^{0}utsiders

[11] Peter Informs Apostles (1-18) : *"Facts" Eleven* + 1 : I^{1}nforms I^{1}eaders

Antioch's "Christians" (19-27) : *Aps Allegin "Christians"I* : 1^{1st} I^{1}abelled "Christians"

Agabus: "Famine Coming!" (27-30) : *Ag Allegin / Slack Levels* of food : I^{1}ess I^{1}ettuce/I^{1}egumes/I^{1}ivestock

[12] Herod Kills James with Sword (2) : *Ap Run Through/ Stabs "Twelfth"* (12 Apostles) : I^{1}anced T^{2}hrough

Angel Frees Peter (6-18) : *Ap Helped*: I^{1}oosens T^{2}ies

Angel Kills Herod (20-23) : *Whacked: Felled* by angel : I^{1}ord T^{2}erminated

[13] Paul and Barnabas Set Apart for Travel (1-3) : *Aps Journey* : I^{1}eave F^{3}lock

Paul Blinds Magician Elymas (4-12) : *Mag's/Elymas Blurring* : I^{1}ndicts m^{3}agician / I^{1}llusionist H^{3}andicapped

Paul Recaps Israel's History (16-46) : *"Caps"/Tracks Journeyings* from Egypt : I^{1}srael's H^{3}istory

"Light for Gentiles" (47-52) : *Flash Stirring* Gentiles : I^{1}ighten H^{3}eathen

[14] Iconium Divides over Paul (1-6) : *Ap Warring/Discording* : I^{1}conium M^{4}eetings

OT **Acts** **NT**

[14] **Lystra Divides over Paul** (8-23) : *Ap Warring/Discording* :
I¹ystra M⁴eetings

We See Gods as Men! (11) : *Aps Forming men* : I¹ords
E⁴mbodied/M⁴en

God Testified: *Acts informing men* : "I¹eaves W⁴itness" *in
every generation* (17)

Jerusalem Council: Circumcision (1-35) : *Fact iffing* : I¹f
S⁵aved *need to be circumcised?* / J¹erusalem S⁵ynod // *Pack
The Knife* away! : I¹aw S⁵aves? *No!* I¹aw S⁵laves!

[15] **Paul and Barnabas Separate** (36-41) : *Aps Splitting* up :
I¹eave S⁵eparately

[16] **Spirit Blocks Bithynia** (6-8) : *Pass "Bithing!"* : I¹ay-off/
I¹gnore b⁶ithynia

Macedonia: "Help us!" (9-10) : *Mac/Ap: "Come Fix us!"* :
I¹end b⁶elievers *a hand!*

Lydia Converts (11-15) : *Acts of Lydia* : I¹ydia b⁶elieves

Earthquake > Jail Guard Believes (16-40) : *Cracks The
Bricks* > I¹ookout b⁶elieves

[17] **Paul Reasons with Thessalonians** (1-9) : *Ap Severing
arguments* : "I¹ogicking" T⁷hessalonians/I¹ntrosuming/
I¹nvolving ... L⁷ogic

Berean's Nobility (10-15) : *Ap "Checkining" against
scripture* : I¹nspect T⁷estaments/T⁷orah

Athen's Lifeless Idols (16-21) : *Ath's Dumb Deafened idols*
: I¹dols L⁷ifeless

OT   Acts   NT

[17] Unknown/God (23) : *Lack the Sovereign*: I[1]gnore *L[7]ord*

God Overlooked Times of Ignorance (30) : *Passed Dumb Deafened Times :* I[1]gnorance *T[7]imes*

God Now Commands Everyone Everywhere to Repent (30) : *Have/Act repenting!* : I[1]nformation *T[7]urn!*

Resurrection Rejected (32) : *Ax Heavenly bodies—no such thing* : I[1]ifting *L[7]ifeless is impossible*

[18] Aquila the Tentmaker (1-3) : *Aq's Making tents*: I[1]aces B[8]ivouacs

Aquila Trains Apollos in Word (24-28) : *Aq/Ap Training* : I[1]nstruct B[8]ible

[19] Spirit-less "disciples" in Ephesus (1-19) : *Lack The Sign* : I[1]ack [Holy] g[9]host / I[1]n Ep[9]hesus

Sceva's "Exorcist" Sons Attacked (11-20) : *"Hacks" Maligned/Maligning by evil spirit* : I[1]eaping g[9]host (16)

Demetrius's Idol Trade (24) : *Crafts A Shrine (Artemis)* : I[1]ayers g[9]ods *with silver* (24)

[20] Paul Successful in Macedonia and Greece (1-3) : *"MacPlenty"* : n[2]o O[0]pposition *for 3 months*

Eutychus Naps into Unconsciousness (9) : *Naps Plenty* : n[2]aps O[0]ut *at Paul's sermon*

Spoke Whole Counsel of God to Ephesus (27) : *Facts Plenty* : T[2]otal O[0]rated / n[2]othing O[0]verlooked

<u>OT</u>   **Acts**   <u>NT</u>

[21] Agabus Hinders Paul (10-12) : *Ag To Shunt* Paul : "n^{2}ot J^{1}erusalem, *man!*"

Gentile Prohibitions (25) : *Acts To Shun* : n^{2}ew O^{0}bligations

[22] Paul Preaches Jesus of Nazareth to Jews (1-21) : *Facts To Jews / "Naz Truths" Jews* : n^{2}azarene (8) T^{2}eachings

[23] Paul Escapes Council by Night (23) : *Acts/Tracks To Free* Paul : n^{2}ight F^{3}light

[24] Felix Backs Jew's Illegal Condemnation of Paul (1-27) : *Backs Jews' Tort* (27) : n^{2}ot W^{4}arranted

[25] Paul Appeals to Caesar Before Festus (11-12) : *Ap To Thrive* under higher court : T^{2}o S^{5}enate *of Roman Republic*

[26] Agrippa To Ship Paul to Rome (1-32) : *Agrippa To Ship* him : V^{6}atican-b^{6}ound

Paul Almost Convinces Agrippa (28) : *Ag's Truth Fix*ation : n^{2}early b^{6}elieved

[27] Paul's Shipwreck (1-44) : *Craft's To "Wreckin"* near island : V^{2}essel L^{7}ossed

[28] Paul's "Snake-off" (3-6) : *Smack To Snake* : V^{2}iper B^{8}eaten-off/B^{8}uffeted

Paul's Residence in Rome (16) : *Ap To Stay* there : n^{2}ew B^{8}oardinghouse

<u>OT</u>   **Romans**   <u>NT</u>
[*ō* : *Home* [with God]**-Man** and *Roam* [from God]**-Man**]

[01] Paul Longs to Go to Rome (8-15) **: *Moans Some* : I¹**onging

Righteous Live by Faith (16-17) **: *Home-Man From*** faith to faith **/ *Home-Man's One*** Faith **: I¹**oyalty *(trust, belief)*

Creation Reveals God (19-20) **: *Show Man Sun* : I¹**nvisible *attributes*

God's Wrath on Sin (18-32) **: *Roam-Man Stunned* : I¹**ashed

[02] Conscience and Law (1-29) **: *Show Man Truth* : V²**oice *of conscience*

[03] No Man Seeks God (9-20) **: *No Man Seeks*** God **/ *Rome-Man Flees*** God **: F³**lees *God*

Righteousness Through Faith (21-31) **: *Home-Man's*** be***lief* : F³**aith

[04] Abraham: Father of Faith (1-12) **: *Role-Man For*** faith **: A⁴**braham

Promise to Abraham's Faith—Offspring (13-25) **: *Home-Men Born* : A⁴**braham's**/E⁴**state**/A⁴**uthor *of faith*

[05] Justified by Faith (1-18) **: *Home-Man's Right*** with God **: S⁵**traight *with God*

Peace with God (1) **: *Home-Man's Strife*** is gone **: S⁵**rife-less

Adam and Christ (12-21) **: *Roam-Man's Strife* / *Home-Man's Life* : S⁵**trife**/S⁵**trifeless **// S⁵**lain *(death in Adam)***/S⁵**aved *(life in Christ)*

[06] Slave to Sin (20) **: *Roam-Man's Pick* : b⁶**ondage *to sin*

Romans

[06] Slave to Righteousness (22) : *Home-Man's Pick* : b^{6}ondage *to God*

[07] Law of Sin (1-25) : *Roam-Man Servin > L^{7}aw of sin* (25)

Law of God (1-25) : *Home-Man Servin > L^{7}aw of God* (25)

[08] Mind of Flesh > Death (1-11) : *Roam-Man's Brain* : B^{8}elief

Mind of Spirit > Life and Peace (1-11) : *Home-Man's Brain* : B^{8}elief

Conformed to Christ (9-30) : *Home-Man's Fate* (28-30) : B^{8}ecome *Christ-like*

Creation Groans/Moans for Redemption (19-23) : *Groan/ Moan State* : B^{8}easts/B^{8}ondage

[09] Children of God (8): **Promise/Elect/Remnant** (1-33) : *Home-Man's Kind* : g^{9}od-like

Children of Flesh: Rejected/Sand of Sea (8) : *Roam-Man's Kind* : g^{9}od-less

[10] Preach to All (5-21) : *Sow-Men Sent* : l^{1}aunched O^{0}ut

[11] Remnant of Israel (1-18) : *Home-Man "Left-in"s* (1-5) : l^{1}imbs l^{1}eft *in vine*

Gentile Branches Grafted (11-24) : *Home-Man "Cleft-in"s* : *severed* l^{1}imbs l^{1}nserted

All Israel Saved (25-36) : *Home-Men Leavenin* (spreading) : All^{11}

Mercy on All (32) : *Home-Men "Leavenin"* : All^{11}

[12] Living Sacrifice (1-2) **:** *Home-Man's Selfless* **:** I[1]iving V[2]ictim

God's Gifts (3-8) **:** *Home-Man Helps* the Church **:** I[1]mprove T[2]emple *of God*

Overcome Evil with Good (9-21) **:** *Grow-Men Help* the *wicked* **:** I[1]ove V[2]illains *(<u>not</u> help the wicked be wicked)*

[13] Submit to Government (1-7) **:** *Home-Man Concedes / Home-Men Juries* **:** I[1]egal H[3]angings (4)**/**F[3]ees *(6: taxes)*

Love Neighbor (14) **:** *Home-Man Spurring good deeds* **:** I[1]ove N[3]eighbor

[14] Help the Weak in Faith (1-22) **:** *Home-Man Shoring up/ Supporting the weak* **:** I[1]ntensify**/**I[1]nvigorate**/**I[1]mprove … W[4]eak *(strengthen them)*

[15] Self-Denial like Christ (1-21) **:** *Home-Man's Living* **:** I[1]iving S[5]acrifice

Paul Plans to Visit Rome (22-33) **:** *"Rome-Man" Shifting to Rome* **:** I[1]ong S[5]eparation *from friends* (24) **/** I[1]onging [to] S[5]ee *them*

[16] Paul's Greeting/Farewell (1-27) **:** *Home-Men "Blissing" /Kissing goodbye* (16) **:** "I[1]ove ya, b[6]ye!"

<u>**OT**</u>   **1 Corinthians**   <u>**NT**</u>
[*or*]

[01] Unity Vs. "I am of Paul" (10-12) : ***Form One*** *body!* : **1**[1] *body*

Christ—Wisdom and Power of God (18-29) : ***W[o]rd/Force One*** : **l**[1]ogos

[02] Christ Crucified/Risen: Gospel (1-5) : ***Corpse To*** *rise* : **V**[2]ictor **/ T**[2]riumph **/ T**[2]idings **/ n**[2]ews *good (gospel)*

Hidden Wisdom Imparted (6-16) : ***W[o]rd New*** : **n**[2]ew/**T**[2]ruth/**T**[2]idings/**T**[2]old

[03] Divisions in Church body (1-23) : ***Corps Cleaved*** : **F**[3]ractured/**F**[3]ellowship

Christ Foundation (11) : ***Lord's F**[3]ield* (9) : **F**[3]oundation

[04] Apostles' Ministry (1-20) : ***Corp's/Core Force*** (cf. Eph. 2:20) : **A**[4]postles/**M**[4]inisters *to the body*

[05] Deliver Fornicator to Satan (1-13) : ***"Forn" Life*** : **S**[5]exist *to* **S**[5]atan *for* **S**[5]laughter *of* **S**[5]arx (flesh) *so* **S**[5]pirit **S**[5]aved *at* **S**[5]econd *Coming* (5)

[06] Believer Lawsuits (1-11) : ***Court Trips*** : **b**[6]eliever/**b**[6]reaches

Flee Fornication (12-20) : ***Forn Quit/Skip/Rid!*** : **b**[6]reak *with it because you were* **b**[6]ought *with a price!* (20)

[07] Marriage & Divorce (1-16) : ***Cords Savin/Severin*** : ***L**[7]ove* or ***L**[7]eave spouse criteria*

Live as Called (17-24) : ***Forward Savin*** : ***L**[7]ive as called*

Divided/Undivided Devotion (25-40) : ***For Several/For Heaven L**[7]oyalties*

[08] Weak Conscience (1-13) : *Morals Lame* : **B⁸**ackslidden

[09] All Things to All Men (1-26) : *More Kinds to save all* (20) : **g⁹**enerous

[10] Idolatry Destroyed (1-22) : *Forms End* : **I¹**dolatry **O⁰**verthrown **/**

   OT Types: *For End-age people* : **I¹**nstruction **O⁰**urs (11)

   Do All for God's Glory (23-33) : *Moral End* (purpose) : **I¹**ord's **O⁰**bjectives

[11] Head Coverings (1-16) : *Shorn Levels none!* (5-6) : **I¹**ong **I¹**ocks *preferred*

   Lord's Last Supper (17-33) : *Lord Left this Memorial for us* : **I¹**ord **I¹**eft *it*

[12] One Body, Various Spiritual Gifts : *Corps Helps* : **I¹** [Body] **V²**arious *parts*/**I¹**ord's **T²**reats/**T²**alents/**T²**reasures

[13] Love Defined by Lord (1-13) : *Lord's referring* (definition) : **I¹**ove's **m³**eaning/**F³**ormulation

   Love Endures (8, 13) : *Amor enduring/Lord's Enduring* : **I¹**ove **K³**eeps

[14] Tongues/Prophecies: Signs (1-24) : *Lord's Tongues For unbelievers* : **I¹**ingual/**I¹**nformation **M⁴**anifestations/ **E⁴**vidence

[15] Resurrection (1-58) : *Corps/Corpse Revive!* : **I¹**iven **S⁵**lain!

[16] Gifts for Jerusalem (1-4) : *For Gifting Jerusalem* : **J¹**erusalem **b⁶**ounty

OT   2 Corinthians   NT
[*to* + *or*]

[01] **God of Comfort** (1-11) : *To In"Sure" One* : I^{1}nsure/I^{1}ord

[02] **Forgive/Comfort the Sinner** (5-11) : *To In"Sure" Doomed* : T^{2}ranquilize/T^{2}ransgressor/T^{2}respasser

    Two Aromas' Effects (14-16) : *Two Force-Fumes* : T^{2}wo/ n^{2}asal *effects:* n^{2}ourish *(life)* and n^{2}oxious *(death)*

[03] **Minister New Covenant** (1-18) : *New Glor-y* (9-10) : N^{3}ew

[04] **Preach Christ as Lord, not Selves** (5) : *To "Lord" Lord* : M^{4}essage/A^{4}nnounce /E^{4}vangelize

    Treasure in Clay Jars (7-15) : *To Store Lord* in us : M^{4}anifest *Jesus' life* (11)

    Temporal/Eternal (16-18) : *Two More Forms* (18) : E^{4}nding/ E^{4}ndless

[05] **Eternal Body** (1-10) : *ImMortal Life /* : S^{5}empiternal/ S^{5}ustained S^{5}oma *(body)*

    Ministry of Reconciliation (11-20) : *To Pour Life* into others */ Lure Lives* : S^{5}ave *others*

    Made Sin > So We Live (21) : *Slew For Life* : S^{5}in > S^{5}aved

[06] **We Commend Ourselves** (4-10) : *To Form List* of credentials : b^{6}ravos, b^{6}eatings, etc. (5)

    Temple of Living God (14-18) : *True Lord Lives* in us : b^{6}ody *of Christ*

    Unequally Bound/Yoked (14-18) : *Two: Poor Mix* : b^{6}ad/ b^{6}onds

[07] Two Kinds of Sorrow (2-16) **:** *Two Sore affections/ regrettins* **:** L^7aments**:** *one* L^7ethal, one L^7ife-giving

[08] Give Generously (1-9) **:** *To Pour/Poor Aid* **:** B^8enefactors

Lord Poor So We Rich (9) **:** *You Poor Made us rich* **:** B^8eggar > B^8eneficiary/B^8illionare/B^8ountiful

Paul Commends Titus (16-24) **:** *To Score "A" / To Orate about Titus* **:** B^8est!/B^8ravo!

[09] Generous Cheerful Giving (1-15) **:** *Do More Kind acts* **:** g^9enerous/g^9lad/g^9iving

[10] Paul Defends his Ministry (1-18) **:** *To Forfend accusations / Shoot Foreign thoughts* **:** I^1llegitimate O^0bjections *to him* (5)

Weapons not Flesh but Power (4-6) **:** *To Forfend conjecture / Shoot Foreign thoughts* **:** I^1iquidate O^0bjections = I^1ofty O^0pinions (5)

We Boast in the Lord (17) **:** *To Lord's Splendor* **:** I^1ord O^0nly *boast*

[11] False Apostles (1-14) **:** *"To-Lure" Leaven* (5, 13) **:** I^1ying I^1eaven/*Satan an Angel of light* (14) **:** I^1ying I^1ight

[12] Ascent to 3rd heaven (1-10) **:** *To Lord's Dwelling* **:** I^1ord's T^2hird heaven / I^1ifted T^2o *3rd heaven*

Thorn in the Flesh (7) **:** *Two-Thorned Welt?* **:** I^1imb T^2horn? / I^1nquired T^2hree times *for removal*

[13] Examine Your Faith (5) **:** *Prove Belief* **:** I^1nspect F^3aith

OT   Galatians   NT
[*a + ā* *āsh*]
Grace vs. Case (Law)

[01] **False Gospels** (6-10) : *Fallacious Ones* : l¹ies / l¹egalism

Paul Called by Grace (11-23) : *Gracious One* (calling) / *Gracious Son* appeared : l¹ord/l¹ight appeared

[02] **False Apostles** (1-6): *Mendacious/Fallacious/Predacious/ Rapacious/Voracious/Dissuasive Dudes* : T²hreats to Church

Apostles Finally Accept Paul (7-10) : *Veracious/Tenacious Dudes* / Paul is *Persuasion Dude* : T²ruth provers

Circumcise Gentiles, Peter? No! (11-14) : *Gracious/ Vivacious Wound?* No! : T²rim saves Gentiles? No way!

Grace Through Faith (15-21) : *Gracious Truth / A Grace Through* faith content : T²rust/T²ruth

[03] **Foolish Galatians** (1-9) : *Galatians deceived* : F³oolish

Righteous Live by Faith (10-14) : *The Faith "Vive"s/ Vivacious Feed* (source) : F³aith/F³eeds

The Law:

Does not Void Promise (15-18) : *Promise is Negate-Free* : N³egateless

Tutors to Faith in Christ (21-29) : *The Faith Frees* from Law : F³aith/F³rees / *The Claims Lead* to Christ : F³orensics N³urture faith

[04] **Slave Wards > Heir-Sons** (1-7) : *A Slave Ward > An Heir Born* : E⁴nslaved > E⁴state // W⁴ards > E⁴statees

OT   Galatians   NT

[04] Why Do You Want to be Slaves Again? (8-20) : *A Slave re**store**/**More**/**Form?*** : **E**[4]nslaved *again?*

Two Women Covenants (21-30) : *A Slave Ward* > *An Heir Born* : **W**[4]oman > **W**[4]oman

[05] Christ Set Us Free (1-15) : *Gracious Life / Galatians Thrive!* : **S**[5]laves *no more!*

Fruit of the Spirit (16-18, 22-25) : *Gracious/Sagacious Life / Galatians Thrive* : **S**[5]pirit/**S**[5]uculents/**S**[5]trawberries

Works of the Flesh (19-21) : *Salacious/Vexatious Life / Galatians Strive against* : **S**[5]arx *(Greek: flesh)*/**S**[5]trife

[06] Bear Burdens (1-10) : *Vexations Rid* : **b**[6]ear/**b**[6]urdens

OT Ephesians NT

[*ee* * ees* * eesh* *each* + *in* or *un*]

[01] Chosen and Predestined Sons in Christ (1-9) : *Leashin Sons* : I^1eashed *(predestined)* : I^1n *Him*

All Headed/Summed Up in Him (10) : *Cohesion One* : 1^1 / I^1n *Him*

Paul's Unceasing Intercession (15-23) : *Ceasin None to pray* (16) : I^1ntercession

Christ Fills All in All (23) : *Inhesion One* : I^1nflates *All*

[02] Made Alive—Grace Through Faith (1-10) : *Freeing You from death* : V^2ivified/T^2hrough/T^2rust

Jew/Gentile: 2 > 1 New Man (11-21) : *Breaching Two* : T^2wo > On^2e/n^2ew

[03] Mystery of Gospel Revealed (1-13) : *Secretion Treats/ Leakin Treats* : H^3idden > H^3ighlighted/H^3anded *over*

Prays, Bows Knees for Power (14-21) : *Beseechin Knees* : K^3neels *for* F^3orce *(power)*

[04] One Lord, One Faith (1-6) : *Adhesion Core beliefs* (5) : A^4ccord with *Jesus as Chief Cornerstone*: M^4onotheistic/ M^4onolithic = *One Stone* (2:20)

Many Gifts for Church (7-17) : *Each One's for Church* : M^4any/E^4ndowments

Spiritual Life Actions (17-32) : *Each One's Morals* : M^4orals /A^4ctions

[05] Imitate God (1) : *Teachin/Speechin Life / Meme One's Life* : S^5imulate/S^5avior

<u>OT</u>   **Ephesians**   <u>NT</u>

[05] Children of Light (8) : *Teachin Light to the world* :
S[5]tarlight

Speak Psalms, Spiritual Songs (19) : *Speechin Life* :
PS[5]alms**/S[5]**piritual**/S[5]**ongs

Submissions (21—6:5) : *Leashin Life to others!* :
S[5]ubmissions *(voluntary)*

Purify Wife (26-38) : *Bleachin Wife* : S[5]anctify *to* S[5]potless

[06] Bring Up Kids (1-4) : *Teachin Kids* : b[6]ring *up/*d[6]iscipline
(4) **/ b[6]**ehavior

Don't Provoke : *Teasin Kids? No!* : b[6]adger**/b[6]**elittle *not!*

Whole Armor of God : *Beatin/Breachin/Defeatin Sticks* :
b[6]attling *Satan*

Sword of Spirit > Word of God (17) : *Preachin/Teachin
Stick*er : b[6]ayonet**/b[6]**lade**/b[6]**ible

Philippians
[*ill*]

[01] Paul Thanks God for their Love (3-11) : *Philippians' Love* (11) : l[1]ove/l[1]auded/l[1]aden *with fruit* (9, 11)

God Perfects Us Until the Day of Christ (6) : *Till Done* : l[1]abors *until* l[1]ord's *coming* (2:13)

Preaching Motives: The Will (16-17) : *Filled / ill ones* : l[1]ove / i[1]ll

To Live is Christ (19-30) : *Filled Ones* : l[1]ife *is* l[1]ord

[02] Christ Empties Himself (1-8) : *Dilutes Himself* : V[2]acates/ n[2]ullifies/n[2]egates/n[2]ils *Self*

Every Knee will Bow (10) : *Will Stoop* : T[2]high/Kn[2]ee

Every Tongue Confess (11) : *Will Cue/"Truth" that Jesus is Lord"* : T[2]ongue *the* T[2]ruth

God Works in Us to Will/Do (12-13) : *Will, Do* : V[2]olition *and* V[2]erbs *(actions)*

Lights in our Dark World (15) : *Fill Gloom with light* : T[2]orches *to* T[2]wisted *age*

Sending Timothy/Epaphroditus to Look After You (19-30) : *"Will Look after you"* (2) : **"**T[2]ake *care of you"*

Epaphroditus was Sick : *ill To death* : *"*T[2]erminal*" almost*

[03] Lose World, Gain Christ (8) : *Will Seek Christ / Will Heave all things* : H[3]eave *Things* > H[3]ave *Christ*

Upward Call (12-21) : *Hilly Call* : H[3]illy *Call*

Philippians

[03] **Jesus will Transform our bodies** (20-21) **:** *Will Heal* our bodies **:** H³eal *them* **/** *Will Treat them to immortality*

[04] **Cast Anxiety on Him; Peace of God will Calm! :** *iLL Core* > *"STILL" (Quiet) Core* (6-7) **:** A⁴nxiety **>** A⁴ppeasement **/** E⁴motions > E⁴irenes *(Greek: peace)*

    Think Pure things (8) **:** *"Will"/Build Pure thoughts* **:** M⁴ind**/** M⁴editate **//** M⁴erit**/**M⁴orality**/**E⁴xcellence**/**the W⁴ord

OT   Colossians   NT
[*oss* *osh*]

[01] Colossian Fruit (6) : *Colossian Plums* : l^1imes/l^1ndustrious

Paul Prays for Them (3, 9) : *C[a]lls Son* : l^1ntercedes

Darkness > Son's Kingdom (13) : *Closet >> Son* : l^1ucifer > /l^1ightless >> l^1ord/l^1ight

Christ's Preeminence:

Image of God (15) : *Colossal/Class One* : l^1mage *of God*

Fullness of God (19) : *Colossal/Class One* : l^1aden *with God*

First in All Things (15, 18) : *Colossal/Class One* : #1/1^{1st}

Reconciled All Things (20) : *Colossal/Class One* : l^1inked *All to God* / 1^1

United Things : *Cross-"Oned" together Jew-Gentile, Master-Slave, etc.* / *"1^1-ed"*

Hidden Mystery Revealed (24-29) : *Colossal Mum revealed* : l^1ntrigue > l^1lluminated/l^1ightened

[02] Philosophy Empty (8) : *"Philoph's" Fools / Foolish/Moot* : V^2oid/n^2ul *thinking*

God's Fulness Bodily (9) : *God's Son Full of Deity* : T^2otal / *implies* T^2rinity

In Christ we are:

Circumcised in Heart (11) :*"Crossed" [crucified] Root (Old Heart)* : V^2entricle/V^2ascular >> T^2ossed/T^2ransformed

OT   Colossians   NT

[02] In Christ we are:

    Buried: Old Man Dies (12) **:** *"Crossed" Coot* (Old Man) **:** V^2eteran **>** "T^2d!" *(Crucified: "T" symbol)*

    Raised in Him (13) **:** *Cross Boosts* us up **:** V^2ivified

    Debt Cancelled (14) **:** *"Crossed"* **Dues** **:** T^2ossed **>** n^2otes

[03] Mind Things Above (1-4) **:** *Colossals Seek* **:** F^3ocus *on* **/** m^3ind *above-things*

    Put Off Old, Put On New (5-17) **:** *"Cross" Mean / Gloss Clean* **:** F^3ilthy **>** F^3resh **//** F^3aithless **>** F^3aith **//** F^3iend **>** F^3riend **//** m^3ean **>** m^3oral

    Submissions: Wives, Children, Slaves (18-22) **:** *Boss Treat* well **:** H^3umility

[04] Open Door for Gospel (2) **:** *Colossal Door* **:** W^4ide open **/** A^4jar/E^4vangelism

[*ess*]

[01] Chosen by God (4-5) : *Vested/Blessed Ones* : I^{1}oved *by God*

Faith Imitators (6-9) : *Best Ones* : I^{1}mitators *of us*

Jesus Rescues Us from Wrath to Come (10) : *Rescued Ones* : I^{1}ifeline

[02] Our Good Conduct Toward You (5) : *Blessed You* : V^{2}irtuous/n^{2}oble/*Dressed You* like nursing mother (7)/ n^{2}ursed *you*

Word of God, not Men (13) : *Blessed Truth* : n^{2}on-human

[03] If You Endure, We Live (8) : *Endure Test* >> We *Be* : F^{3}ortitude >> H^{3}ang *in there* / K^{3}eep *on going*

[04] Please the Lord! (1-11) : *Bless Lord!* : A^{4}dore/E^{4}xalt *Him!*

Rapture: Dead Snatched First (13-18) : *Wrest Corpse!* : W^{4}rest/A^{4}scend *to Lord (Rapture = Seize, Snatch, Wrest)*

[05] Day of Lord = Thief in Night (1-11) : *Wrest Lives* suddenly : S^{5}neak/S^{5}urprise *attack*

Rebuke Idleness (14) : *Redress "ide"s* : S^{5}cold/S^{5}luggards

Don't Quench Spirit (19) : *Less Strife/Stifle* : S^{5}tifle/S^{5}pirit

Test Everything (21) : *Test Lives* : S^{5}creen *Lives*

OT   2 Thessalonians   NT
[*oo* + *ess*]

[01] **Christ Returns :** *To Bless/Stress/Redress* (7, 10)**:** l**¹**iberate/
l**¹**nflict

[02] **Man of Sin Restrained** (1-12) **:** *Stressed/"Pressed" Dude*
: T**²**ethered

    Stand Firm (13-16) **:** *To Press To* perfection **:** T**²**rudge *on*

[03] **Pray for Quick Growth** (1-5) **:** *To Bless Speed* of Word
(1) **:** H**³**urry!/F**³**ast!

    No Work, No Eat (6-14) **:** *To Less Deeds >> To Less Eats* **:**
F**³**reeload > F**³**amish

1 Timothy
[*im* *in*]

[01] False Teachers (3-11) : *"Spin" Ones* : l¹iars/l¹ecturers

Law is for Lawless (9) : *"Whim" Ones* : l¹aw *for* l¹awless

Christ Came to Save Sinners (12-20) : *Sin Ones* > *Win Ones* : l¹iberate > l¹awbreakers

"Of Whom I am the Chief" (15) : *Sin #1* : l¹ord *of sinners*

[02] Pray For All for Peace (1-8) : *Him To grant peace* : T²ranquility *for* T²otal

God Wills All to be Saved (4-6) : *Him To will all saved* : V²olition *for* T²otal

Women Teachers (12) : *Women "School"?* : T²each/T²utor?

Saved Through The **Childbearing** (15) : *Women 's Use* : *Saved* T²hrough / *T²he* *T²eknogonias* (**The** *Child birthing >* *definite article may refer to the Messiah*)

[03] Overseer (1-7) : *Him Lead/"Seer"* (5) : F³oreman/H³eadman /m³anager (4)

Deacon (8-13) : *Him "Deacs"* : F³ootman/H³enchman

Jesus: Flesh-Mystery (14-16) : *Him Seen in flesh by angels* (16) : F³lesh/m³ystery

[04] Apostate (1-5) : *Him Scorns doctrine for doctrines of demons* : A⁴postate

Good Servant of Jesus (6-16) : *Him Chores for Lord* : A⁴ttends *to God's people*

[05] True Widows (3-10) **:** *Been Wives* **:**

S[5]urvivors—has children (4)
S[5]ingle (5)
S[5]ets *hope in God* (5)
S[5]ixty *or older* (9)
S[5]ingle *(one) husband* (9)
S[5]aint *foot-washer* (10)
S[5]erved *afflicted* (10)

Younger Widows (11-15) **:** *Whim Lives* **:**

S[5]ensual (11)
S[5]inful – *abandoned faith* (12)
S[5]landerers (13-14)
S[5]cuttlebutts/**S**[5]chmoozers/**S**[5]landerers/**S**[5]hoptalkers –
    gossips (13)
S[5]noops – Busybodies (13)
S[5]atan-**S**[5]trayers (15)

Salute Good Elders! (17-19) **:** *Him "High/Five!"* **:** **S**[5]alute!

Shame (Rebuke) Bad Elders (20-22) **:** *Him Chide* **:** **S**[5]hame
/**S**[5]cold

[06] Honor Masters (1-2) **:** *Him Give* honor **:** **b**[6]osses/**b**[6]estow
honor

Contentious Teacher (3-5) **:** *Him Bickers / Him Rid* from
Church **:** **b**[6]ickerer

Godly for Gain (5) **:** *Skim Rich(es) from Church* **:** **b**[6]lameless
for worldly **b**[6]enefits

Fight the Good Faith Fight (11-20) **:** *Tim, Kick/Inflict* the
enemy! (12) **:** **b**[6]elief-**b**[6]attle

2 Timothy
[*oo* + *im* or* in*]

[01] **Inflame Your Gifts** (4) : *To Kindle them* : I^{1}nflame

Spirit of Power, not Fear (7) : *Too Timid One?* : I^{1}nfluence, *not* I^{1}ntimidation

Life and Immortality to Light (10) : *Truth Into light* : I^{1}ife/ I^{1}mmortality > I^{1}ight

Guard What was Entrusted (12, 14) : *To Instruct/[E]ntrust* : I^{1}ogos *to* I^{1}oyality

[02] **Good Soldiers Endure** (1-7) : *To [E]ndure* : V^{2}irtuous V^{2}ets *are* V^{2}ictorious, *so are* V^{2}irtuous V^{2}ignerons *(grape farmers) and* V^{2}aulters *(athletes)*

Endure for Elect's sake (10) : *To [E]ndure* : V^{2}ictorious *for the* V^{2}oted *(elected)*

Endure > Reign with Him (12) : *To [E]ndure > To Him Rule* : V^{2}ictory > V^{2}iceregents

Approved Worker (14-24) : *Proved Him True* : T^{2}ested/ T^{2}rue/T^{2}eam-player

God Grants Repentance > (25-26) : *To Him/Win Truth* : T^{2}urns *to* > T^{2}ruth

[03] **Last Day Godlessness** (1-9) : *To Sin Deep/Mean/Greed* : F^{3}iends/F^{3}und-lovers

Scripture Inspired (10-17) : *To Him: "Breathed from God" (God's Opinion of His Word)* : F^{3}aith/F^{3}acts // F^{3}or *profit to the man of God*

2 Timothy

[04] Urgently Preach the Word (1-8) **:** *To Implore* with Word **:** E⁴xhort**/W⁴**ord

Apostates (10, 14-16) **:** *To Ignore* Word**/To Import** words of their own **/** *To Immoral* words they go **:** **W⁴**ord *distorters***/** **A⁴**postates

Lord Brings Us to Heaven (18) **:** *To Import* us **:** E⁴xtricate *us from all evil*

OT   Titus   NT
[*ite*]

[01] Elder Qualifications (5-16) : *Right Ones* (upright: 7) :
I^{1}mpeccable *//* *Qualifications are **Tight Ones***

[02] Sound Doctrine (1-10) : *Right/Tight Truths* : T^{2}ight/T^{2}ruths

Salvation to All men Brought (11) : *Light To all* : T^{2}o *all*

[03] Ready for Every Good Work (1-4) : *Ripe Deeds* : F^{3}it *and*
F^{3}ueled

Mercy Washed us (5) : *Bright Clean* : F^{3}avor F^{3}reshened *us*

Spirit Renewed Us (5-7) : *"Right" Cleaned* (justified) :
H^{3}olied/F^{3}reshened/N^{3}ewed

Philemon

[01] Escaped Slave Restored : *Flee M[a]n restored* : -L^{7}emon's
*slave **L^7**oosed himself*

<u>OT</u>   Hebrews   <u>NT</u>
[*ee * + *ooz* or *oos*]

[01] Jesus' Supremacy (1-14) **:** *"He-Rules" Son* **:** J[1]esus/l[1]ord

[02] Neglect Salvation (1-4) **:** *Refuse Truth* **:** T[2]ruth/n[2]eglect

Man will Rule All (5-18) **:** *He Rules Tout* (French**:** *"all"*) **:**
V[2]ictor

Tastes Death For All (9) **:** *He Chooses Tomb* **:** T[2]astes
T[2]omb *for* T[2]otal

Perfected through Suffering (10) **:** *He Grew Through* it **:**
V[2]ictim > V[2]irtue

[03] Jesus Rules God's House (1-6) : *He Rules "Keep"/as King* **:**
H[3]ouse/K[3]ing/K[3]ingdom

Sabbath Rest (7-11) **:** *We Choose Sleep* (rest) **:** H[3]oly
H[3]oliday *ahead*

Wavering Hearts don't Enter Rest (12-19) **:** *We Choose
Reel*ing > *We Lose Peace* **:** F[3]luctuating/H[3]earts

[04] God Swore: Don't Enter Rest (1-13) **:** *He Who Swore* **:**
E[4]nter *not my* E[4]ase

Word: Living Sword (11-13) **:** *He Fused Truth-Sword* **:**
W[4]ord-W[4]eapon

[05] Priest Sacrifices Self (1-7) **:** *Refuses Life* **:** S[5]acrifices S[5]elf

Obedience through Suffering (8-9) **:** *He Loses Life/He
Chooses Strife* **:** S[5]uffer/S[5]uffering > S[5]ervant

[06] Apostasy > Recrucify Christ (1-12) **:** *Refuse Him/His >
"Recrucifix"* (6) **:** b[6]ackslide > b[6]rad *(nail) Jesus again*

OT   Hebrews   NT

[06] **We Hope Better Things for You** (9) : *Deduce This* from *your works/We Choose* this : **b⁶**etter *things from you*

God who Can't Lie Vows (18) : *Refuses Fibs/Myths/He Chooses Stick* to His Word : **b⁶**onafied

[07] **Abraham Tithes to Melchizedek** (1-10) : *He Proves Zedek's* superior status : **L⁷**evitic/**L⁷**oin/**T⁷**ithes to Abraham

Enduring Priest (1-29) : *He Rules Ever* : **L⁷**asting *priesthood*

[08] **New Covenant's Altar/blood (6-13)** : *Renews Faith/Place* of worship : **B⁸**ooth/**B⁸**lood of Christ

[09] **Old Blood** (lamb/goat's) > **New blood** (Jesus') : *Renews Kind* of blood : **g⁹**oats > **g⁹**uy

[10] **One Sacrifice** (1-18) : *Jes[u]s Ends* offerings : **1¹ O⁰**ffering for all time

Apostate (26-31) : *He Chooses End-*Faith : **l¹**eaving **O⁰**ne departs from the true faith

Perseverer (19-24, 32-39) : *He Chooses Clench-*faith" : **l¹**asting **O⁰**nes stick with the true faith

[11] **Hall of Faith** (1-39) : *Reviews The Sons* of God / *The True Sons* of God : **l¹**oyal/**l¹**egends

[12] **Jesus: Author of Faith** (1-2) : *He Chooses Self* sacrifice */Refuses Self/Help* on cross : **l¹**mpeccable **T²**rust

True Sons are Disciplined (3-17) : *He Bruises Whelps* : **l¹**nstructs **T²**ots/**l¹**nflicts/**l¹**nculcates **T²**ots // **l¹**llegitimate **T²**ots if not disciplined

OT   Hebrews   NT

[12] **We've Come to the City of God** (18-29) **:** *We Who Dwell there* **:** I**¹**ord's T**²**emple**/**J**¹**erusalem n**²**ew

[13] **Jesus—Always the Same** (8) **:** *He Who's "Turning" never* **:** I**¹**ord's F**³**ixed **/** I**¹**mmutable K**³**ing

   No Lasting City Here (14) **:** *We Lose Serene places of this world* **:** I**¹**mpermanent H**³**omes**/**H**³**ometowns

   Sacrifice of Praise (15) **:** *We Choose Cheering God* **:** I**¹**ips H**³**onor *God*

OT   **James**   **NT**
[*ame* *ain*]

[01] Faith Testing (2-12) : *Pains One* : l¹itmus/l¹oyalty

Temptation Internal (13-15) : *Blames None* outside because > : l¹ust is the problem/l¹nternal issue

Hearers Only (19-27) : *Feign Ones* : l¹isteners, not doers

[02] Some Favor the Rich (1-13) : *Fame Snoots* : T²oadies

Workless Faith > Dead (14-26) : *Feign Truth* : T²ruthless > T²ombed

[03] Bridling the Tongue (1-12) : *Tames/Trains/Aims Speech* : F³etters/H³obbles/H³inders/H³ampers the Tongue

Two Wisdoms (13-18) : *Brain Feeds* : N³orms—

F³rom *above* or *below* / One F³aith one F³lesh
From H³eaven or H³ell / H³oly or H³ellish
F³riendly or F³iendish

[04] Passion > War (1-12) : *Flames Wars* : W⁴ars/W⁴ithin us

Boasting of the Future (13-17) : *Fame For* me! : A⁴rrogance / rather we should say "If the Lord W⁴ills we will live and do this or that.

[05] Warning to the Rich (1-6) : *Blames "Thrive"* : S⁵tashers (hoarders: 3) / S⁵lave-drivers (4) / S⁵elf-indulgers / S⁵lay the righteous (6)

Patient Suffering (7-12) : *Tames Strife* : S⁵erene/S⁵uffering

Faith Prayer Raises Sick (13-20) : *Lame/Maimed Rise* : S⁵aves/S⁵ick

OT   1 Peter   NT
[*ee* + *er*]

[01] God Rebirths us (3) : *Breeder One* : I**¹**ivens us/I**¹**iving *hope*

"Little While Faith Trials" (6) : *Griever Ones* : I**¹**ittle/I**¹**itmus *tests*

Prophets Inquire (11) : *Seeker Ones* : I**¹**nquirers

"Be Holy as I Am" (16) : *Cleaner Ones* : "I**¹**mmaculate *ones*

Jesus Foreknown (20) : *"Seer"/Breeder One* (the Father) : J**¹**esus/I**¹**aid-out *(humanity planned)*

God's Word Forever (24-25) : *"E[e]ver" One* : I**¹**ecture/ I**¹**ong/I**¹**asting *Word* **// *"Unceaser" One*** (Word)

[02] Holy Priesthood (5) : *Priester-Hood* : V**²**icars

Submit to Authorities (13-24) : *"Caesar Rules"* : V**²**oluntary

[03] Wives be Subject to Husbands (1-7) : *Leaders—Treat with respect* > : F**³**ollow/H**³**usbands/H**³**umility

Suffer for Righteousness (8-17) : *Beater Treatments* : H**³**ostility/H**³**arrasment/H**³**ounding/H**³**ardship/H**³**atred

Christ Suffered (18) : *Leader Beat* : K**³**illed *for sins and* H**³**armed *along the way to the cross*

Preached to Spirits in Prison (19-22) : *Preacher Reached* > : H**³**ell/F**³**allen m**³**en *or* H**³**eavenly *creatures (angels) or both*

[04] Speak God's Oracles (11) : *Speakers: Oracles* : E**⁴**vangelize

Fiery Trials (12) : *Heater Courts* : M**⁴**elt-*you-down Trials*

[05] **Shepherd the Flock** (1-5) **:** *Sheep Are "Drived"* **:** S⁵hepherd

Devil: Lion Seeking Prey (8) **:** *Eat Her "Live"!* **:** S⁵atan/ S⁵imba/S⁵eeks *prey*

OT   **2 Peter**   **NT**
[*oo* + *ee* + *er*]

[01] **Assure One's Calling** (1-15) **:** *To "Meter" One's* call **>** **:**
I¹ncrease *spiritual qualities*

"Hear My Son!" (16-19) **:** *Listen **To Leader Son** :* I¹isten *to*
I¹ad (17)

Prophecy from Spirit (20-21) **:** <u>*To Seekers **From*** *Spirit* **:**
I¹nspired/I¹nterpretation *not* I¹ (one = private)

[02] **False Prophet/Teacher Fate** (1-19) **:** *To Preacher/Teacher*
> *Gloom/Doom* **:** T²ruthless/T²eachers/T²erminated/
T²artarused *(4: wicked angels)*

Dogs Return to Vomit (19-22) **:** *Puke-Eaters' Doom* (22) **:**
V²omit

[03] **Lord is the Night Thief** (1-13) **:** *To "Dreamer" Thief* **:** F³lash-
coming/N³ight-time/F³ast/F³righteningly *on unbelievers who
sleep* (1 Thessalonians 5**:**4)

God will Burn Heaven (7, 10) **:** *To Be Her Heat* **:** H³eaven/
F³ire-*reserved* (7)

God will Create New Heaven (13) **:** *To Be Her Peace* **:**
H³eaven/N³ew/ H³oly/H³onest/H³umble

Twist Word to their own Destruction(16) **:** *Truth-Beaters
Cease* **:** F³alsify/F³inagle *Word* **>** F³inished/H³ell-*bound*

OT   **1 John**   **NT**
[*ers* + *on*]

[01] Word (Logos) of Life (1-4) : *Verse/Words On Son* : l^{1}ogos/
l^{1}ife

Walk in the Light (5-10) : *Verse/Words On Sun* : l^{1}ogos/
l^{1}ight

[02] Christ Our Advocate/Propitiation (1-2) : *Versed On Suits*
(lawsuits) : V^{2}indicator

Jesus' New Command (1-14) : *Verse/Words On New* love
for brothers : n^{2}ew

Do Not Love the World (15-17) : *Turn On Loot* : n^{2}atural
world perishes

Antichrist Denies Jesus' Flesh (18-27) : *Turns On Truth/*
Foot : n^{2}egates *his human nature/body parts like foot*

No Lie is of the Truth (21) : *Turns on Truth* : n^{2}egate/V^{2}oid
/V^{2}eto/V^{2}illify/T^{2}ruth

Anointing: No Need for Teacher (27) : *Nursed On Truth/*
: T^{2}eacherless/T^{2}ruth/n^{2}o/n^{2}eed *for teacher*

[03] Born of God's Word (28-29) : *Nursed On Seed* (9) : F^{3}ilial
relation

Love One Another (11-24) : *Be First On Sweet* : F^{3}irst *on*
N^{3}ice/F^{3}riendly/K^{3}ind

Don't Hate like Cain (12-15) : *Curse On "He"* (Genesis 4:11)
: H^{3}ated *his* K^{3}in *(brother)*/K^{3}iller

[04] Spirit of Antichrist Rejects Jesus' Flesh (1-6) : *Turns On*
Form (body) : M^{4}an

[04] God is Love and One who Loves is Born of God (7-21) **:**
God AMor / God-Born **:** A[4]lmighty/A[4]gape (8, 16): One *who loves* is **born** *of God* (7)

[05] Overcome the World (1-5) **:** *Burst On Life!* **:** S[5]urmount/
S[5]ociety

Life is in Christ (6-12) **:** *Nursed On Life (His)* **:** S[5]on >
S[5]ucceed

Words Written to Know You Have Eternal Life (13) **:**
Words On Life **:** S[5]criptures/S[5]iempre-life

<u>2 John</u>
[*oo* *on*]

[01] Truth Forever (2**)** **:** *Truth Long Run* **:** I[1]nformation *that*
I[1]asts

Antichrist Denies Jesus' Flesh (7) **:** *Denies God's* **Truth On Son** **:** I[1]owliness

<u>3 John</u>
[*ee* + *on*]

[01] Support Visiting Brethren (8) **:** *Heed! On Fund*ing **:** I[1]end

Imitate Good (11) **:** *Heed! On Love* **:** I[1]ove

<u>Jude</u>
[*ū*]

[01] Faith Once For All Given (3) **:** *Truth "Onced!"* **:** I[1]aid-*down*
for Saints

Jude

[01] Bad Angels Jailed (6-7) **:** *Doomed/Gloomed* **:** I¹mprisoned

False Teachers (3-5, 8-16) **:** *"Pseud"/Shrewd/Doomed* **:** I¹iars/I¹ecturers

Persevere in Faith and God's Love (17-23) **:** *P[u]sh ahead!* **:** I¹abor/I¹ast

OT   Revelation   NT
[*ev* *Rev* for Reveal or Revelation]

[01] Seven Churches (11, 20) **: *Sev-un* :** l[1]ampstands

The Son of Man Appears (9-20) ***Rev**[eal]* **Son :** l[1]ord

[02] Jesus Reviews the Churches (2—3) **: *Rev-views*** *churches* **:** V[2]aluator

Ephesus : Left First Love (4-5) **: *Left True*** *Love* **:** T[2]op *love*/ n[2]umber-one *love*

Smyrna : False Jews: Synagogue of Satan (9) **: *Dev**il **Jews*** **:** n[2]on-*Jews of* T[2]empter

Pergamum :

Satan Kills An[2]tipas (13) **: *Dev**il **Slew*** **:** T[2]empter/ T[2]erminates/AnT[2]ipas

Satan's Throne (13) **: *Dev**il **Rules*** **:** T[2]empter's/T[2]hrone

Teaching of the Nicolaitans (15-17) **: *L[e]ver Dudes* :** n[2]icolaitans/V[2]ictors *(Nicolaitan means "people conquerors")*

Thyatira: Jezebel (20) **: *Dev**il's **Shrew*** **:** T[2]emptress/V[2]amp

[03] Sardis : Thief in the Night (1-3) **: *Heav**en's **Thief*** **:** N[3]ight/ N[3]abber

Philadelphia : Kept from Trial (10-12) **: *Every*** *perseverer guarded* **:** K[3]ept

Laodicea : Neither Hot Nor Cold (15-19) **: *Leav**ened **Heat*** **:** N[3]either H[3]ot N[3]or F[3]rigid *but* ω[3]arm

OT   Revelation   NT

[03] Knock At Door—Dine With Jesus (20-22) : *Reveals Himself for Revelry* : **F³**east *with* **K³**ing

Door to [Rev]eal Future (1-6) : *Reveal Door* (1) : **E⁴**ntrance

[04] Four Living Creatures Worship Continuously (6-11) : *Ever Four* : **4⁴/W⁴**orship: *Holy, Holy Holy—***W⁴**orthy *to receive* **M⁴**ight (11)

Created All things For His Pleasure (11) : *Every Form/For Him* : **A⁴**ll *things* **W⁴**illed *for His* **M⁴**erriment

[05] Scroll and Lamb with 7 Eyes (1-9) : *S⁵even Eyes* : **S⁵**croll

Ransomed From Every Tribe (9-10) : *Every Tribe* : **S⁵**aved/ **S⁵**ects

All Creatures Worship (11-16) : *Every Life* : **S⁵**um/**S⁵**erve

[06] Seven Seals (1-17) : *Seven Kicks* (*judgments*) :

    b⁶ow ... *and arrows?*
    b⁶attle *conqueror*
    b⁶readless *famine*
    b⁶easts *led by Death and Hades*
    b⁶odies *martyrs*
    b⁶lack *sun/***b⁶**lood *moon/***b⁶**ury *us!*

[07] 144,000 Sealed (1-8) : *Every Servant of Israel* : **T⁷**ribes/ **L⁷**evi + *11*

Saints from Tribulation in Heaven (9-17) : *Heaven's Servants* : **T⁷**ribulation *saints/***L⁷**anguages *all*

[08] Seventh Seal: Silence (1-5) : *Seven Tame?/Safe?//Sedate?* : **B⁸**reathless/**B⁸**ecalm **B⁸**efore **B⁸**eStorming?

OT   Revelation   NT

[08] Seven Trumpets (6-13) **:** *Seven Blares* **: B⁸**lares**/B⁸**lasts**/**
  B⁸ugles

  B⁸urning hail**/B⁸**lood on *earth, trees, grass* (7)
  B⁸urning Mountain *on sea, creatures, ships* (8-9)
  B⁸itter ("Wormwood") Star *on rivers, springs* (10-11)
  B⁸lackness *on third of sun, moon, stars* (12)

[09] Seven Trumpets (1-21) **:**

  g⁹reat *Furnace* **:** *Rav[i]ne* (1-12)
  g⁹reat River Euphrates **:** *River Binds* angels (13-19)

[10] Little Scroll from Heaven Opened (1-11) **:** *Heaven Scroll*
  : l¹ittle **O⁰**pen *Scroll*

  Seven Thunders (3-4) **:** *Seven/Seven Bolts* **: l¹**oud
  O⁰utburst

[11] Two "Lampstand" Witnesses (1-14) **:** *Heaven Elevated/*
  Levitated **: l¹**ampstands (4)**/l¹**evitated (12)

  Seventh Trumpet: Kingdom Lord's (15-19) **:** *Seventh*
  Trump Trumps evil **: l¹**ord **l¹**nstalled *king* (15)

[12] The Woman with 12 Stars (1-6) **:** *Heaven's Twelve* **:** **12¹²**

  Son Ascends (5,10) : *Heaven Dwells* **: l¹**ord "**V²**erticals"

  Michael Fells Dragon From Heaven (7-9) **:** *Heaven-Felled*
  Dragon **: l¹**ucifer **T²**umbles**/n²**ose-dives**/T²**oppled *by*
  Michael—**l¹**ucifer-**V²**ictory

[13] Lion-Mouthed <u>First</u> Beast from Sea (1-10) **:** *Reveal One*
  Beast/From Sea/From Deep // Marine **: l¹**ion-**m³**outh**/**
  F³anged (2) **/ l¹**ion **F³**irst *beast* **// l¹**eaves **ω³**ater

[13] Head Death-Wound Healed (3-4) : *Reveal One Healed* :
l¹ethal ω³ound *healed* / l¹njury H³ealed

Lamb-Horned <u>Second</u> Beast from Land (11-18) : *Reveal One Beast/From Beach?* : l¹amb-H³orn (11)/F³ollowing *first* : l¹eaves m³ud (rises)/l¹and F³oundation

[14] Lamb's 144,000 on Mount Zion (1-5) : *Heaven's One Four* : 14¹⁴4,000 / l¹amb W⁴orshippers (4) / l¹ie-free/l¹nnocent M⁴ouths (5)

Three Angels Shout Three Messages (1-11) : *Heaven's Sons Roar* : l¹oud A⁴ngels/M⁴essages

Eternal Gospel (6-7) : *Heaven's W[o]rd* : l¹nformation E⁴ternal

Babylon Falls (8) : *Sever The Whore* : l¹evel W⁴hore

Beast-Worshippers Tormented (9-11) : *Every One Torched* : l¹nflict W⁴orshippers *of Beast*

Blessed Those who Die in Lord (13) : *Heaven Comfort* : l¹ifeless M⁴erry/E⁴lated / l¹ifeless E⁴ase

Two Harvests Sickled:

Good-Corn Harvest (14-16) : *Sever The Moral/Corn* : l¹ngather M⁴aize

Bad-Grape Harvest (17-20) : *Sever Stubborn* : l¹ngather W⁴rath-grapes

[15] Seven Angels with Seven Plagues (last) : *Seven Blights* : l¹ast S⁵courges/S⁵trikes/S⁵curvy?/S⁵mallpox?

<u>OT</u>   **Revelation**   <u>NT</u>

[15] Sea of Glass and Fire (2) : *Heaven's Fire* : **I**^{1}nflamed **S**^{5}ea

   Moses/Lamb's Victory Song (3-4) : *Heaven's Pride/Vibe* :
   I^{1}aw/**I**^{1}amb's **S**^{5}ong

[16] Seven b^6**owls of Wrath** (1-21) : *Sevun Kicks (again)* :
   I^{1}ndignation **b**^{6}owls/**I**^{1}mage-**b**^{6}east *sores* (1-2)/**I**^{1}ick **b**^{6}owls?

   Seven b^6**owls of Wrath (1-21):**

   I^{1}iquid *(sea)* > **b**^{6}lood (3-4) > **I**^{1}iving **b**^{6}easts
   I^{1}iquid *(rivers, streams)* > **b**^{6}lood (4-7)
   I^{1}ight **b**^{6}urns *hotter* (sun**:** 8-9)
   I^{1}ight > **d**^{6}arkness : *throne of beast* (10-11)
   I^{1}ast **b**^{6}attle : *Armageddon* (12-16)
   I^{1}ast **b**^{6}owl (17-21) : **I**^{1}t's **d**^{6}one! (17)/**I**^{1}evel **b**^{6}abylon/
   I^{1}slands **d**^{6}issappear/**I**^{1}arge **b**^{6}oulders *from heaven*

[17] Prostitute of Babylon : *Rev*eal *Seventeen* heads and horns
   : **17**^{17} = **7** *heads* + **10** *horns* : **I**^{1}ewd **L**^{7}ady. *One* with **7** heads =
   7 mountains = 7 kings **:** *5 fell, one is, one to come, then an 8*th

[18] Babylon Falls (1-3) : *Leav*ened *The Great* ones of earth :
   I^{1}mmoral **B**^{8}abylon

   Kings Fornicated with Her (3, 9-10) : *Leav*ened *Mating* :
   I^{1}mmoral **B**^{8}edding

   Merchants Grew Rich (3) : *Leav*ened *Trading* : **I**^{1}mmoral
   B^{8}usiness

   Babylon Judged (4-24) : *Level The Great whore!* : **I**^{1}evel
   B^{8}abylon

   Trade Destroyed (11-19) : *Rev*enue *Waining / Lev*el
   Trading : **I**^{1}ose **B**^{8}usiness

OT   Revelation   NT

[19] Prostitute Destroyed (1-4) : *Revenge Timing* : I^1ash P^9rostitute

Marriage Supper of Lamb (6-10) : *Heaven's Binding* : I^1amb's g^9room/g^9amos *(Greek: marriage)*

Beasts Cast into Lake of Fire (17-21) : *[E]vil/Devils Confined* : I^1ake P^9yre

[20] Satan Sent to Abyss (1-3) : *Devil Sending/To Hole* *(Bottomless Pit)* : T^2artarus O^0pened/n^2o O^0utlet

First Resurrection (4-6) : *Heaven Empties graves* : V^2ivifies O^0wn *people*

1000-year Reign (4-6) : *Several To Thrones to rule* (4) : T^2hrones O^0ccupied

Satan Released (7-10) : *Devil To Go out* : T^2o O^0btain *army*

Satan Cast into Lake of Fire (10) : *Devil To Go in* : T^2ortured O^0ngoingly

[21] New Heavens/Earth (1-7) : *Heavens—New Ones* : n^2ew I^1aunch

New Jerusalem (1-4, 9-26) : *Heaven's New One (city)* : n^2ew I^1odging / n^2ew I^1ight *to nations* (24) / n^2ations' I^1ight

[22] River of Life (1-5) : *Heaven's New Fleuve* : V^2ital T^2orrent

Tree of Life: *Heaven's New Root* : n^2ew T^2ree *of life along River's banks* (2)

Don't Add to Words (18) : *Revelation: New Truths? No!* : n^2o n^2ew *truths after Revelation*

www.ingramcontent.com/pod-product-compliance
Lightning Source LLC
LaVergne TN
LVHW051046080426
835508LV00019B/1727